Freud
Insight and Change

Freud
Insight and Change

İlham Dilman

Basil Blackwell

Copyright © İlham Dilman 1988

First published 1988

Basil Blackwell Ltd
108 Cowley Road, Oxford, OX4 1JF, UK

Basil Blackwell Inc.
432 Park Avenue South, Suite 1503
New York, NY 10016, USA

British Library Cataloguing in Publication Data

Dilman, İlham
  Freud : insight and change.
  1. Freud, Sigmund 2. Psychoanalysis
  I. Title
  150.19'52   BF173.F85

  ISBN 0-631-16119-8

Library of Congress Cataloging in Publication Data

Dilman, İlham
  Freud, insight and change.

  Bibliography: p.
  Includes index.
  1. Psychoanalysis 2. Psychotherapy.
  3. Freud, Sigmund, 1856–1939. I. Title.
  RC506.D55 1988   616.89'17   87–35461
  ISBN 0-631-16119-8

Typeset in 10 on 12pt Plantin
by Alan Sutton Publishing Ltd, Gloucester
Printed in Great Britain by Billing & Sons Ltd, Worcester

Contents

1

Introduction: Problems about Psycho-analytic Therapy

Psycho-analysis is two things: a way of understanding man and a 'treatment' of 'pyschological ailments', and it sees the two as interconnected. For the treatment aims to promote 'insight' or 'self-understanding', and the 'cure' for which the 'patient' seeks analysis is supposed to flow from this understanding. The understanding in question involves coming to face one's feelings and inclinations, and other aspects of oneself, taking account of them in one's appraisal of where one wishes to go, and acquiring a better appreciation of what one is up to in the preoccupations and activities that fill one's life.

This statement of what psycho-analysis is begs many questions and I have indicated the terms in it that are problematic by putting them in inverted commas: what is a psychological ailment and what does it mean to treat such an ailment or to treat a person for it? How far does the medical model help us to understand what is in question? How far does it influence the conduct of psychotherapy for good or ill? What we are concerned to understand is the *practice* of psycho-analysis, and that cannot be detached from the psycho-analyst's view of it: his view of what he is doing and his view of that to which his practice is directed.

What distinguishes psycho-analysis from other forms of psycho-therapy is that it confines itself to promoting self-understanding in the patient and avoids any form of psychological manipulation of him. But what is this self-understanding or insight into oneself and how can it be imparted by another person? If what is in question is something each person has to win through for himself what role can another person play in the process? If, further, this insight is shunned and resisted by the patient or analysand, how can imparting it be free from the taint of manipulation? Secondly, what kind of connection is there between the change in understanding which constitutes insight into oneself and the change in will, change in the direction in which one is facing, which constitutes a change in the self – change in oneself? How are we to understand the notions of truth and authenticity in terms of which the former change is assessed and the notions of growth and autonomy in terms of which the latter is understood?

Why should the change that a person must allow in himself in gaining self-understanding be 'therapeutically beneficial' or in the direction of 'personal growth'? Is there not some further change, which involves the patient's will to a greater degree? It is a presumption in psycho-analysis that a gain in self-understanding is automatically a change in the direction of greater autonomy: 'truth is inevitably liberating'. In other words, the patient or analysand is 'guided' towards greater autonomy without any intervention aimed at the redirection of his will. The idea is that the analyst does no more than guide him towards 'greater truth', helping him to find this himself, by showing him his resistances and enabling him to dispense with them. In this way he is enabled to choose for himself in which direction he wishes to move. But what does 'choice' mean in this context? Does the patient reach the position from which he changes simply by shedding what has so far shackled him (*per via di levare*) or does he find it, partly at least, by growing up to it ('emotional learning')? In the latter case, does not the analyst make a more 'positive' contribution to the patient's change – positive in contrast to merely acting as a 'mirror' in which the patient can see himself? If so, something of the kind of person the analyst is and the kinds of value he holds must play a role in the therapy.

These are the main questions I propose to discuss in this book. The distinction between a psycho-analytic conception of man and the practice of psycho-analytic therapy is, to some extent at least, an artificial one. For, historically, the conception has grown out of the search for a therapy of psychological ills, and it has, in turn, informed the procedures which constitute a therapy. Yet, for practical purposes, questions have to be taken one at a time, and I have already discussed some questions regarding the psycho-analytic conception of man and the workings of his mind in my two earlier books on Freud.[1] So in this book I shall concentrate on the kind of therapy which is a

[1] Dilman, *Freud and Human Nature*, 1983, Blackwell, and *Freud and the Mind*, 1984, Blackwell.

legacy of Freud and on the way it has changed our understanding of man's relationships and the problems with which these present him.

I have deliberately avoided the term 'neurosis' just now as this is one of the terms that begs many questions: what is a neurosis? What kind of 'causation' does it have? What might be meant by a 'psychogenic cause'? Should we think of a neurosis as an illness at all? How is what is neurotic to be distinguished from what it not – neurotic problems from problems of life, neurotic reactions and misery from 'normal' reactions and what Freud called 'real unavoidable suffering' (1949b, p. 320)? What is a 'normal' reaction? How is a neurosis, an 'illness of the nerves' in its original meaning, to be distinguished from a mental illness or psychosis?

There are those, of course, who deny that what are called mental illnesses are to be understood in medical terms. They sometimes express this point by saying that they are not illnesses at all and that there is no such thing, therefore, as a mental illness: 'mental illness is a myth' (Szasz, 1967). But the question of whether what are called mental illnesses are illnesses properly speaking is distinct from the question of whether neuroses are illnesses: illnesses of what?

Whether or not a 'neurotic person' can be considered as ill, one thing can be said at the outset: whatever it is that people seek psycho-analytic treatment or help for, it is something which is part and parcel of their very being: they are 'internally related' to it. Somehow or other the person himself is at the root of the problems in question. So he cannot leave the treatment to the analyst and simply undertake to comply with 'doctor's orders'. To try to do so is for him to shirk his responsibility for these problems and to avoid participating in the treatment. Without such participation psycho-analytic treatment cannot exist.

This, of course, does not mean that the pscyho-analytic patient has to be his own doctor and carry out his own treatment. That, too, would be a form of evasion. There are patients who find it difficult to put themselves into the hands of their therapist and insist on running the show themselves. They are afraid to open up to another person, to take on board anything new that comes to them from outside, anything that calls for a fresh response. They are afraid to allow the analyst his full role as therapist. But if that role is not that of the active physician in orthodox medicine, or his psychological counterpart of mentor or adviser, then what is it?

I said that the problems for which people seek psychotherapy involve them as persons. A treatment that is directed to these problems cannot, therefore, by-pass the person. It is also true that what makes people seek help for such problems varies from person to person. Some people seek help too readily, others have a great reluctance to do so. Those that are reluctant are not necessarily those who are afraid of the temptations of a dependent relationship. Some people genuinely believe that 'one ought to deal with one's problems oneself'. But dealing with them does not exclude accepting help from another person. So what form must this help take for it to leave the person to deal with these problems himself?

Once a person embarks on an analysis, his aims and his expectations from the treatment cannot be taken as read. In medical treatment the patient's and the doctor's aims and objectives coincide: to get rid of the infection, to restore the injured organ to its proper function, etc. But the psycho-analytic patient may, and usually does, have unrealistic aims: he may seek treatment as a means to ends that are embedded in his phantasies and neurosis. What he seeks from the treatment may turn out to be the perpetuation of the very aims and attitudes that lie at the root of his problems, those for which he seeks treatment. His aims and expectations when he says 'I want help' or 'I need treatment' will, therefore, have to be scrutinized analytically as part of the treatment and come to be modified in the course of it. One possibility is that he may come to accept and learn to live with what he complained about at the outset of his treatment. His 'cure' may consist of just this. His view of it may so change that it no longer bothers him, or his conception of life may so change that he is able to endure it without complaint. Certainly, a treatment that works in part by changing the patient's needs and norms of what he finds acceptable is a very different kind of treatment from the one we find in orthodox medicine.

People choose to undergo psycho-analytic treatment for a variety of reasons. Often even some of their tangible complaints lose their importance for the patient in the light of what the analysis uncovers. Therefore, 'cure' is one of those words for which there is hardly a clear use in psycho-analysis, and this greatly confuses those who wish to compare the 'success rate' in psycho-analytic therapy with the 'success rate' in other forms of psychological treatment. When the treatment has advanced sufficiently the question 'am I cured?' loses much of its meaning for the patient. He may say, 'I think I can now manage well enough on my own'. If he is deceiving himself, the analyst will warn him of it.

But if he is right, does this mean that he has been 'cured'? After all, he may have been 'cured' of his complaining and not of what he was complaining about: he may have learned to make the best of a bad job. Is this the kind of thing one could call a cure? One could say that the psycho-analysis has worked for him, though the way in which it has done so is very different from his original hopes and expectations. One could point to the ground he has covered in the analysis, the 'emotional work' he has done in the course of it. There is much else that one could say by way of expanding and supporting these claims. One could describe what was the matter with him in a way that is now acceptable to him, how he has become different in the course of the analysis, how his life has become richer and more satisfactory in his own estimate. But these are relative terms, and 'cure' implies something more definite. It implies a change and benefit on which there is fairly general agreement in relation to which the patient's own estimate fades into relative insignificance.

This doesn't mean that it makes no sense to talk of 'mental health'. But can we say that psycho-analysis is concerned with its improvement? Or should we say that it relies on the degree of mental health enjoyed by the patient in helping him to deal with his problems? But what is 'mental health' and what constitutes its breakdown?

I spoke of the analytic patient who says 'I think I can now manage well enough on my own'. I stress the 'well enough': there is no end to the road on which he has been travelling as the notion of cure suggests. But for that same reason if he says 'I want to go on with analysis' this does not mean that 'he is still sick'. Nor need it imply that he has resisted the treatment and so remains unchanged, or that he has become dependent on the analysis and is unwilling to grow up. Someone else in his place may have stopped earlier. But he may feel that he has further to go and is willing to work for it.

Both the patient's judgement and will have to come into a third person's assessment of the 'result' the analysis has achieved for him, although both are subject to deception and, therefore, to correction. In the end it is a matter of what the patient himself wants out of life and what he can realistically expect from himself. The success of the analysis cannot be assessed independently of what the patient himself thinks and what he wishes to do. There is no 'objective' judgement to which this is irrelevant, as in medicine.

That there is this difference should not be surprising when in one case it may be the lungs that have been treated for tuberculosis, whereas in the other case it is the person himself. Consequently, the term 'treatment' itself must mean something different in the two cases, even if there are comparisons to be made. But what does it mean in psychotherapy?

It *may* be best to drop the terms 'treatment', 'cure' and 'illness' here and speak of 'help' and 'problems and difficulties' – difficulties, for instance, a person finds or creates in his personal and social relationships. The word 'help' would emphasize the participatory character of what is sought and the 'problems' would have to be specified, characterized and distinguished from others.

In more than one place in his writings Freud speaks of the transformation in analysis of 'neurotic misery' into 'everyday unhappiness' (Freud and Breuer, 1950, p. 232). It is certainly part of Freud's conception of life that human life is inherently problematic, that problems and difficulties are endemic to life. But what problems life presents a person depend partly on chance and partly on his receptivity or sensitivity. There are, of course, problems that are of a man's own making, and these are the ones which psycho-analysis tends to regard as 'neurotic'. But in what sense are they of his own making?

There are problems that one avoids by good luck, by 'management', or by insensitivity. The management in question is what psycho-analysts call 'defence', and they see it as shutting out life. No one, of course, can avoid life's problems altogether, but those who avoid some of them by good luck need not be insensitive to the stings of life, and they can be compassionate with those who are exposed to them. Those who have a thick skin, on the other hand, or those who guard themselves against such problems, miss some of life's offerings. Sometimes the dissatisfaction or depression with which this leaves them is just what makes them seek psychotherapeutic help. This is what makes Freud say that much will be gained in transforming the patient's neurotic misery into 'everyday suffering': the latter cannot be altogether avoided and the attempt to do so diminishes life and creates new problems.

One philosophical problem here concerns the distinction between 'neurotic difficulties' and what I called 'problems of life'. For instance, someone keeps grieving over a loved one he has lost; he is inconsolable. Has he lost his ability to make a 'come back'? Was his relationship one of identification so that without the loved one he has no identity and so no self on which to fall back? Or is the fact that nothing consoles him an indication of the depth of his love? There are genuine differences here, but no abstract words or general criteria can capture them. So there is the danger of simplifying the distinction or even of denying it altogether: 'all inconsolable mourning is melancholia' (see 1950, vol. v). This can blunt the kind of perception needed in psycho-analysis.

Our philosophical problems concerning the practice of psycho-analysis thus fall roughly under three heads: (i) *Neurosis*: the character of the kind of trouble which psycho-analysis purports to treat or help the patient with, its relation to the person who seeks help, and the sense in which it is an expression of something 'wrong' with him: how far can this be understood in terms of medical categories? (ii) *Psychotherapy*: the character of the treatment appropriate to such trouble: how much does it differ from a medical response to disease and physical illness? (iii) *Insight and change*: how does psycho-analysis promote self-understanding? How does this bring about changes in the person that help him with his special problems?

Our problems are *philosophical* in that they are all concerned with the categories appropriate to understanding the distinctive features of what is in question: the conduct and objectives of psycho-analytic therapy, and the nature of what it is directed at, namely personal problems and neurotic suffering. This is a field in which conflicting pulls on our understanding make it difficult for us to obtain a clear vision of things, conflicting pulls which make themselves felt in psycho-analytic thinking itself. Freud's views were not immune from such conflicting pulls. Therefore, a philosophical discussion of Freud's views of neurosis, its causation and treatment, cannot avoid being *critical* of Freud himself.

Freud revolutionized our understanding of certain forms of 'mental trouble' and their treatment. The kind of work that led to his discoveries obviously does not belong to philosophy. So it does not fall within the province of philosophy to tell Freud, or any other psycho-analyst, how to proceed. Yet in this matter of appreciating Freud's discoveries and the concepts he developed philosophy does have a positive role to play, provided it remains well informed. Since, however, philosophy can alter the practitioner's *understanding* of what he is doing and the character of what he is working on, it can actually influence, albeit indirectly, the development of the *practice* in question. Naturally, to do so is not part of the philosopher's brief, and it would be presumptuous of him to aim at it. Nevertheless, this may be an *effect* of his reflections when he is sufficiently in touch with that practice to be taken seriously by those who engage in it.

2

Medicine and Illness:
Physical and Mental

1 BODY AND MIND: PHYSICAL ILLNESS

What is an illness? What kind of interest does medicine take in those who consult a physician?

It is primarily a *person* who is said to be ill, even though we extend the notion to animals we treat as pets. An organism may be diseased, including human organs, but it is a person who is ill. It is more natural to speak of an animal as sick. This has to do with the fact that a person can *say* he is ill, in the first person, can be aware that all is not well with him, that there is something *wrong*: 'things with me are not as they *normally* are, as they *ought* to be'. The judgement in question is normative.

Wrong in what way? He may feel hot or feverish, limp or weary, standing up may be an effort, his head may be aching, he may feel dizzy. *Normally* standing up, walking, moving, breathing, focusing one's eyes, are things we do without effort or difficulty. They do not require our attention. Indeed, this unawareness is an expression of our well-being.

When something goes wrong with us, when we have an infection, inflammation or disease, we feel ill. One can, of course, feel ill without being ill, such as when one has sun stroke, and one can be ill before one feels ill. But usually when one feels ill one is ill, and this is something accountable to 'objective' criteria. The person himself has no special say in the matter, and such things as his body temperature and blood count are decisive in settling the question.

What is wrong with a person in this way affects his well-being. We say that he is not 'in good health'. He may cough, suffer from aches and pains, and he may have a disease. If he is 'healthy', however, he will have the reserve and resources to fight off the illness.

Healthy or not, when a person feels ill the illness affects him in a particular way and follows a particular course regardless of who he is. We identify it on this basis and say that he has mumps or measles, jaundice or tuberculosis. Illness and disease do not always coincide. I may feel ill with a severe local infection, but if this doesn't cause fever, fatigue, drowsiness, and the like, it is not an illness. Pryorrhoea, for instance, is a disease of the gums, but it is not an illness.

A physician treats diseases, often specializing in diseases of particular regions of the body. But this is not the only thing he does. A general practitioner is concerned with different aspects of the well-being of his patients – primarily their physical well-being. What he finds wrong with them may not amount to an illness or disease. A person may suffer from a vitamin deficiency or the lack of some mineral in his diet, so that he is anaemic, lacks energy or is susceptible to colds. He may suffer from high or low blood pressure, which may, in the future, have consequences detrimental to his health. His physician will take measures to correct his condition or to keep it under control.

Someone may consult a doctor for obesity, which is not an illness but may affect health adversely in the long run. The doctor may find the cause of this in the patient's diet or in a malfunctioning of glands, and will accordingly advise a change of diet or prescribe some medication that will correct or compensate for the malfunction. In a different case a man may go to see the doctor because he has injured an eyelid, broken a limb, swallowed a fish bone, eaten something that has gone bad or breathed toxic vapours. The effect of some of these conditions may not last; the injury or broken bone may heal by itself without medical intervention. But medical intervention may speed up the healing process, and in any case it will relieve the discomfort.

In short, one goes to the doctor to get a remedy for what is wrong, and what is wrong need not be an illness. There are different ways in which things may be wrong with a person in a way that threatens or affects his health, and there are different kinds of treatment and remedy. If the correction of what is wrong, the eradication of its cause, proves impossible, then the doctor seeks to contain or control it. One also seeks relief from pain, comfort in the short or long term. The conditions for which one seeks a remedy are conditions which affect one's well-being, cause pain and suffering, restrict one's actions, lower the quality of one's life or even threaten to shorten it. Medicine is interested in that aspect of people's well-being which constitutes their health. It is concerned to restore and preserve it.

The doctor may treat the infection, mend the broken bone, apply medication to the injured organ, but he may also treat the *man* for the condition which affects his health. He may recommend a diet that will build him up, prescribe rest from his work, or even fresh air away from the polluted atmosphere of his everyday environment. Rest in a sanatorium thus combines both these aspects of medicine. That aspect of the treatment directed to building up the person's strength may also take the form of nursing.

Nursing includes attending to the patient's comfort, relieving his pain, helping him with elementary tasks of hygiene and medication, which in his restricted condition he is unable to perform on his own. From this there is no sharp line to considering the patient's anxieties. Whoever is nursing him may take the time to comfort him, respond with understanding to the anxiety he feels about his helplessness, treat him in a way that will make him feel less helpless. This may include keeping him informed about his illness and its treatment. While all this is part of responding to another human being in pain, discomfort and, perhaps distress, one who has had to relinquish some of his autonomy, it is also directed towards letting the healing process take its course. In that sense the nursing in question is part of the treatment, or at least supplementary to it.

When a person is ill it is his whole life that is affected; he is affected in 'body and mind'. The body, we could say, is an intricate machine much of which we are hardly aware of when we are in good health. Then we enjoy physical exercise and all the riches with which we are regaled through our senses. When in good health we and our bodies are one and the same. There is no sense then of any dependence on our body as something other or apart from us.

It is when our health fails or something goes wrong with some part of our body that it becomes a burden. Our limbs begin to ache, we feel too weary to move them, and find no pleasure in exercising them. We have to take care of our body, attend to parts of it, take pills to avoid giddiness, inject ourselves with insulin to avoid high blood sugar, even carry out regular dialysis of the kidneys. The body thus 'takes over' and becomes something that makes demands on our time and attention. We have to take care of it in order to be able to carry on at all. Yet this care and attention restricts our activities and leaves us less able to enjoy life. We become aware then of our dependence on our body, on its good health, as a condition for enjoying all that life has to offer.

Thus, having a serious illness or suffering from a severe incapacitating condition is a case for concern. A person in such a condition has something to cope with and adjust to. It would be the same, in some ways, if he were sent to prison, lost some of his rights and privileges, or if his environment underwent a sudden transformation and ceased to offer him the support, sustenance, contact and pleasures around which he has built his life and that he has come to take for granted. Having a severe illness and submitting to its treatment thus involves a loss of autonomy and calls on special mental resources in a person. An inability to put up with its demands and restrictions usually interferes with the 'healing process'.

For this reason, if for no other, medical treatment has to pay some attention to the patient's mental condition, to direct itself at the whole person: 'body and mind'. The point is that while physical and chemical manipulation of specific localities of the body and physiological processes takes place as part of the treatment, the physician and his supporting team need to remember that they are dealing with a person for whom this situation presents problems, a person who is suffering and has feelings about what is happening to him. This dimension of the treatment of physical illness is not, of course, psychotherapy, but part of the humanity integral to medical treatment. It is also plain medical good sense.

When a person's physical health breaks down, as we have seen, his body becomes something 'external' to him. His part in the treatment, therefore, is a *passive* one. He needs to *submit* to the treatment, which may be difficult or painful, to *comply* with its requirements, as directed by the doctor. The causes of his condition are outside him, and the treatment is concerned with removing or counteracting these. Since they lie within his body he has to *consent* to the treatment. This is the extent of his responsibility.

What the patient expects from the treatment, its objective, is usually something specific and definite. Realizing this objective is what returning him to physical health constitutes. By and large most people agree on this and regard it as good. For it is a fundamental aspect of a person's well-being, fundamental in the sense that his enjoyment of life and his capacity for the activities which make it up depend on it. For most of this it may not be sufficient, but it is at least necessary.

2   MENTAL ILLNESS: IS IT A MYTH?

A physical illness then is the condition a person finds himself in as a result of some part of his body not functioning properly, however that may come about. It constitutes a breakdown of his physical health. We have seen the sense in which this is fundamental to his well-being as a person and the way its breakdown affects him 'body and mind'. It is, nevertheless, his *physical* health that is in question since it is maintained by the proper functioning of parts of the *body*.

When a person enjoys good physical health his body is not as vulnerable to disease and physical illness, and if he does fall ill his body can counteract its causes more easily so that he can make a quick recovery. Indeed, some of the symptoms of his illness, even when they are unpleasant or painful, are the result of the resistance or fight which his body puts up.

How much of a parallel is there to all this where a person's *mind* is concerned, that is, his mental powers or capacities? Can we justifiably speak of a person's mental health? Can we speak of an illness of the mind? Are what we call mental illnesses really illnesses?

We have noted that there are those who answer this last question in the negative. There are different considerations which incline them to do so, although people who have held this position have not all been impressed by the same ones.

One of the major considerations is concerned with a person's relation to what constitutes his 'mental illness' and the way this differs from his relation to his physical illness. An illness, the argument goes, is something *external* to the person who suffers from it, even when he is responsible for getting it. He is related to it as to a shoe that pinches his foot or restricts the circulation of his blood. He can inspect the shoe, remove it to ease the discomfort or have the shoe altered to eliminate the defect.

It is otherwise with those personal characteristics and patterns of behaviour which enter into the constitution of what we call mental illnesses. An enlarged liver or high blood pressure, like an aquiline nose, a medium height or cauliflower ears, are not aspects of a man's 'mode of being' or 'manner of existence' in the way that his impulsiveness or weakness of will, his courage or cowardice are. So we cannot imagine any of these being different without the man himself changing.

Thus Wittgenstein suggested (though I am reading this into what he actually said in *The Blue Book*, 1969, pp. 66 – 7) that when I am said to have a broken arm or a bump on my forehead, or to be six feet tall, the sense in which I have or am these things is different from the sense in which I have thoughts, intentions and pains. I am the subject of my thoughts; they are not something I can survey or manipulate while I think them. Whereas in respect of having a broken arm or bump on my forehead I am an object. I can be mistaken about whether the broken arm I see at my side after an accident is mine or my neighbour's. I can look into a mirror and mistake a bump on his forehead for mine. I can also take my arm to the surgeon in the hope that he can mend the break. I can apply cold compresses to the bump to try and make it go down.

To treat my thoughts in this way is to take a 'schizoid' attitude towards them. It is as if I had nothing to do with the thoughts in question, as if they were the thoughts of another person. This is to treat myself as an object.

Similarly, Sartre has pointed out that I am not thoughtful or impulsive in the sense in which I am tall and have blue eyes, or in the sense in which the table top is hard and flat. In *that* sense I am *not* a coward or, to put it less misleadingly, a coward is not what I *am*. There is nothing that is what I am. I am only what I make of myself. I sink into a relatively thing-like existence when I acquiesce in my personal characteristics passively, when I neither endorse nor repudiate my greed, envy or cowardice. I do so when, for instance, I take on the characteristics that people project onto me, conform to their expectations, adopt their norms without criticism, positive or negative.

Now, in what is called a mental illness, such as schizophrenia, I may sink into just such a thing-like existence, or at any rate move some way towards it. But even then there is no necessity for me to exist as a thing. Indeed, being thing-like is no more what I *am* than being greedy or a coward. In so far as I believe it I am deluded. This is a delusion that is part of the schizophrenia itself. Ultimately it is up to me whether or not I continue in this mode of existence and so continue to delude myself.

I say 'ultimately' because in the short term I cannot divest myself of it in the same way as I may change my clothes. Nor do I *believe* I can do so, since I am deluded. But if I suffer and my life is greatly impoverished, so that a psychiatrist such as R. D. Laing wishes to help me out of this mode of existence, he needs to understand my reasons for having taken this path and kept on it, and to appreciate what it is I get out of it despite the pain and disadvantages I suffer as a result. He must try to piece together the complex situation, partly real and partly fictitious, to which I respond in this way and perhaps partly perpetuate, by persisting in this thing-like existence. Only thus can he help me retrace my steps and undo the web that keeps me from changing direction. But if he is to succeed I need to have or find the will to do so.

This is the outline of one argument for denying that mental illnesses, as we call them, such as schizophrenia, are illnesses, genuine illnesses on the model of a physical illness. It establishes, to my mind conclusively, a radical difference between mental and physical illnesses. But the question is whether this difference, although radical, is fatal to our notion of mental illness. May there not be other similarities which justify the extension of the term to mental cases?

I shall mention, briefly, two supplementary arguments which are also to be found in the work of R. D. Laing. What we popularly call 'madness' may itself be a 'curative process', a salutary method of dealing with serious problems pertaining to damaging relationships which have been foisted onto one. Thus, in a book entitled *Freud's Unfinished Journey*, Professor Louis Berger argues this very convincingly in connection with Dr Schreber, of whom Freud wrote a case study. The gist of what he brings out is that as a boy Schreber had become the 'good', frightened boy which his father had forced him to become, extremely eager as an adult to please and comply with authority. 'Schreber's psychosis proper [Berger writes] may be understood as the break-up of the personality complaint with the internalized rules of his father. It was a revolt against the tyranny experienced as a child – a tyranny that had continued within the adult personality . . . Schreber [had to] regress to his painful childhood in order to free himself from the long-lasting effects of his traumatic upbringing' (1981, pp. 95 – 6). The implication is (though we find this in Laing and not in Berger) that what is a stage in a movement out of a very unsatisfactory mode of existence cannot justifiably be described as an illness. What is in question is what Freud diagnosed as a case of paranoia.

Someone who is impressed by this argument may fully admit the extent to which many mental illnesses and neuroses in part represent, or are expressions of, a person's struggle with adverse psychological conditions, but continue to use these terms. He may point out that what this argument emphasizes is equally true of physical illnesses. It should not, therefore, be made to count against the application of the term 'illness' to mental conditions. High temperature, for instance, which we generally regard as a symptom of physical illness, is often part of the body's struggle with what is inimical to its integrity. As Jung puts it, talking of neuroses: 'Neurosis is by no means only negative, it is also positive. Only a soulless rationalism could and does overlook this fact' (1953, p. 84).

In a book entitled *Wisdom, Madness and Folly* John Custance speaks in a similar vein. He emphasizes the value there was for him in his experience through a long manic-depressive illness. He makes a plea for his 'manic consciousness' and says that he does not wish to return to normality if that means dismissing it as a tissue of delusions. He means, if I understand him rightly, that what he experienced during his illness contained genuine perceptions of himself, the kinds of perception we do not allow in our everyday, 'normal' conceptions of human existence. He protests that to be bound by such conceptions would be for him to return to a narrower, poorer life.

This leads to the second supplementary argument, namely that normality assessed in statistical terms is not necessarily preferable to what those who are normal in this sense ('the average man', *l'homme moyen sensuel*) call madness. But if this is true, what right has anyone to describe those who are mad as 'ill', thus implying that there is something wrong with them?

Certainly it may be true at certain times and in certain places that those who would pass as 'normal' in a culture have restricted lives and restricted contact with what belongs to the spiritual realm. This may even be true more generally: 'human kind cannot bear very much reality' (T. S. Eliot, 'Burnt Norton', 1955, p. 8). All that follows from this, however, is caution: we should not be ready to regard deviation from the average, or from what is regarded as normal, as mental illness. Normality is no criterion of mental health.

The fact that normality is no criterion and that the term 'mentally ill' can be misused, and even abused, in ways depicted by Thomas Szasz and others, does not mean that there are no *clinical* criteria. This brings me to the second major consideration that leads people to question the idea of mental illness. It focuses on these criteria and finds them arbitrary. This leads to the claim that in contrast to physical illnesses the diagnosis of a mental illness has no objective basis: the criteria are not clear-cut and there is no general agreement in their application.

I would reply by agreeing and adding that it should not be surprising that things are as claimed here. For the kind of assessment that is in question has to do with people's *mental* condition. The identity of the condition identified is, therefore, bound to be logically dependent on the surroundings in which it is embedded, namely the rest of the personality in which a mental illness is diagnosed and that bears its imprint. Assessing a mental condition is, in this respect, like assessing personality or character, that is, a judgement as to what a person is like. Such judgements are often not easy to make, those who make them often disagree, and may support the same judgement by what appears to be contradictory evidence. So they, too, have been dismissed by some people as 'subjective'.

Professor John Wisdom has commented on the differences between such judgements and claims as that a man possesses a gold watch – and, may I add, a club foot, a broken bone or an inflamed appendix – which make the former seem logically suspect:

Suppose someone asks 'What is the character of the Englishman? Is he simple and honest like a bull-dog, or is he very foxy?' It is not easy to answer this question. In the first place, there are Englishmen and Englishmen and Englishmen. Some are comparatively simple and honest like dogs, some are *very* foxy, and many are mixed. In the second place, even in the case of an individual Englishman it is not easy to say what character he possesses as it is to say whether he possesses a watch of gold or any other object. We may of course guess that a man possesses a watch from the many occasions on which he arrives on time for pleasant appointments and ten minutes late for unpleasant ones. But besides observing those incidents in a man's life which may well be due to his possession of a watch, there is a quicker and surer way of telling whether he has a watch or any other object, namely, looking to see. But with his character, his motives, and his meaning, there is not. There is no better and surer way of ascertaining what character a man possesses or what motives drive him than observing and remembering those incidents in his life which are due to his possession of that character. To study these is to study his character and the driving forces of his life. (1965, p. 94)

Compare Wisdom's questions here with the questions: 'What is schizophrenia?' or 'What is it like, what is its character?' and 'Does he have schizophrenia?' or 'Is what he suffers from schizophrenia?'

Many psychiatrists have pointed out that schizophrenia takes many different forms, indeed, that what we have here are diverse patterns of mind and conduct that are rather loosely connected. One could make the point in an extreme form by saying that schizophrenia has as many different faces as there are individual schizophrenics. This is a paradoxical way of putting it since it suggests that there are no limits to the application of the term. Obviously, this is not what one wishes to say, but certainly what one is wishing to bring out is not true of mumps, measles or tuberculosis. Consequently, when we ask of a particular person whether he has schizophrenia we are asking how he stands in relation to individuals who are themselves rather loosely related. There is no clear-cut paradigm to act as our litmus paper,[1] and indeed there could not be. But does it follow from this (i) that we should not talk of schizophrenia at all, and (ii) that we should not classify it as an illness?

In a paper, 'The Reality of Mental Illness' (*Philosophy*, 1981), where he argues for the legitimacy of the notion of mental illness, Steve Champlin points out a connected logical difference between the concepts of mental and physical illness. The pattern of the symptoms of a physical illness is established within a short duration of time, its identity is relatively insensitive to the before and the after, whereas it takes the stretch of a fair chunk of life to establish a pattern of schizophrenia or any other mental illness. As he puts it: 'Many physical illnesses are trivial and of short duration. Whereas mental illness is a serious thing, and cannot last two or three days from onset to recovery . . . [In this respect] mental illness shares the temporal logic of political conviction, not of physical illness' (p. 476).

Wittgenstein made the same point about love and grief: 'Why does it sound queer to say: "For a second he felt deep grief?" Only because it so seldom happens?' (1963, p. 174). For this very reason a person has to have come some way in his development, reached a certain mental age, before he can be mentally ill – before we can

---

[1] The two questions 'Is the liquid in this test tube acid and what is its pH?' and 'Does this man have a watch in his pocket?' are answered differently. But in both cases there are fairly definite criteria, and what satisfies them appears within a relatively short duration and is identified independently of the surrounding circumstances.

intelligibly attribute a mental illness to him. As Champlin puts it: 'It would make no sense for the midwife to wonder whether the baby she had just delivered has a mental illness, even if it runs in the family' (p. 476).

Consequently Ian D. Suttie is right to regret that the study and treatment of mental illnesses have been left in the hands of the medical profession. There such a study 'has yielded little more in a century than a descriptive classification of "syndromes" . . . It was a study of the less profound disorders (i.e. hysteria and neurasthenia) that yielded a clue to the "method' which is now believed to underlie all "madness" (1948, pp. 183–4). He then goes on to point out that 'such conditions as scarlet fever, gastric ulcer or appendicitis offer to research a group of comparable cases facilitating the discovery of a common cause' whereas mental illnesses 'cannot be distinguished from each other in this way'. Indeed medicine's attempt to try to do so is the cause of the sterility of its descriptive classification about which Suttie complains.

These then are some of the weighty objections to the notion of an illness of the mind. They do really point to important differences between the physical and the mental cases. But these differences do not seem to me to be fatal to the case for talking of mental illness. I have indicated why I think not. What they show, to my mind, is that mental illnesses do not fall squarely in the province of medicine, as has been assumed in much of psychiatry, and that their treatment is a very different kind of thing from the treatment of physical illnesses.[2] This, and the abuses committed in the name of medicine, are the main reasons why some anti-establishment psychiatrists have denied the existence of mental illnesses. As Laing puts it in a recent autobiographical book, *Wisdom, Madness and Folly, the Making of a Psychiatrist 1927–57* (1985):

> I have never denied the existence of patterns of mind and conduct that are excruciating. I have never called myself an anti-psychiatrist . . . However, I agree with the anti-psychiatrist thesis that by and large psychiatry functions to exclude and repress those elements society wants excluded and repressed. (pp. 8–9)

---

[2] There are, of course, physical methods of treatment for mental illness. These are directed at the nervous system and yield some success. But their application raises some questions on which I will comment in the next chapter. My main concern, however, will be to understand what is involved in the *psychological* treatment of neuroses and I shall concentrate on psycho-analytic therapy.

The claim is that physical and chemical methods of treatment aim at removing something that is an intimate part of the patient's personality, regardless of what it means to the patient, simply because the psychiatrist and those whose interests he represents do not 'like it'. 'Madness' does have a point of view and medical psychiatry, in common with common sense, is dismissive of it. Laing writes:

> There are many people who have been psychotic . . . who want people to know what it is like to be completely out of the ordinary, common sense, shared world, and into some other hell-world of sheer horror, terror and torture. There is no doubt that there are enormous differences between states of mind, between different 'realities'. I am not trying to gloss over or minimize these differences. The question is: what sort of differences does this sort of difference make? What sort of difference does it make to 'us'? (1985, p. 7)

3   MADNESS: WHY AN ILLNESS?

That there are extreme cases, 'patterns of mind and conduct that are excruciating', is not in question. Given the differences on which I have commented, what justification is there still for talking of illnesses of the mind?

If we have any justification at all it would have to turn (it seems to me) on the possibility of claiming that something has gone *wrong* with the mind of the person in question – much in the way in which we speak of there being something wrong with a person when an organ of his body does not function properly so that the workings of the rest of his body ('integrity of the body') are affected in ways that are detrimental to his well-being. Here we have to tread carefully, however, and not let our moral judgements determine what we are going to call 'wrong'.

Plato talked of evil in the soul as a 'spiritual sickness' and compared the punishment of such a person to the treatment of an illness – a treatment of the soul aiming to cure it of the wickedness that has entered it. I can understand this way of talking and I have written about it elsewhere (see Dilman, 1979). Plato regards goodness, or love of the good, in contrast with indifference to it, as essential to a person's *spiritual* health or well-being, and this inevitably involves certain moral judgements. We, on the other hand, are here concerned with the *mind*, and our question is: what could constitute its health, 'balance', 'equilibrium' or sanity? Whatever is in question, it lies in a different dimension from wickedness, even though remorse for his wickedness can drive a person 'out of his mind'.

Let us be clear that when we speak of 'the mind' here we are speaking of a person's mental capacities – his capacity to think, reason, remember, judge, understand what is going on around him and respond to it on that basis. We should, perhaps, also include his capacity for self-awareness, that is awareness of himself as a being distinct from his environment, with interests of his own, and his capacity to appreciate his dependence on this environment for survival and for the fulfilment of his interests, and so to take an interest in it, and even feel some fellowship for others, fellow human beings, in the same position. One or more of these capacities may be impaired in a person, or have failed to develop altogether, affecting the exercise of the others in such a way as to throw the mind 'out of balance'. Where it is simply a matter of the lack of development, retardation or arrest, especially where the person's intelligence is concerned, we have idiocy. Where his capacity to communicate and respond to others is severely retarded we have autism. Neither of these are instances of insanity; they are deficiencies or incapacities that restrict human life in such basic ways that it is reduced to a lower grade. What we have here is the *lack* of something fundamental to human life as we know it rather than a *disturbance* in the common exercise of the interdependent capacities of mind which constitutes its 'balance'.

In the latter case there is a *regression* in the use of the person's mental capacities. The capacities themselves are not absent. Indeed, they are very much in evidence in the experiences and sufferings of mad people or psychotics: sensitivity, imagination, intelligence, conscience. Yet these take on a warped appearance, they are exercised without proper restraint, the person exercising them shows a complete lack of sense of proportion, with excruciating results: utterly unfounded doubts; suspicions and fears; anguish, dejection and depression, or elation and excitement not commensurate with the person's circumstances. The delusions, whether of grandeur or persecution, are not simply unfounded. There is some logic in them, one which echoes our own, but *we* cannot make sense of it. From where we stand, it seems as if such a person 'has lost his reason', 'is no longer in touch with reality', 'is living in another world'.

All this is certainly an expression of the way he is in his *mind*. We say that he is 'out of his mind'. He can no longer exercise it 'responsibly'. Indeed, he is no longer himself, he is too 'fragmented' in himself to be able to act sensibly. Sense no longer prevails in his assessments and responses, and we cannot ourselves make sense of these. If we describe him as 'alienated', we have in mind the point of view from which his judgements and reasoning strike us as 'irresponsible' and his responses as 'incommensurate with his circumstances'. His alienation from such a point of view and his lack of cohesiveness in himself are the two sides of the same coin. Nothing holds him together and so his conduct and assessments seem to have their source in an alien, perverse will: he is 'out of his mind'.

This is no more than an indication of the way madness (e.g. extreme schizophrenia) looks to *us*, who have a coherent point of view, from the outside. The sense of our descriptions is bound up with this outsider's view of it and its lack of comprehension. If the mad can be reached at all, as some who are trying to help them claim they can be, they certainly cannot be reached from where we stand when we describe them as 'mad'. There are serious philosophical problems here: how can the insane be reached at all? The problem is more acute than the one concerning 'understanding a primitive society'. But this is not our problem at present. We are trying to understand whether and how madness can be characterized as an illness.

From what we have seen so far it is clear in what sense the mad or insane have been affected in their *mind*, and why *we* would say 'adversely': 'something is *wrong* with him in his mind'. Such a person seems unable to exercise properly mental capacities that are fundamental to human life as most of us understand it, so he is cut off from communication with others, unable to co-operate with them, look after his own interests or even consider them. A whole sphere of pleasures and activities that enrich human life is closed to him. Indeed, he may even be unable to look after himself and so need to be taken care of. He is incapacitated, in ways that are reminiscent of the ways in which those afflicted with a serious illness are incapacitated, and so need to be taken care of and nursed.

Furthermore, his experiences are often anguishing. He may be tormented by doubts, fears, guilt, dejection and depression. These anguishing experiences are the mental counterpart of the physical pain and suffering we find in physical illness.

What is in question may or may not be the result of a disease of the brain. It is clear, however, that it constitutes some justification for talking of mental illness. In the former case we would say that it has a physical basis, that it is the result of a physical disease. It would then be treatable by physico-chemical means and this clearly falls within the province of medicine. Furthermore, since some mental illnesses have a physical cause their diagnosis, though not necessarily their treatment, would always have to involve medical expertise.

Some people argue that since 'the mind has a physical basis in the brain', mental illness is always treatable by physico-chemical means, so that psychiatry *as a whole* is a branch of medicine. But this, even if it is put forward as a medical opinion, is based on a philosophical assumption which is, at the least, questionable.

I return to the question of whether a mental illness is a genuine illness. We have reviewed some of the arguments against thinking of it as an illness and found that while each brings out something important, none of them establish their claim. We have also seen what kind of justification there is for the opposite claim, on the affirmative side. Such justification is not, of course, conclusive.

What is in question is the extension of the use of the word 'illness' to new territory. There is, therefore, bound to be some conflict between the reasons for and those against doing so. Perhaps among the reasons on the negative side the one that carries the greatest weight for me relates to the differences in the kind of 'treatment' appropriate to the phenomena in question, given their distinctive character. Such treatment is based on communication and involves reaching or making contact with the patient rather than consisting of the mechanical or chemical manipulation of processes to which he is directly or indirectly subject. But can what is so treated be called an illness? And is such treatment 'treatment' in the medical sense of the term?

It was, at least in part, an historical accident that brought madness or insanity within the province of medicine. Previously people suffering from madness were simply shunned and neglected, or locked up and flogged. They were thought of as being possessed and some of the practices to which they were subjected were aimed at exorcising their demons.

Medicine changed this way of thinking; exorcism and punishment gave way to treatment. As Ian D. Suttie puts it: 'The failure to distinguish the symptoms of brain disease from the symptoms and consequences of social and interest disturbances, left the study and treatment of mental "diseases" in the hands of the medical profession' (1948, p. 183). But its materialistic bias 'retarded the appearance of a psychological medicine by nearly a century'.

4 MADNESS AND SPIRITUALITY

So in madness we have 'patterns of mind and conduct that are excruciating'. There is, therefore, no danger of confusing them with what is 'normal'. Our problem was: can we characterize them as expressions or symptoms of illness – mental illness? But states of mind and patterns of conduct that are far from ordinary need not amount to madness. They may represent human responses and sensibilities that are exceptional and extraordinary – genius, eccentricity, deep spirituality. Our problem now is: how are they to be distinguished from insanity? How is a person to be diagnosed as insane and treated accordingly when he may be a saint or a genius? Who is to do the diagnosing and can there be an expert in this field? These are the questions Dr Drury addresses in a paper entitled 'Madness and Religion' (1973).

He considers examples from case histories taken from the records of the hospital where he worked. The first was diagnosed as 'involutional depression', the second and third as 'mania' with states of elation and delusions. All three were treated successfully by electro-chemical means. The fourth case is described as 'unusual' by Drury. He was given no treatment. Drury gave him a good breakfast on the morning after the day of his admission to hospital and discharged him. 'I learnt more from talking to him', he says, 'than he did listening to me' (p. 124).

The first patient was a priest, Father A, who began to lose his faith, sleep and appetite and could not carry out his religious duties. He insisted that his condition was a *spiritual* one. He was given a brief course of electro-convulsive therapy; his sleep and appetite returned and his spiritual problems disappeared. Does that mean that his condition was not a spiritual one, that his problems were unreal, a product of his illness? If one claims, as Father A did, that his problems were spiritual and, therefore, 'real' in that sense, does it mean, as he insisted before the treatment, that 'no doctor could aid him' (p. 117)?

Drury puts the case of Father A side by side with Tolstoy and Father Gratry, whose words he quotes. There is a remarkable parallel. Tolstoy went through a similar state of depression, and he emerged a deeper man and believer, and is in our debt for making a permanent contribution to European culture. Drury asks: 'Can we differentiate between madness and religion? Can we say of one such state: "This is a mental illness and is the province of the psychiatrist"? And of another: "This is a spiritual experience sent by God for the advancement of the soul and is the province of a wise director"?' (p. 121)

He does the same with the other two cases and raises the same question in connection with them. They, too, were successfully treated by Drury, as I pointed out, while he dismissed the fourth man, who one morning heard at Mass the words of the Gospel, 'Go and sell all that thou hast and give to the poor and thou shalt have treasure in heaven, and come and follow me', and *he acted on them*. 'His wife', Drury says, 'had no sympathy for what she regarded as a morbid religiousness' (p. 124). Drury obviously didn't think there was anything *wrong* with him. He describes him as 'a man of great piety' (ibid.).

On this last man Drury's opinion differed from that of the man's wife. Was this because he could see what the wife could not, namely the man's clear spirituality and the depth and sincerity of the convictions upon which he acted? Or was it because he could find no independent signs of a mental illness which he had been trained to detect as a psychiatrist? He had shown no hesitation in treating the other three people despite the fact that their states of mind and conduct seemed to show some resemblance to those of men and women whose *spiritual authenticity* is not in doubt. Indeed, Drury says: 'No psychiatrist can read the Bible without sometimes hearing a disturbing echo of what he has just heard said to him on his ward round' (p. 125). All this raises for Drury the question of the distinction between mental illness and authentic spiritual experience.

He considers four answers, of which he finds the last the most attractive. But he rejects them all – and, I think, rightly so. He rejects Freud's answer that religious belief is an illusion and that religion is a pathological phenomenon.[3] He then rejects Jung's answer that 'madness is religion which has not yet come to an understanding of itself' (p. 129). He rejects the third answer that

---

[3] I am not concerned now with an accurate statement of Freud's position on this question.

'where there is an obvious failure of physical well-being then we may diagnose morbidity and not spirituality' (p. 130). The bodily disturbances 'are not a constant feature in all mental illness' and in any case they are 'secondary phenomena . . . Remove the depression, subdue the excitement, get rid of the hallucinations, and sleep and appetite and physical health are restored too.' Furthermore 'the lives of the saints are not free from just these same disturbances of physical health' (ibid.).

The fourth answer says that you have to wait and see before you can decide on which side of the line you are to place a particular case. We can look back on what Tolstoy describes in *A Confession* in the light of what we now know it flowered into. But Drury gives a counter example which throws doubt on the confidence one may feel even in retrospect. What is in question are the conflicting opinions of Pascal's 'night of pentecostal fire': was it an authentic spiritual experience or a mental aberration or breakdown? Those to whom Pascal's *Pensées* are 'a source of depth and wonder' will have no doubt. But the author of a recent history of mathematics, whom Drury mentions, thinks otherwise.

Drury emphasizes that in order to be able to appreciate the authenticity of a spiritual state one must oneself have some under-standing and sympathy for the tradition to which it belongs and also possess some degree of spiritual discernment. One must have attained some inwardness oneself. One need not share the beliefs in question. One need not think, with Drury, that what is in question may be 'a spiritual experience sent by God for the advancement of the soul', but one has to be capable of respecting it. Thus, Freud, for purely theoretical reasons, would have dogmatically dismissed the possi-bility of authentic religious experience. Drury's historian of mathe-matics, in his concern with the assessment of advance in mathe-matics, is not tuned to seeing anything of value in the *Pensées*. The state of soul in which these thoughts have their source strikes him as an aberration. He can only see it as the thing that diverted Pascal from the discoveries he was on the brink of making in mathematics.

It is the same with the fourth person, Mr D's wife. She must have found it sorely trying to live with this civil servant after his retirement. As a result, she saw his conduct under the aspect of morbidity. No doubt he *was* trying to live with – or at least he may have been. Certainly most church-going people would not doubt the seriousness of the words of Christ that Mr D heard at Mass. But how many of them would not describe as mad a man who took it upon himself to act on these words?

May be, in most cases, they would be right to do so. For it would take a great deal to act on those words, and *very* few people have it in them to be able to do so. There is a big difference between taking the first few steps on that path and following them through in the rest of one's life. Unless one is prepared to go the whole way and take the consequences one would indeed be 'mad' to throw everything to the winds. Think of an ordinary mortal who thinks of himself as a saint: is he very different from one who believes himself to be Napoleon?

To throw oneself into what is being asked of one in Christ's words without fear shows great courage and deep spirituality, but only if one knows what one is doing and is moved by compassion. To do so without realizing the enormity of what is being asked of one is foolishness. To minimize it, or think of oneself as equal to the task, is arrogance that borders on madness. Such a person is 'out of touch with reality' and his actions have their source in what is only a caricature of spirituality.

I am not suggesting this was the case with Drury's man, Mr D. It is quite possible that his wife did not have the greatness of soul to see that he was in earnest and not merely oblivious of what he was letting himself into. My point is that there is a difference, there are different possibilities.

Does Drury reject this? His position *seems* to be this. Of course there is a difference between sanity and madness, and of course there is a difference between genuine and false spirituality. There are difficulties in making either distinction in a particular case, but a psychiatrist need not be concerned with the spiritual condition of his patient. What is important is that he should treat him or her with respect and never assume that his or her mental condition reflects on his or her spiritual state. For mental illness does not exclude spirituality, and the diagnosis of the former is *independent* of the assessment of the latter.

I am not sure that I have not misrepresented Drury's position in the view that I have just attributed to him. For on this view the diagnosis of a mental illness is a purely *medical* and, therefore, 'objective' matter. And yet there is much in Drury's lecture which *seems* to contradict this view: who is to judge whether Pascal suffered a nervous breakdown on the night of 23 November 1654 or underwent an authentic spiritual experience? 'It is not possible to adopt a detached and purely theoretical attitude in these matters' (see pp. 132–3).

I said '*seems* to contradict'. But does it? The logic of Drury's position may be summarized as follows: mental illness *or* authentic spiritual experience? This question cannot be decided from a detached, theoretical point of view, because the question of the spiritual authenticity of an experience is not a theoretical question. If you had to rule out authentic spirituality before you could establish mental illness then you could not establish mental illness from a detached, theoretical point of view. But you can do so since the two categories are not exclusive.

The question which Drury rejects is: mental illness *or* authentic spiritual experience? He seems confident in his diagnosis of mental illness. Thus, he gave Mr D no treatment not because he judged him to be a saint but because he judged him not to be mentally ill. His answer to the question 'Should I give treatment to this man referred to me as a psychiatrist?' is 'Yes, if he is ill, and no, if he is not'.

Drury is, of course, absolutely right to suggest that 'it is not possible to adopt a detached and purely theoretical attitude in these matters' (p. 133). For the matters he refers to concern the difference between appearance and reality in the realm of the spiritual, between what is an imitation or even a caricature and what is authentic here. And to appreciate that one has to have certain qualities of soul oneself, to have been touched by life, and no amount of psychiatric training can give one that.

But does this not apply equally to the diagnosis of mental illness? It is notorious how much, to anyone immersed in the practicalities of everyday life and busy defending his own corner, great spirituality can take on the aspect of the mad. As Drury himself puts it: 'every religious belief and practice where it is deep and sincere is madness to those who trust in themselves and despise others' (p. 136). If so, can the psychiatrist's pronouncement on this matter be neutral between the conflicting viewpoints? Can there be a medical viewpoint on 'madness' that is above this conflict? Or is the word 'mad' being used differently in such locutions as 'It would be madness to put all your capital in these shares' and 'It is folly to put your trust in man'?

Drury does not say '*seems*', he says it *is* 'madness to those who trust in themselves'. To speak like this is to emphasize the radical, uprooting character of what spiritual religions demand from the believer. It is to emphasize the break between worldliness and spirituality. Thus, if we wish to say that the worldly person is 'deceived' or 'blind' in his judgement of who is 'mad', we are *not* speaking from a standpoint that is neutral between us. As far as *these* judgements are concerned there is no neutral viewpoint and psychiatry had better come to terms with this fact.

There is another point here. You cannot judge or diagnose mental illness as a physician diagnoses physical illness, that is, without regard to the forms of life in which it appears. How can a Western psychiatrist be confident that the state of mind and pattern of conduct of a person from an alien culture is a symptom of mental illness? He does not have the means to make sense of it.

Drury, we have seen, is eager to emphasize that spirituality does not exclude mental illness and that madness itself can be a spiritual experience. On this I wholeheartedly agree. He writes:

> It is a common prejudice . . . that a mental illness is a degradation of the total personality; that is renders the sufferer to some degree subhuman. Thus many people would feel that if Tolstoy really suffered from melancholia his challenge to our whole western way of life would be largely blunted and nullified. And if Joan of Arc was a schizophrenic she could not at the same time be a saint. But these are prejudices. A mental illness may indeed utterly disable the patient for the daily commerce of social life, but the terrifying loneliness of such an experience may make him more aware of the mysteriousness of our present being. (pp. 135–6).

What this says is that a mental illness itself can give the sufferer a spiritual vision that he may not have had without the illness.

But though it *can* do so, it need not. The spirituality of someone who is mentally ill may be perfectly genuine, but it may also be a grotesque caricature of the real thing. In the latter case it is only a form his illness takes, a vehicle for the expression of his illness. He is thus differently related to what is in question, and this, to a large extent, is what makes the difference between genuine spirituality and a false imitation of it.

So there is a distinction to be made here to which a psychiatrist needs to be alert. Drury does not deny this distinction. But though he would agree that a psychiatrist needs to be alert to it in his response to the person he interviews or treats, he does not agree that it is relevant to his diagnosis of mental illness: madness and spirituality are not exclusive categories, they can overlap – 'that distinction we spent so much time looking for was nothing but a will-o'-the-wisp' (p. 136).

I agree with Drury that they may indeed overlap and even coincide in the manner he suggests. Where they do, the diagnosis of mental illness would have to be an independent judgement. Here the question is: what sort of judgement? Drury does not tell us. Why did he treat Father A and not the retired civil servant Mr D? Because the former's physical health was affected and his condition was incapacitating in basic ways: he didn't want to eat, he could not sleep, he seemed to be giving up life, whereas this was not true of Mr D? Would Drury have treated Tolstoy at the time he suffered an 'arrest of life'?

Furthermore, while madness and spirituality may overlap, may not also madness mock and caricature spirituality – as it can mock other things too? When that is so, is not the recognition of the inauthenticity in question also a recognition of the madness?

So, in Drury's view, in the realm of the spiritual, what matters, as far as the psychiatrist is concerned, is whether a person is suffering mentally and whether his physical health has been affected as a result. Where this is the case the psychiatrist's duty is clear: he must relieve the suffering and restore mental health, thus allowing physical health to follow suit. The distinction between the real and the sham in the realm of spirituality is irrelevant to his duty as a psychiatrist. 'A doctor who attempts to shorten and relieve the suffering of the mentally ill in no way diminishes the lesson of madness' (p. 137).

But mental suffering in itself is no sign of madness, or of anything wrong with the person – not even if others in his place would not have suffered. Surely what matters is not that someone is suffering, but how he is suffering and how this suffering affects the rest of his life: how he copes with it. Neither the excess nor the length of his suffering need show an impairment in his 'balance of mind' – even if it finally drives him out of his mind. And if his physical health suffers, he loses his sleep and his appetite, this may be nothing more than the result of the intensity of his suffering.

I return to Drury's rejection of the distinction between madness and spirituality. Supposing a man, say, for example, Raskolnikov in *Crime and Punishment*, were suffering from remorse, the kind that makes a man long for the river or the noose. Is his condition spiritual or medical? To call it 'medical' suggests that there is something *wrong* with him for feeling the way he does. But can this be decided without considering the spiritual content of his condition? Would Drury have given him a course of electro-chemical treatment to remove his suffering were it in his power to do so? Let us consider each answer, 'yes' and 'no'.

If Drury were to remove the man's suffering and hence his remorse, for the two are one and the same, he would have removed at the same time the person's recognition or awareness of the evil that had entered his soul through his action. It could be argued that one can only know evil through direct acquaintance and that remorse is one form of such acquaintance. To remove his remorse, as opposed to giving him a chance to work through it and make amends for what he has done, is to deprive him of the moral growth that this entails.

It is surely a mistake to treat mental and physical pain as if they were logically equivalent. Mental pain, such as anguish or guilt, is a person's response to the significance of what he has done or what has been done to him or to someone near or dear. It may also be a response to what is purely imaginary. But to be impervious to mental pain is to be insensitive to or shut off from a dimension of the significance of human action and intercourse, to the possibilities of good and evil in them. To treat it like physical pain is, therefore, to take lightly that dimension of life.

Consider now the negative answer: 'I would not remove it, since what we have here is the person's response to something real.' Yes, but does this not reopen the question of the distinction between what is real and what is delusory in the sphere of the spiritual? Can a psychiatrist, in all conscience, decide whether or not to treat the person in question by physico-chemical means before deciding what he is suffering from – whether it is a genuine moral or spiritual response, a response to something real?

To return to Tolstoy. The experiences he describes as an 'arrest of life' in *A Confession* lead to a change in his life. The pain and doubts that afflicted him were his response to the way he had lived, seen from a new perspective. For how could he view his life, being what it was, from this new perspective and go on with it as before, with no qualms and no pain? Therefore, if you removed the qualms and doubts that arrested his life, instead of giving him a chance to work through them, he would simply revert to his old life. This is what happened to Father A in consequence of his treatment. He lost his doubts about his faith and work and returned to his previous life. He did not come to a deeper faith.

Certainly, the treatment did not lessen the possibility of Father A learning from what he went through. But there is a difference between learning from one's affliction, from the helplessness to which it reduces one, and learning from the confrontation of oneself in one's doubts and anguish. Tolstoy depicts this kind of learning in the case of Father Sergius in a moving story by that name. There is no suggestion in the story that Father Sergius is in any way mentally ill. Yet supposing he were and that a physico-chemical treatment turned him from the monastery to his previous life in the army, changed him back from Father Sergius to Kazatsky. Would he not have missed out on the lessons Tolstoy depicts him as learning?

I am making two points. The first one is that even here, in this very difficult area of spirituality, there is a difference between madness and sanity, even though there is a large borderline area where the two overlap. Certainly, there is no neutral, theoretical point of view from which the distinction is applied in any particular case. Thus, a psychiatrist to whom Father Sergius' spiritual struggles mean nothing would think that when, in the story, Sergius chops off his finger, and when he later comes to the brink of suicide, 'the balance of his mind must have been disturbed'. He would not appreciate that what is in question has little to do with 'the balance of his mind' and everything with the strength of his temptations and the depth of his convictions. In both of these, and in the way Sergius struggles with the conflict between them, we see the expression of a strong, resourceful and healthy personality.

My second point is that there is a radical difference between physico-chemical methods for treating mental illness and psycho-therapeutic methods that involve making contact with the patient. Mental illness is a serious affliction and I would not speak against its relief by physico-chemical methods of treatment. In any case, the patient may be inaccessible to contact. What I am concerned to point out is that what we have in the two forms of treatment are not two different means to the same end.

Even in the realm of the body there is a difference between curing a toothache by pulling out the tooth and doing so by filling in the cavity that is causing the trouble – though sometimes the dentist has no choice but to pull out the tooth. The cure of mental pain by physico-chemical means is the removal of the person's *awareness* of what he finds painful on account of its particular significance. It is thus a narrowing of consciousness rather than an enlargement of it. But this is a question to which I shall return later.

3

Neurosis and Mental Health

1 NEUROSIS: A NERVOUS ILLNESS?

In the last chapter we considered the notion of mental illness: how are mental illnesses related to physical illnesses? Are they sufficiently like physical illnesses to deserve being called 'illnesses' and to be treated as such? Under the title of 'neurosis' we are concerned with something more common. Indeed, it was Freud who pointed out that the difference between those who are neurotic and those who are not is a difference of degree and not one of kind.

In his *Introductory Lectures on Psycho-analysis* he points out, in general terms, certain similarities between 'neurotic' and what he calls 'healthy' persons: the same facts account for the production of dreams and neurotic symptoms, in both neurotics and healthy persons we find repressions, and both 'have to expend a certain amount of energy to maintain them'. Thus the minds of both 'harbour repressed impulses which are still suffused with energy', and 'a part of the libido is in them also withdrawn from the disposal of the ego' (p. 382). Freud concludes that 'the healthy man too is therefore virtually a neurotic', that 'the difference between nervous health and nervous illness (neurosis) is narrowed down to a practical distinction . . . [namely] how far the person concerned remains capable of a sufficient degree of capacity for enjoyment and active achievement in life. The difference can probably be traced back to the proportion of the energy which has remained free relative to that of the energy which has been bound by repression, i.e. it is a quantitative and not a qualitative difference' (pp. 382 – 3). He adds that 'this view provides a theoretical basis for our conviction that the neuroses are essentially amenable to cure' (p. 383).

He says this because he believes that a cure comes from the mobilization of what is 'healthy' in the neurotic patient, namely the healthy aspects of his ego. In a late (1917) paper, 'Analysis Terminable and Interminable' (1950, vol. v), he returns to this question in sombre mood:

> We know that the essence of the analytic situation is that the analyst enters into an alliance with the ego of the patient to subdue certain uncontrolled parts of the id, i.e. to include them in the synthesis of the ego . . . If we want to make a compact with the patient's ego, the ego must be normal. But such a normal ego is, like normality in general, an ideal fiction. The abnormal ego, which is of no use for our purpose, is unfortunately no fiction. Now every normal person is only approximately normal: his ego resembles that of the psychotic in one point or another, in a greater or lesser degree, and its distance from one end of the scale and proximity to the other may provisionally serve as a measure of what we have indefinitely spoken of as 'modification of the ego'. (p. 337)

These two passages raise more questions than I can discuss at once. The two main questions raised in them that interest me now are: (i) Even if the line between 'mental health' and neurosis is not a sharp one, how is it drawn? (ii) Even if we grant that mental health is an 'ideal fiction', a point on the scale never actually reached, so that those who pass as mentally healthy are all to some extent neurotic, what is Freud claiming about them when he says this? What is it to be neurotic, even if only to some degree? What is a neurosis? I shall take these two questions in the reverse order, leaving the discussion of the first one to the third section of this chapter.

What, then, is a neurosis? In the passage from his *Introductory Lectures* Freud speaks of neurosis as a 'nervous illness'. Here the words 'nerves' and 'nervous' are being used metaphorically. When a person is described as 'nervous' this may mean that he is anxious, jittery, on edge. This has nothing to do with his nerves in the literal, physiological sense. The suggestion is that he is not in control, that he has something to hide and is feeling uneasy, something he is trying to keep under control and is anxious it may get out of hand and, consequently, that he is not quite himself. What are being referred to are the person's emotions and his uneasy relation to himself. Thus he may have bottled up his emotions, his anger for instance, and he may feel at once anxious about being taken over by it and frustrated for not giving vent to it. When such a person does show his anger, it is often strangulated. We get the impression that there is more to it than meets the eye, and that what has roused his anger contains much that comes from him. The significance he sees in it is charged by the 'projection' of his own bad feelings.

The 'symptoms' of 'nervousness' in this sense are such things as cold or shaking hands, a dry throat, a breaking of the voice, stammer, blushing, specifice inhibitions, insomnia. It is as if something in the person, some part of him, is objecting to, feels unhappy about, disapproves of, is dragging its feet over or takes a different view of what he is up to and what he faces. In other words, there is more to what he is up to than he is willing to admit to himself. He is afraid that it will get out of hand and lead him in a direction which he finds unacceptable or, in the opposite case, that it will take over and crush the life out of him. The nervous symptoms in question are thus, in Freud's terminology, expressions of a conflict between the ego and the id in the first case, and between the ego and the super-ego in the second case. What we have here, in its milder varieties, is fairly common.

It is clear that this kind of nervousness concerns the person's division in himself. If the particular situation that faces him makes him 'nervous' or 'anxious', this is because, given the significance he attributes to it, it rouses in him conflicting inclinations. The nervous symptom represents the person's partial yielding to both of these at once, and so Freud characterizes it as a 'compromise formation'. He emphasizes that in such cases what the person is nervous about is not primarily the 'external' situation but *himself* – that part of himself which comes alive in the temptations which the situation puts in his way.

One can, of course, be nervous about the situation that faces one without being apprehensive about oneself. Not to be nervous at all, in certain circumstances, is to have something missing in one. Just as foolhardiness is not the same thing as courage, so, similarly, a lack of nervousness in certain circumstances is not the same thing as having mastered the situation that poses a threat. It is not the expression of strength and self-confidence, but rather a lack of intelligence or sensitivity. Still, the important distinction is between cases where a person's nervousness emanates from a lack of inner certainty and is directed to the possibility of falling apart in himself, and cases where the source of the danger that threatens him lies outside.

In the latter case the particular occasions on which a person becomes nervous will remain unconnected. We would not speak of him as a nervous person. But where nervousness emanates from inner conflict there is an invisible thread that ties together the different situations that make him nervous. For they all touch the same inner conflict in him. His attempt to get away from the anxiety and nervousness that this awakens in him burdens his response to these situations and creates new problems for him. These are 'secondary', neurotic problems, 'problems of his own making' in the sense that he has them not so much because of the situations that face him as because of what he does in the face of what they touch in him. It is not simply that these problems have their source in him, but also that he has them because of what he *does*, this being concerned with keeping things a certain way, maintaining a particular pattern of responses.

It is here that the difference between 'ordinary nervousness' and 'neurosis' is to be found. In the case of a neurosis ordinary situations become problem-ridden. The person can no longer find sustenance in them, no longer respond to them with the pleasure or anger that sustains his self-integrity. It is this that gives a foothold to the notion of illness here: 'illness of the nerves', though I do not find that notion contributes greatly to our understanding. What is in question, whether flagrant or silent, is rooted in the personality and 'accompanies' the person through his life unless he can change in himself and make a break with it.

Sometimes the reverse is the case and we speak of a person having a 'nervous breakdown'. He gives up what keeps him together under the pressure of certain stresses and strains – conflicts with people to whom he is close or on whom he is dependent, inability to get on with them, frustrations and privations, excessive demands on his time and attention, failures, disappointments, guilt and shame. He comes to the limit of whatever it takes for him to carry on in the way he does, he feels he can no longer go on with what he is engaged in. He gives up what holds him together, what keeps him going – going on in the way he does with the diverse activities and relationships in which he has built up the identity by which people recognize him, the identity in which much of his inner security is rooted.

So under pressure that he can no longer take he 'opts out' instead of changing. He washes his hands of the responsibilities of life as an adult: having to strive, to be patient, to care, to put himself out, to consider, to put up with what is disagreeable, to have to answer for what he does. He 'regresses' to a childish, dependent mode of behaviour.

What is this a 'breakdown' in? One could say that it is a breakdown in the person's 'adult personality', in 'what holds him together', so that he can no longer act in a way that takes account of his interests and concerns and of all that needs negotiating in the pursuit of his objectives – means to be utilized, obstacles to be surmounted or circumvented. It takes a certain 'integrity' or 'cohesion of self' to act responsibly, to avoid precipitousness, to take stock of things, to endure uncertainty, to tolerate what one finds painful.

Where what holds a person together is primarily 'defensive' then to that degree his identity will be 'false'. In such a case the pressures which will have led to his nervous breakdown will, in the main, be 'internal': the increasing price he has to pay in terms of a loss of sense and satisfaction in order to maintain this false self or identity for the sake of inner security. In such a case his nervous breakdown is at the same time a 'breaking out'. It is true that he has lost a relatively coherent manner of acting and he can no longer manage to 'get on' in the adult world where he has established an identity commensurate with his age. But since his manner of acting has been an 'act', the 'cover up' of a somewhat fragmented, immature and insecure self, it could be said that what has 'broken out' is just such a self. On the other hand, this 'breaking out' can be seen in a more positive light, as the expression of an impulse towards something more genuine: what was blocking the way to a development towards greater authenticity has been given up. Still, for this to constitute a 'break through' much work will have to be done.

But why is a breakdown in what holds a person together a 'nervous' breakdown? Because it involves a failure of 'nerve'. Given the psychological pressures to which he is subjected, internal or external, he can no longer cope with the situation from which these pressures emanate. Such pressures, as I have mentioned, exacerbate his 'nervousness' to breaking point. Were he more collected, with less to hide or avoid coming in contact with, less burdened with defensive measures he must keep up, more reconciled to himself, the pressures on him would not have been as great. At any rate, he would have a greater capacity to withstand them, to carry on under pressure.

This does not mean that he would go on putting up with what he finds intolerable, but that he would not run away from it. He would rise up to it, put himself into the equation and attempt to negotiate a change in the circumstances. In contrast, the person who has a breakdown is one who is panicked into beating a hasty retreat. He jettisons or abandons what he considers valuable, he sacrifices his needs. In his 'nervousness' he loses sight of their importance. He fails to remain collected, to look for a way of keeping what is important to him. Part of the reason for his failure to do so is that underneath he is divided in himself and so ambivalent towards what he regards as important.

We see that what Freud calls a neurosis has two faces: (i) the face it takes when a person builds defences against his 'nervousness' with the aim of accomodating it in the life he wants to lead, or of reconciling that life to his 'nervousness', and (ii) the face it takes when he fails to do so, when he can no longer maintain these defences and carry on with the life they are aimed at facilitating for him. A psycho-analysis which aims at 'making the unconscious conscious' by enabling the patient to dispense with his defences may bring about just such a breakdown in the course of the analysis: 'transference neurosis'. Here the patient's hidden neurosis becomes manifest and amenable to analysis. It is acted out within the setting of the analysis, in response to its demands, opportunities and frustrations, real and imaginary. This is the form in which it becomes manifest even if the patient has to go back in time, that is, regress, in order to find it. What he finds, and hopefully works through, is all that his particular 'nervousness' comprises, all that he had built up defences in his adult life to protect himself from. Finding it is reliving it, letting it once more become the person he is.

Seeing this face of one's neurosis, its inner core, living or reliving it, can be a harrowing experience. It has its own momentum, and while it is in full swing it absorbs a person, leaving him unable to take much interest in what is going on around him, except in so far as it reflects his inner turmoil and so merges into what he is going through. Working through it is living it out so that one can move away from it.

A neurosis, we see, is marked by an impairment of a person's autonomy. While this is more severe in the case of a mental illness, one difference between the two on which Freud remarked is that while a person's powers of judgement and reasoning are affected in a mental illness, they remain intact in a neurosis. Indeed, a neurosis is not a *mental* illness in this sense.

In a psychosis, Freud said, the person is 'torn away from reality';

in a neurosis he is torn away from himself – 'Neurosis and Psychosis' (1950, vol. ii). In other words, the psychotic is alienated from and out of touch with reality – what counts as reality in the culture to which he belongs. He lives in a different world, a world of his own. A neurotic, on the other hand, is out of touch with himself, a self from which he has turned away, left behind, and allowed to remain stunted and immature: the ego is in conflict with the id or the super-ego. Freud, therefore, sees the task of psycho-analytic therapy as bringing the neurotic patient in touch with those parts of himself which he finds unacceptable so that he can resolve his inner conflicts, allow himself to grow and to learn in the process.

2   NEUROSIS AND PERSONALITY

Human beings are vulnerable to a great deal of what human life itself throws in their way. They are often thrown off balance by what they meet and have to call on their inner resources to pull themselves together. How they meet such a situation and what kind of balance they return to affects, positively or negatively, their capacity to participate in the activities that make up their life, to contribute to these and to find fulfilment in doing so. The range and nature of their vulnerabilities depend on what has gone on before in their lives as well as on certain innate capacities and predispositions – intelligence and sensitivity for instance. How they respond to what touches their particular vulnerability depends on what they have met in their lives and what they have made of themselves in their response to it. Our paths and our options are largely determined by the earlier turnings we have taken, some of these leaving us with a wider range of options than others.

If, for instance, our earlier experiences leave us anxious to avoid pain, perhaps because we have been unable to overcome certain hurts, unable to do so in turn because we have not been given love and support when we needed it most, in our childhood, then we may wish to avoid such pain and invest in certain safeguards that clutter up our life and hamper our enjoyment of it. Or again if, for instance, certain privations in early life leave us with clamouring needs, the urgency with which to seek their satisfaction may destroy our very opportunity to do so in our present life. Again, our sense of inferiority, which gives us the need to keep up certain appearances, may hamper our spontaneity and openness to experience. What we miss out as a result may leave us dissatisfied with our life in a way that increases our sense of inferiority. Or again, what has left us with the need to settle old scores that keep reappearing in the current situations of our life may leave us unable to take an interest in much that life has to offer us. Engrossed in fighting these old battles life may pass us by leaving us empty-handed.

The patterns in question are very various and much more intricate than I have managed to suggest. I have stressed the negative aspect of the patterns through which our personality comes into being and our character emerges since our interest here centres round the notion of neurosis. Freud has made us aware of the extent to which these patterns stretch back into the past, indeed into our childhood and even infancy, and the combined role of our activity and passivity, of intention and chance, in their formation. What we thus play a part in the formation of is at once a ladder that gives us access to new experiences and a spider's web in which we get caught. In so far as it is the latter, the more we struggle the more we entangle ourselves in it. Karen Horney has spoken of this as the vicious circles of neuroses (1937). To get free we have to undo the whole structure, going from one knot of the web to an earlier one that holds it in place.

What has thus been constructed is a structure of a person's personality. Under one aspect he feels at one with it; it is his perspective on the world, that in terms of which he lives his life and experiences the bitter and the sweet in it. Under another aspect it takes on a partially instrumental character, and though it furthers schemes that are his it hampers his spontaneity and contact with life. This is the neurotic aspect of a person's personality. It may simply constitute part of his character, or take on the appearance of something to which he succumbs or against which he struggles.

When I spoke of the instrumental character of this aspect of the personality I was referring to the *defensive* aspect of a neurosis. The defence is against the pain, distress and discomfort of experiences which the person cannot assimilate. He cannot assimilate them because of their originally *traumatic* character or because he lacks the toughness to do so. He may be more easily shaken, more sensitive to humiliation. As a result, like upaid debts or unsettled scores, they don't let go of him, or he won't let go of them. They survive in the unconscious, they continue to haunt him down the years and become the nucleus around which the defensive structure of the neurosis is built. While this nucleus provides the ultimate rationale of the defensive structure, the defensive structure itself becomes a protection of this nucleus, helping to support and keep it going. They are 'dynamically' interdependent.

These, then, are the two aspects of a neurosis, its inner aspect, which embodies painful conflicts that divide a person in himself and incapacitate him, and its outer aspect, in which a person attempts to ward off the pain, compensate for the incapacity and contain the damage. However, these attempts create new problems for him in his dealings with his environment, of which other people constitute the most prominent aspect, and these problems in turn, given his particular personality, drive him to take new measures. These layers of measures, together with the fragmented, vulnerable self they aim to protect and thus keep alive, constitute a neurosis. Yet what is in question is none other than the person himself, the form and structure of his personality. When aspects of the conflicts contained break through the defensive measures we have what Freud calls 'neurotic symptoms'.

Despite the painful and incapacitating character of neurosis I do not myself feel any great pull towards calling it an illness. I believe that it was largely an historical accident that led Freud to think of it as such, namely the fact that the symptoms of the hysterical patients to which he first attended were *imitations* of genuine medical conditions.

3 PROBLEMS OF LIFE AND NEUROTIC DIFFICULTIES

Freud, we have seen, speaks of mental health as an 'ideal fiction'.[1] 'Every normal person is only approximately normal' (1950, vol. v, p. 337). In his *Introductory Lectures* he expresses this more strongly: 'the healthy man too is virtually a neurotic' (1949b, p. 382).

I would expand the thought behind this statement as follows. However good our parents may have been to us in our early childhood when we particularly needed their attention, affection and care, none of us could have escaped some occasion on which they failed us. Besides, no human being and no child is free from some

---

[1] Although Freud uses the term 'normality' he does not mean it in the statistical sense of 'average'. How could that be an 'ideal fiction'?

degree of selfishness, greed and anger, and none could have avoided some envy and jealousy in his relations to his parents and siblings. Human development is not problem-free and involves wrestling with problems. Each of us fails in some respect and to some extent in this struggle. Development towards greater autonomy inevitably involves some struggle. None of us moves from one stage of our development to the next without collecting some psychological handicap. We, therefore, face the problems of the next stage with some disadvantage and go on acquiring further handicaps.

Human personality is an attainment, something that we acquire through a continuous process of formation. The degree of unity and wholeness it comes to possess is an achievement. It is not something from which the neurotic person falls away, but something towards which each of us has to move. Inner conflicts which no one can escape have to be resolved to achieve such wholeness.

We are all, therefore, in the same boat and progressing along the same path. Some of us make further progress, move a little further along: that is all. While a lot can be achieved that many fail, in some degree, to achieve, irreconcilable pulls remain to pose some threat even to those who have achieved most by way of wholeness.

A neurosis, then, unlike a physical illness, is not something which some people catch or fall prey to, while those who are lucky manage to avoid altogether. Indeed, what I earlier called 'the inner core of a neurosis' is something which we all have to work our way out of in the course of our emotional development ('infantile neurosis'), and none of us succeeds in doing so completely.

This is certainly what Freud would have said and it is certainly why he says that we are all to some extent neurotic. This claim received confirmation in Freud's experience of people and, of course, of himself too – as it would for any of us who have their eyes open. For people who seem paragons of stability and maturity very often turn out to be flawed in these respects when we can see them from closer quarters, in the cut and thrust of personal intimacy. We appreciate this as we come into contact with aspects they have not exhibited to us before.

Someone may agree that we all have some 'neurotic' problems or difficulties but add that this does not make us all neurotic. In his little book *De la Psychothérapie* Karl Jaspers speaks like this: 'Some neurotic phenomena may appear among normal people . . . This does not mean that everyone is a little neurotic, but that such phenomena, isolated and transitory, may be produced in healthy soil' (1956, p. 50 – translation mine). But does this amount to anything more than a difference of emphasis?

Obviously the term 'neurotic' depends for its sense on its having an antithesis: a person is 'neurotic' in so far as he lacks 'mental health', and 'mentally healthy' in so far as he is not 'neurotic'. But it does not follow from this that we cannot all be neurotic – to some extent. The term 'mentally healthy' must have an application, certainly, but it would have an application if some people could be said to be mentally healthy to some degree. This precisely is what Freud is saying: the most mentally healthy of us is healthy only up to a certain degree, and so we are all to some extent neurotic. Mental health is an 'ideal fiction'.

Jaspers seems to reject this: mental health is perfectly well realizable and is realized in particular cases. The fact that a person reacts or behaves in a neurotic way on isolated occasions doesn't make him neurotic. It does not mean that such a person is mentally healthy only to a certain degree.

I don't think that the difference between Freud and Jaspers is merely one of emphasis; there is a difference in conception. For Freud is saying that even when the neurotic reaction is transitory and confined to isolated occasions it is not without significance. It is indicative of certain inner conflicts that are normally fairly well contained, weak spots in the personality which in the normal course of events in the person's life cause no trouble. You can call such a person 'mentally healthy', but you must not delude yourself into thinking that he has nothing in common with the person you call 'neurotic'.

Jaspers could reply that if it is just this sort of person we describe as mentally healthy, then this is surely what the word does mean. It is confusing to say that even he leaves something to be desired. What is it that he could have had but lacks? Is it not misleading to imply that he lacks something?

Someone may say that part of Freud's point is that you can only talk of 'neurosis' and 'mental health' in degrees – like 'hot' and 'cold'. Something that is hot is to that extent not cold, but it can always, inevitably, be hotter. There is nothing that is so hot that it cannot be made hotter. That is what anything that is hot lacks: a greater degree of heat. Similarly, that is what anyone we correctly describe as 'mentally healthy' lacks: a greater degree of mental health.

One could reply, however, that there are certain limits beyond which the greater degree of mental health that it seems any person could logically be able to have turns his mental health on its head. These are themselves logical limits specific to what we mean by the term. Freud, one could say, is warning us against the idea of such 'perfect mental health'. A person possessing it is imagined as impregnable to all psychological pressure or hurt. He is thought of as possessing such inner unity as would not crack up under any circumstances, so that he is radically different from 'the neurotic'. It is such 'perfect health' which Freud describes as 'ideal fiction', for in imagining it we exaggerate certain tendencies in our ways of thinking about mental health, indeed about all human goods, until the notion is turned into a self-contradiction.

John Wisdom brought this out in connection with our concept of goodness: 'No man is good – not even St Francis.' Or, to put it in the Freudian idiom: 'Goodness is an ideal fiction.' One who says this 'may be using the word "good" so that nothing which has an evil desire is good and nothing which doesn't overcome an evil desire is good. And then plainly nothing could be good.' One who says this, Wisdom continues, 'speaks misleadingly'. 'But this doesn't make what he says meaningless. For in his caricature of our idea of goodness he has brought out the conflicting elements in that idea by accentuating them until the hidden conflict becomes a contradiction and sweet perfection wears a foolish smile' (1952, pp. 257 – 8).

What are the conflicting temptations to which Freud's use of the term 'mental health' is vulnerable? Well, on the one hand, Freud is himself tempted to think that no one who has any vestige of inner conflict, however unconscious, can be said to be in perfect mental health. On the other hand, he wishes to say that mental health is something we attain by resolving our inner conflicts. However, he also holds that nothing in the mind is ever completely erased: 'every earlier stage of development persists alongside the later stage which has developed from it . . . the primitive mind is, in the fullest meaning of the word, imperishable' (1950, vol. iv, p. 301).

Each of these temptations comes in part from the perception of something important.[2] Yet try to bring together the pull which each represents and you cannot move: they leave no logical room for the application of the word 'mental health'. So when Freud says that

---

[2] I have discussed what there is in Freud's view that 'the primitive mind is imperishable' in Dilman, 1983, chapter 4.

mental health is an 'ideal fiction' he is to some extent giving in to such pulls and identifying the notion of mental health he uses and wishes to keep with the notion of 'perfect mental health' which he warns us against and, rightly, wishes to reject. So when he says that we are all virtually neurotic and that the most healthy among us is only approximately healthy, his words contain some confusion. We should not, however, let this obscure from us the penetration to which they give expression. It is this which I have been concerned to bring out.

In *An Autobiographical Study* Freud agrees with Jung that 'neuroses have no peculiar content which belongs exclusively to them but that neurotics break down at the same difficulties that are successfully overcome by normal people'. He then adds that this is at one with his conception of depth-psychology as 'the psychology of the normal mind': 'Our path had been like that of chemistry: the great qualitative differences between substances were traced back to quantitative variations in the proportions in which the same elements were combined' (1948, p. 102). Freud is here making the point that the workings of the minds of 'neurotic' and 'mentally healthy' people are commensurable and their responses to the situations that face them are to be understood in the same terms. Although he thinks that this step in the development of his thought follows a pattern familiar in the sciences, it is a step which takes abnormal psychology out of the sphere of medicine, which is an applied science. Clearly, what Freud is saying provides a refutation of those who claim that his explanations of 'abnormal behaviour' are radically different in character from our everyday explanations of ordinary purposive behaviour (see Peters, 1958). They are not.

The idea that 'neurotics break down at the same difficulties that are successfully overcome by normal people' is important and brings to a head the problem of understanding the contrast marked by the words 'neurotic' and 'mentally healthy'. In a perceptive book that owes much to Freud's ideas on this subject, entitled *The Mind Alive*, Harry and Bonaro Overstreet express this same idea as follows: 'He [the neurotic] does not belong to a race apart. He is simply a human being that has exaggeratedly failed to resolve certain key emotional problems that every human being wrestles with and that no one ever resolves completely' (1954, p. 89).

We have already seen the sense in which Freud denies that the neurotic 'belongs to a race apart'. He is not someone visited by something from outside – a disease that he contracts. He does not suffer from a condition that sets him apart – such as leprosy or tuberculosis. He is not subject to external causes – a virus, toxic substance or radiation – with effects that interfere with the normal course of his life. Where, for instance, a person has been subjected to excessive radiation, the resulting degeneration of cells in that locality, the pain and other effects constitute the 'peculiar content which belongs exclusively' to the disease he contracts, namely cancer. In contrast, the neurotic's worries, doubts, distress, feelings of guilt, his inhibitions, compulsions, obsessions, sense of isolation, are all part of the texture of human life with which we are familiar at first hand.

Still, there is a problem about the claim that neurotics break down at *the same difficulties* that every human being encounters in his life – 'problems of life'. This is partly true and partly not. Certainly, what they find difficult to manage can present difficulties for most people, and certainly, what they find difficult to take or recover from are things that hurt everyone: the disappointments of life, loss and rejection, the inconsiderateness of others, their treachery and cruelty, temptations and frustrations, failures and more. But in the case of those who are neurotic these things assume an additional significance in that they touch old sores, reactivate unresolved conflicts, revive past feuds, stir up dormant fears and anxieties. Indeed, this is in part what makes Freud talk of them as neurotic. Besides, in allowing themselves to be driven by their anxiety to take defensive measures and evasive action, neurotics complicate their own lives and often create new problems for themselves – problems which they would not have had but for their neurosis. They find problems where most other people find none. Or, at any rate, they have additional problems to contend with.

So, yes, what they encounter in themselves by way of weakness, pain, inadequacy, anger and resentment, and suffer on that account, is nothing with which any human being is unfamiliar in his life. Yet what they see in the situations to which they respond in these ways is determined to a larger extent by the way they feel in themselves, independently of these situations, than in the case of those who are less neurotic. For instance, a neurotic person of a certain kind may see a snub in an innocent remark. But even where the remark is not innocent, the offence he takes, while outwardly the kind that is appropriate to a snub, may have a dramatic quality which reflects the precariousness of his own esteem of himself. So what he encounters here is not the same as that encountered by someone who has a greater acceptance of himself when he is similarly snubbed. The neurotic and he are not faced with the same difficulty.

Of course, there is an overlap and the differences beyond that are differences of degree. *Any* human response to a particular situation involves an appraisal of the situation plus one's own individual affective orientation, that is, what a situation of the significance appraised means to the individual personally. But here there is an important distinction to be made. What the situation means to the individual personally may be largely an expression of his commitments, loyalties and convictions, or it may be largely determined by his weaknesses, vulnerabilities and defences. It is in the latter case that Freud speaks of 'neurotic difficulties' and 'neurotic responses'.

The distinction is not easy to characterize in general terms, nor always easy to apply in particular cases. For instance, one may be inclined to say that a neurotic reaction is 'exaggerated', 'excessive', 'over the top'. But do we have any yardstick for determining what is 'appropriate' or 'normal' on which everyone agrees? Someone's reaction may strike me as exaggerated because I fail to see what he sees in the situation to which it is a response. Or it may seem exaggerated by comparison to what I take to be the 'normal' response because he has greater sensitivity, a deeper perception than the average person. This may indeed be the reason why life is more complicated and problematic for him; not any inner instability or excessive touchiness. Certainly, this is not something on which one can form an opinion until one comes to know the person. But unless one has his sensibility and imagination one will be in danger of misjudging him.

Take, for example, the person who is unable to get over a broken heart. There is, of couse, nothing neurotic about a broken heart itself, about the vulnerability for which it is an expression. A person who is immune to it could hardly undergo the experience of love. A lack of vulnerability, as I have already pointed out, is not necessarily a sign of inner strength or an expression of mental health. It may be a sign of coarseness and insensitivity or, alternatively, of a very raw spot in the person over which he has developed a thick skin to hide and protect it. Getting over a broken heart quickly means that the person's feelings did not go deep. On the other hand, where the grieving 'drags on' there will be more to the person's experience than what makes us speak of a broken heart.

The question is: has he been hit so badly because of what the beloved who has deserted him had come to mean to him in the depth of his love for her and in terms of the extent to which he had given himself to her? Or is it because of the significance she had come to assume for him in meeting his needs, in playing a part in holding him together? In the latter case what he calls a 'broken heart' is a loss of inner cohesion, a loss of self.

Here the devastation goes beyond the desertion he has suffered. That has reopened an old wound which had never healed properly. It is this old wound from which he is finding it difficult to recover. His problem, therefore, is not simply that of getting over a broken heart. It is the long-standing problem of finding a separate identity so as to be able to accept the dependency of love without so losing himself in it that when the love is lost he is lost too. Only when he has been able to establish such a separate identity can he have the shattering experience of losing the love of the person he loves without being shattered in himself.

His long-standing problem is thus one of the 'key emotional problems' that every human being meets in the course of his development. But, given the extent to which he has failed to resolve it, it persists in his present life to spoil or impoverish his relationships. This is what makes his problem 'neurotic'. In so far as it conditions his response to eventualities that arise in his current relationships his response and conduct may be characterized as 'neurotic'. That is how Freud used the term.

For him a 'neurotic' person was one who had been unable to solve the emotional problems of his early childhood, had evaded doing so to a greater degree than others, so that they persisted in his present life, together with his evasions, to complicate and mar it. What persists in this way, however, is not a remnant of past years, but the person who lived them, and who is continuing to do so, taking evasive and defensive measures in the present. Each person is, according to Freud, 'neurotic' in this sense to a certain degree. For what makes him so, unlike an illness, is not something he can escape if he is fortunate. What he does escape, if he is fortunate, is a childhood with additional burdens – neurotic, even severely disturbed, parents, a weak constitution, debilitating conditions, or more than his fair share of physical illnesses, traumatic chance circumstances. But, otherwise, as we have seen, Freud thought of the individual's development through childhood and human life as inherently problematic and he did not believe that most of these problems have a 'complete' or 'final' solution. Some people come to terms with them 'better' than others – 'better' meaning that what they do to reach an accommodation is not at the expense of their autonomy and authenticity, present or future – and some attempt to evade doing so. That is all.

4 MENTAL HEALTH AND MORAL STRENGTH

We have seen the difficulty in drawing a line between neurosis and mental health, between what is neurotic and what is not – 'neurotic and ordinary unhappiness', 'neurotic and normal responses and behaviour', 'neurotic difficulties and problems of life and of growing up'. Everything that one can say in general can be turned on its heads and needs to be balanced – as is the case with much else that can be said in psychology. Further, it is not a matter of indifference who draws the line. One could say that the sensitive and the coarse, the imaginative and the shallow do not live in quite the same world, and we are not touched by the same things. Therefore, to the shallow person the highly sensitive man's problems may appear 'neurotic', or 'of his own making'.

But sensitivity may fade into over-sensitivity, indeed into a 'nervous disposition' – thus Proust's narrator Marcel, for instance. Where does the one end and the other begin? Where, for instance, does having high standards and being critical turn into being over-critical, a healthy scepticism into an inability to believe, trust or accept? At what point does conscientiousness turn into over-conscientiousness and an obsessive scrupulosity, a healthy independence into a destructive rebelliousness, politeness into a reactive over-politeness, meekness into an inability to stand up for what one believes in, toughness into invulnerability, mourning into melancholia?

There is no sharp line and no general answer. One has to use judgement and imagination in particular cases. One has to know the person before one can exercise one's judgement; and the kinds of consideration that guide one here can only be illustrated with reference to such cases. And, as I said before, we should not expect to find any large concensus of opinion. For, as Wittgenstein has pointed out, 'there are those whose judgement is "worse", and the difference is not one to be bridged by an expertise one could acquire through formal training (1963, p. 227).

Freud was aware of these difficulties and I think it was his recognition of them that made him impatient when in the passage I quoted from his *Introductory Lectures* he said: 'The difference between nervous health and nervous illness (neurosis) is narrowed down therefore to a practical distinction, and is determined by the practical result – how far the person concerned remains capable of a sufficient degree of capacity for enjoyment and active achievement in life' (p. 382). But these criteria raise the same difficulties as I mentioned before: where does enjoyment of life turn into a merry-go-round of 'good times'?[3] May not both the pursuit and attainment of pleasure as well as that of success in the hedonist and the 'workoholic' themselves by expressions of a neurosis? I am, of course, distorting Freud's intention, caricaturing his words. But my point is that his words themselves are no guarantee against such falsification of meaning.

So I want to carry the discussion of the previous section a little further by asking the question I raised there from the other side: what did Freud have in mind when he spoke of 'mental health'? We saw that he characterized it as an 'ideal fiction' and meant to warn us, in our attempt to give content to the concept, against the tendency to take it to an extreme where it destroys itself. My question then is: what did Freud have in mind when he spoke of the kind of 'mental health' he hoped could be attained by his patients under favourable conditions?

Most psycho-analysts would agree that a person who can be described as 'mentally healthy' in this sense is one who has had a 'good enough' environment in his childhood, 'good enough'[4] parents, to have been able to 'work through' his inner conflicts. He is thus a person whose development has taken place relatively unhampered and thus has not been arrested. Consequently, his give and take with the environment in which he has developed – personal and cultural – will not have been obstructed. He will have learned from these transactions and managed to make his own ('integrate') what he has received. The values he has received will be the source of genuine convictions; when he is loved he will feel loved for himself – he will not have doubts on this score. Similarly, as regards, the praise, regard and gratitude he may be the object of on different

---

[3] I have criticized Freud's 'hedonism' elsewhere, although I do not believe it represents an aspect of his serious thought. See Dilman, 1983, chapter 6, section 1.
[4] This expression is one of W. D. Winnicott's choice.

occasions in the course of his life. As for blame, he will take responsibility for what he is being blamed for if he believes he has done wrong.

He is thus relatively at one with himself and able to find sustenance in his environment. He has the ability to trust it, to trust those others who are part of that environment. He will not burden it with projections, reading his own state of mind and inclinations into it, or idealize it in order to tame and control it. He will not be ready to blame it when things go wrong, or make it into a scapegoat for his own failures.

A person who has 'mental health' is thus one who has the kind of inner unity that gives him a stability which incorporates flexibility, openness and spontaneity; the ability to contain anxiety, tolerate disappointment, surmount grief and trust others; dependability in commitment, the courage to stand up and be counted, to defend what he believes in, and stick up for those to whom he has given his loyalty.

We are talking of a form of inner strength and resiliance. Such a person will not easily 'crack up' or 'cave in'. Yet he will be capable of 'bending', making concessions, adapting to change. His strength is that of conviction rather than rigidity, commitment rather than defence. Such a person is not afraid that if he makes concessions he will not have a leg to stand on. He will not need to resist giving in or bending where no principles are at stake. On the other hand, where his principles and loyalties are concerned, he will not be afraid to stand firm lest he lose other people's support or attract their anger and disfavour.

He is in active transaction with his environment and so open to experience, learning from it and growing in the process. He does not meet or negotiate with this environment from fixed positions established as barricades. His energies are not taken up by the defence of such positions, or by having to keep at bay what these positions aim to contain. Here it is important to distinguish between convictions genuinely held and positions defensively maintained: the former give a person life, the latter drain him of life.

It may be curious that mental health, under the aspect in which we are considering it, is realized in qualities of character that include some which many of us regard as virtues – such qualities as dependability, integrity, courage, responsibility and independence. This is no accident, for these are expressions of 'strength' and 'solidity'. As I have pointed out elsewhere (Dilman, 1983, chapter 8, section 3), these are not 'partisan values' and, indeed, are compatible with different systems of value. One could call them 'formal values' in that they take different contents in different cultures and moralities.

Thus, a person who possesses mental health is not necessarily a good man. But if he lacked mental health his relation to the values in which he believes would be disturbed – just as his relations are to the people for whom he cares. One interesting question is whether a person could be wicked and amoral, that is, without any moral convictions, and at the same time be a person we could characterize as 'mentally healthy'.

In an earlier book (Dilman, 1979), I argued that Archelaus, the Macedonian tyrant whom Plato represents as such a wicked man, was not a man divided in himself, that he was fully behind his wicked deeds. He was thoroughly selfish and completely ruthless, and though he may have lacked something without which human life would be much poorer in most people's estimate, he did not care for what he thus missed and enjoyed what he had. What I did not think through then was what such a man would be lacking in so far as he is thoroughly indifferent to any moral values and cares for nothing outside himself.

No doubt Archelaus enjoyed accumulating wealth and exercising power. No doubt his exploits and successes gave him a sense of satisfaction with himself. No doubt conquering difficulties, sweeping obstacles out of his way gave him a sense of exhilaration and quickened his life in the different activities in which he exercised his intelligence, prowess and power. Is this not a 'full life', one form of full life at any rate, and can the person who lives his life to the full and according to his own lights be said to lack mental health? However treacherous he may have been to others, was not Archelaus to his own self true?

These are difficult questions to answer in the affirmative. It is important not to confuse Archelaus's case with that of Callicles, also in the *Gorgias*, who is represented as a man of courage, prepared to put his own life on the line for what he believed, however outrageous *we* may find his beliefs. He certainly cared for a certain kind of life and, however contemptuous he may have been of most men whom he regarded as 'riff-raff', he was capable of admiring and associating with those few whom he regarded as 'real men'. But what pleasure could a man like Archelaus find in the company of other men? Would he, for instance, be able to share with them the challenge of a difficult task that they were helping him to meet? If all he was interested in was what he could get out of it for himself, then the others helping him would be perceived and treated by him as mere instruments. He would not feel any gratitude for their help; he would not see it as help, since he would not see it as freely given. For him there would be no possibility of co-operation, or give and take, of sharing anything with anyone. Indeed, such a person's conception of others would be seriously defective.

Here I wonder whether his greed and thirst for power is not a consequence of his inability to see in others something to which he could respond positively and find sustenance in? How can a man who is unable or unwilling – the two come to the same thing here – to relate to others in a fully human way be considered to have had an unimpeded development? Archelaus may not have been divided in himself, but his wholeness does not seem to have the fullness we have been considering. The power he sought, attained and enjoyed may not have been a crutch, or even compensation, but I think it filled a void in him left by his indifference to love and his inability to care for others.

Most psycho-analysts would agree that what a person comes to be like in himself is something he reaches in the course of transactions with his environment, of which give and take with other people is the most important aspect. Indeed, and this is a logical point, what he comes to be like in himself cannot be separated from the kinds of relationship he has come to be capable of forming. They reflect what he is like in himself, and conversely what he is like in himself makes possible the kinds of relationship he establishes.

Now, could a man whose relationships are based on using and subjugating other people, one who is incapable of caring for them, have within him anything that would sustain him in failure and adversity? I think the answer is yes. The objective or purpose which his insatiable greed gives him is, in his case, what holds him together and would do so in adversity – remembering that adversity in his case amounts to little more than failure and the frustration of his selfish ambitions.

My question was: can a thoroughly wicked and amoral person, a rascal on whom it is impossible to count, and one who in turn trusts no one, be described as 'mentally healthy'? The answer towards which I have moved is that we would not describe him as lacking mental health, but as being a *psychopath*. Here I would contrast a psychopath with a neurotic person. We have seen the fragility of a neurotic in himself. A psychopath, in contrast, is tough and elusive. He is not vulnerable, and what strength and courage he has comes from his having little at stake, few personal investments. By all accounts Archelaus must have been a clever and successful psychopath.

Psychopathy is a deficiency that results in a person missing certain stages of emotional and moral development altogether. The psychopath is related to the neurotic as the idiot is related to the psychotic. Just as the idiot is not 'mentally ill', so equally the psychopath is not 'neurotic'. What he 'suffers' is a lack of 'nerves' or 'nervousness'.

What I said about mental health earlier raised the question of the connection between mental health and moral goodness. I said that a person who possesses mental health is not necessarily a good man. Indeed, under extreme conditions 'mentally healthy' people may be driven to evil and serious crime. Wickedness is not the prerogative of the 'unbalanced'. But in a mentally healthy person judgement, conscience and regard to self-interest often shape, channel, even restrain, and sometimes transform the evil that is in him in the form of greed, envy, thirst for power, desire for revenge, etc. This is what is lacking in a psychopath. In a neurotic, in contrast, these are not lacking, but conscience, for instance, is exaggerated and distorted by the anger and hatred it has come to embody. That is, it has itself fallen into the service of evil. It is precisely in such cases that Freud talks of a 'harsh super-ego' which a weak ego appeases (see Dilman, 1983, chapter 5, section 2; 1984a, chapter 11).

Physical health, we have seen, involves some 'integrity' of body which gives it the ability to ward off illness, withstand infection, assist the healing of injuries and find sustenance in what satisfies the needs of the body and contributes to its welfare – food, fresh air, exercise. The notion involves some reference to the person's welfare. Similarly mental health, if only by analogy, involves some 'integrity' of the person, which gives him the capacity to withstand psychological stress, to surmount adversity and to get over hurt and injury to the self.

Mental health, we have seen, has more than one pole. Sanity is one pole, the loss of which appears in the form of the different psychoses or mental illnesses. 'Personal autonomy' or 'strength of the ego' (Freud's term) is the nearest I can get to naming that pole of mental health we have considered in this section. Its loss appears in the form of different forms of neurosis. I have expressed some reservation about characterizing what this loss amounts to as an 'illness'.

I have a further reservation. Given the distance Freud travelled from his original conception of neurosis and the greatly increased variety since the early days of his practice among those who seek psycho-analytic help, I doubt whether the term 'neurotic' has much sense left to it as a term of classification. Neuroses are real enough and the term has sense as an instrument for concentrating our mind on a dimension of people's lives. It gives a new aspect to people's problems and difficulties, the one which psycho-analysts bring and keep in focus in the course of the therapies they conduct. But beyond this, in Freud's own view, the term cannot be used as a classificatory label for people to mark a diagnostic category. For if 'we are all virtually neurotic' from whom would the term sort out those to whom it is applied? Its use as such a label is, therefore, invidious, giving the impression that the person to whom it is applied belongs to a minority marked by some weakness or blemish.

It is true that the term 'neurotic' as applied to patterns of conduct does have the power to distinguish one kind of behaviour or response from another. But what it says about it is so general that if this is all we can say about the kind of conduct distinguished we have said very little. However, we can say more and Freud certainly did have a great deal more to say. So, to repeat, if taken seriously the term has the power to concentrate the mind on a dimension of the conduct to which it is applied and thus to enable those who have a developed sense or perception to say much that enriches our apprehension of it.

It is here that the value of the term lies and its meaning is bound up with the corpus of Freud's ideas regarding the child's early relations within the family, his individual development, divisions within the personality and the unconscious.

4

Neurosis: its Causation
and Non-causal Treatment
– Evolution of Freud's Ideas

1 HYSTERIA: A PSYCHOGENIC ILLNESS

Freud once referred to the Cartesian identification of mind with consciousness as 'the first shibboleth of psycho-analysis' (1949d, p. 10), and he argued that there is nothing unintelligible or self-contradictory in the notion of an unconscious mind. It is the Cartesian notion of the mind that needs rejecting (see Dilman, 1984a, chapter 4, sections 1 and 2).

He likewise argued that if we are inclined to reject the idea of infantile sexuality this is because of a common prejudice which makes 'the function of reproduction the kernel of sexuality' (1949b, p. 255). This notion of sexuality needs to be extended 'so as to include the sexual life of perverted persons and also of children'. In so doing, however, he argued, 'we have restored to it its true breadth of meaning' (p. 268). 'I do not consider that these extensions are innovations but rather restorations: they signify the removal of inexpedient limitations of the concept into which we have allowed ourselves to be led' (1948, p. 68 – see Dilman, 1983, chapter 1).

In the case of hysteria Freud took it for granted he was dealing with symptoms of an illness. The symptoms for which many of his patients consulted him were those for which they had quite naturally been to see their physician: paralyses of limbs, disturbances of sight and speech, inability to eat or to keep food down, insomnia, contractures, convulsions, pains. Freud could find nothing organically wrong with these patients. He had, further, seen Charcot produce such symptoms artificially by hypnotic suggestion, and also remove them in this way. Furthermore, he had heard from his friend and colleague Dr Breuer about an hysterical patient Anna O – real name Bertha Pappenheim – whose symptoms disappeared when she related the details of their first appearance. That is, they were removed by mere talking. She herself called this a 'talking cure' and 'chimney sweeping'. As Freud reports in his *Autobiographical Study*: 'A chance observation showed her physician that she could be relieved of these clouded states of consciousness if she was induced to express in words the affective phantasy by which she was at the moment dominated . . . He [Breuer] employed the same procedure for removing her inhibitions and physical disorders' (1948, p. 34). For these reasons Freud concluded that these symptoms had a *psychological* origin, had their genesis in the patient's psychology. Hysteria, therefore, was a psychogenic illness, that is, an illness whose causes were psychological and not organic. Moebius had used the expression 'caused by ideas' (see Freud and Breuer, 1950, p. 134).

But the notion of an illness that is so caused and removable by ideas in a broad sense raises conceptual difficulties just as much as the notions of an unconscious mind and infantile sexuality: can what is so caused be an illness? Is it not at best an 'imaginary illness' or an 'imitation' one, like malingering, as hypochondria and hysteria had been thought to be? In so far as it is not, are we not at least extending the notion of an illness beyond its medical boundaries? Anyway, in what sense is such an illness, if we are to call it that, *caused* by ideas, by unconscious reminiscences, by repressed affects, as Freud claimed?

Freud himself compared hysteria to malingering: 'Dora's own gastric pains proclaimed the fact that she identified herself with her cousin, who, according to her, was a malingerer' (1977, p. 70). He went on a little further down: 'And yet illnesses of this kind *are* the result of intention. They are as a rule levelled at a particular person, and consequently vanish with that person's departure. The crudest and most commonplace views on the character of hysterical disorders . . . are in a certain sense right. It is true that the paralysed and the bedridden would spring to her feet if a fire were to break out in her room, and that the spoiled wife would forget all her sufferings if her child were to fall dangerously ill, or if some catastrophe were to threaten the family circumstances. People who speak of the patients in this way are right except upon a single point: they overlook the psychological distinction between what is conscious and what is unconscious' (pp. 77–8 – see Dilman, 1984a, chapter 5). Freud is saying here that hysteria is both like and unlike malingering. May I add that in so far as it is like malingering it is unlike an illness and *vice versa*. This is precisely, of course, why the extension of the notion of illness to cover cases of hysteria is at once both revealing and troublesome.

Freud was adamant in retaining this extension, but his views on the causation and cure of such illnesses evolved and changed, even though there remained a basic continuity between the views he held at different stages of his career. At least, his early views anticipated his later ones. Alongside the changes in Freud's views on the causation, character and cure of neuroses, psycho-analytic treatment itself extended its sphere of application to cover an increasing variety of complaints. The early conversion hysteria at least aped physical illnesses and disabilities; but the connections or analogies between the states or conditions of later psycho-analytic patients and physical illnesses became more and more tenuous. You could not apply the notion of illness to all these conditions without greatly extending or stretching the notion, perhaps to breaking-point.

The early views expressed in *Studies in Hysteria* already differed from those of Breuer and the French psychologist Janet who had also, like Freud, spoken of the unconscious. Influenced by Charcot, Freud held that the symptoms of hysteria were caused by the repressed memories of traumatic experiences and the painful emotions evoked by them but dammed up or strangulated. Freud remarked on the peculiarity of the causation in question. The cause of the symptoms were not traumas now in the past and, therefore, no longer in existence, but continuing memories of them: 'hysterical patients suffer from reminiscences' (Freud and Breuer, 1950, p. 4). These memories 'cause' the symptoms because they are repressed. They are 'affective memories' (to use a Proustian expression) and the symptoms are symptoms of emotions that have been prevented from spending themselves out. The causal connection here is an 'internal' one. Freud describes it as 'direct' and likens it to the connection between the memory of a painful event, such as the loss of a loved one, and the tears shed by the person feeling the pain, the loss (ibid.). To come to see the connection is to find the symptom an *intelligible* response to the painful, traumatic event which continues to haunt the patient, though he is unable consciously to recollect it (see Dilman, 1984a, chapter 2).

Freud had some brief but interesting comments to make on the intelligibility of the connection in question. At the end of his discussion of the case of Miss Elizabeth von R he gives some examples of conversion symptoms in two cases that came under his care – Miss Rosalia H and Mrs Cecilia M. When young Miss Rosalia H had to swallow an affront by her uncle, on which occasion she repressed her contempt; she later developed choking sensations in her throat. On another occasion her suppressed impulse to punish this same uncle who tried to grab her while she was massaging his back led to her fingers jerking. A remark of Mrs Cecilia M's husband which annoyed her was felt by her as 'a slap in the face', whereupon she developed a facial neuralgia. Freud comments:

> If an hysteric creates through symbolization on a somatic sensation for an emotionally accentuated idea, it is due less to individual and arbitrary things than one supposes . . . Is it not probable that the phrase 'to swallow something', applied to an unreturned insult, really originates from the sensation of innervation appearing in the pharynx when one forces back one's speech, thus preventing a reaction to the insult? All these sensations and innervations belong to the 'expression of the emotions', which, as Darwin taught us, originally consisted of sensible and expedient actions; at present most of them may be so weakened that their verbal expression seems to us like a figurative transformation, but very probably all this was once meant literally, and hysteria is justified in reconstructing the original literal sense for its stronger innervation. (Freud and Breuer, 1950, pp. 131–2)

Professor Hampshire, who develops this idea, explains the sense in which these expression are 'internal' to the emotions in question (see Hampshire, 1961).

In all this the patient is conceived of as largely *passive* in the sense that a person who suffers grief, fear or jealousy is passive. The response is, of course, *his* response, but the trauma to the memory of which his symptom is a response is not something he has sought. It is his misfortune to have encountered it. His activity or agency is confined to the way he has turned away from the pain, repressed the memory of his traumatic experience. It is this which Breuer's treatment by hypnotic suggestion sought to influence: to get the patient to cease fighting the memory, however unconsciously. When the patient is induced to do so, he does not only recollect the event or experience, he relives it affectively. Breuer described this as an 'abreaction' of the affect and called the process 'catharsis'. The patient is thus purged of what erupts in somatic symptoms through being bottled up. Consequently, the symptom disappears. The process may be likened to lancing a boil.

For Breuer the connection remained purely one of 'objective causality'; the idea of its intelligibility did not enter his mind. Thus he relates how, as he found out from Anna O's recollections under hypnosis, her symptoms arose in the course of her father's illness while she was nursing him. One of these, the paralysis of her right arm, came about as follows – I quote from Breuer's 'observations':

> The mother was away for a short time and Anna sat near the sick-bed holding her *right arm* over the back of the chair. She sank into a state of day-dreaming, and saw how a black snake came out of the wall towards the patient, as if to bite him . . . She wanted to drive away the reptile, but felt as if paralyzed. The right arm, which was hanging over the back of the chair, was 'asleep' and was anesthetic and paralyzed, and as she looked at it, the fingers changed into small snakes with skulls (nails) . . . When the snake hallucination disappeared, she wished to pray in her anxiety, but words refused to come. She could not talk at all until she finally remembered an *English* nursery rhyme, and only in this language could she continue to think and pray. (Freud and Breuer, 1950, p. 26)

Breuer makes no further comment. But from other observations he makes it is clear that Anna, though very fond of her father, had some inner conflict about nursing him, she was not whole-hearted in her devotion even though her love for her father went very deep. Indeed, her conflict was an expression of her 'ambivalence' towards her father. Thus one night when she kept vigil at her father's bedside she heard some dance music coming from a neighbouring house. She felt a longing to be there and she immediately reproached herself. From that time onwards 'she reacted with a nervous cough throughout her whole illness whenever she heard very rhythmic music' (p. 27).

That she should have wished to be elsewhere at such a time and enjoy herself with people of her own age, though understandable, was obviously a serious matter *for her*. It was tantamount to disloyalty. What made it so was the fact that her affection for her father, however genuine, had been a tie and bondage to her, and she resented it unconsciously. The natural wish for greater autonomy in a girl of her age was not, therefore, quite so innocent in her case, it was contaminated with her rebelliousness and bad feelings. She could not accept that side of her from which it came. The snake she 'saw' coming out of the wall and moving towards her father was a 'projection' of this side of her which she, herself, called her 'evil ego'. She identified herself with the snake. Indeed, in her projective phantasy, which took the form of an hallucination, it became her right arm, ready to strike at the father she so loved.

She was thus more than just ambivalent towards her father. She was split in herself, much in the way that Dr Morton Prince's Sally Beauchamp was. Her 'evil ego' would not merge with her 'good self' and gave her all the trouble which Breuer was trying to take away from her.

My immediate point, however, is that the paralysis of her right arm was her own attempt to restrain herself from striking at her father. Thus the arm became a vehicle for her inner conflict between her good and bad feelings for her father, her 'good self' and her 'bad self', and the paralysis was an expression of will – her unconscious determination to stand by her father despite her wish for greater autonomy through rebellion. That is why it was open to the influence of ideas. It is in this respect, of course, that Freud likens hysteria to malingering, though the matter is much more complex than this.[1]

Anna O had been Breuer's patient and Freud had not yet come to a conception of psychotherapy as an attempt to help the patient resolve inner conflicts, such as the one I sketched out, by disentangling the different elements that merge together to constitute each of the conflicting inclinations. He did already differ from Breuer, however, in taking a 'dynamic' conception of the matter. He explains in *An Autobiographical Study* that by this he means 'the operation of intentions and purposes such as are to be observed in normal life' (1948, p. 40), except for the fact that they are disowned by the patient, not acknowledged by him, so that they are unconscious.

In the fifth case he discusses in *Studies in Hysteria*, that of Miss Elisabeth von R, Freud brings to the fore the idea of *inner conflict* as being at the root of hysterical symptoms, although he tries to combine this with the idea of a trauma – what I would describe as an attenuated sense of 'trauma'. I say 'attenuated', for a trauma here is reduced to the momentary emergence into consciousness of an

---

[1] Here we have the idea of a symptom as belonging to an unconscious strategy of the patient and not simply as an expression of repressed feelings.

unacceptable wish or emotion aided by the occurrence of some actual event (see Freud and Breuer, 1950, p. 120). There is a single hysterical symptom in this case, namely a pain on Miss Elisabeth's right thigh which interferes with her ability to walk. In the course of the analysis a connection emerges between this symptom and two separate incidents in the patient's life as she recalls them. The first one, as in Anna's case, is the occasion of her nursing her father. She had to repress her feelings for a young man on account of her father's illness. One evening when she went out with him she returned home to find the condition of her father aggravated. As Freud puts it: 'She bitterly reproached herself for having sacrificed so much for her own amusement . . . A conflict, or state of incompatibility, arose through the contrast between the happiness which she had not at the time denied herself, and the sad condition in which she found her father upon her arrival home. As a result of this conflict, the erotic ideas were repressed from the associations and the affect connected with them was utilized in aggravating or reviving a simultaneously (or somewhat previously) existing physical pain' (p. 104).

Freud later goes on to connect the erotic feelings or longing for intimacy with the young man with Elisabeth's father; they were part of her attachment to him. She had tried to transfer them to someone she could have married, but failed. In the course of the analysis Freud found that the pain emanated 'from that location on her right thigh . . . upon which her father's leg rested every morning while she changed the bandages of his badly swollen leg' (p. 105).[2] In Freud's view the intimacy of this contact had a sexual aspect which Elisabeth could not face. It was its repression that led to the pain which crippled her. This pain was itself a form of self-reproach or punishment, though at the same time it kept alive the memory of the forbidden sexual intimacy. It also kept her near her father physically, in space, as well as in spirit through the identity with him it enabled her to assume, thus experiencing her father's crippled condition.

The second occasion with which Elisabeth's pain turned out to be connected in the recollections that emerged in the course of her treatment was her return home from a holiday at Gastein whereupon she suffered the loss of her sister. From these recollections Freud

[2] Compare with Freud's explanation of the way the pressure of Herr K's erect member against her body led to Dora's hysterical symptom. See 1977, p.60.

gathers that her apparently innocent relationship with this sister's
husband was not so innocent and that Elisabeth had developed an
erotic love for him of which she was unconscious (see pp. 110–11
and 118). 'She recalled standing before the bed seeing the deceased
and in the moment of the awful certainty that the beloved sister had
died without having taken leave of them and without having her last
days eased through their nursing – in that very moment another
thought flashed through Elisabeth's brain, which now peremptorily
repeated itself. The thought, which flashed like dazzling lightning
through the darkness was, "Now he is free again, and I can become
his wife" (p. 111). This was an expression of the longing that was at
the heart of her unconscious love and it was as unacceptable to her
then as it had been when her sister was alive. She must have felt at
that moment that her sister's death was part of what she had wished
and that in longing to have her husband she was somehow responsible for her death. It was that which gave the thought that flashed
through her mind as she stood by her sister's deathbed a 'traumatic'
character.

This thought and the longing to which it belonged was unacceptable to her in the same way that her illicit erotic longing for her father
was. Freud does not go into this; he had not yet developed his views
about the Oedipus conflict and the way it forms the kernel of every
neurosis. All he says here is that 'the first conversion took place in
the patient while she nursed her father, at the time her duties as a
nurse came into conflict with her erotic yearnings, and that this
process was the model for the later ones which led to the outbreak of
the disease in the Alpine spa' (p. 121).

The main point I want to stress is that while here Freud is still far
from his later views on the nature of a neurosis and its causation he
is already pointing in that direction, is on his way towards those
views, and he differs from Breuer in significant respects – especially
in his *psychological* interest, approach and flair. Charcot had not
taken an interest in the psychology of Anna O's symptoms when
Freud told him about her, and Breuer had run away from it when,
as her therapist, it touched him personally. Freud, on the other
hand, stayed with it and personally faced the kind of challenge that
Anna O had presented to her therapist. He really wanted to get to
the bottom of it and he devoted his whole life to doing so at great
personal risk.

Already Freud's presentation of the case of Miss Elisabeth von R is full of psychological interest. Freud himself comments how much it reads like a novel (p. 114). This element was to become more prominent in Freud's later case studies. Thus, for instance, in his study of Dora, the relationships between members of Dora's family, including her governess, and those of Herr K's family are presented in all their psychological intricacies. The way minor characters in this family drama are used to cast sidelong light on the major characters is reminiscent of Dostoyevsky. Freud leaves us in no doubt about the relevance of all this to an understanding of Dora's problems, those that are at the root of her hysteria.

In the case of Elisabeth von R, Freud is puzzled at first by what the story of her life, as sketched out by him, has to do with her hysterical symptom: 'If one could forget greater suffering, and wished to read one's self into the psychic life of a girl, one could hardly deny Miss Elisabeth a sincere human sympathy. But what about the physician's interest in this sorrowful tale and its relation to her painful and weak gait: what about the prospects of explaining and curing this case by the knowledge which we may perhaps obtain from these psychic traumas?' (p. 102) He complains in the next paragraph that he cannot see how the patient's history explains the causation and determination of the hysteria in question (p. 103). 'But I continued my analysis [he writes] because I felt sure that an understanding of the causation . . . of the hysterical symptoms could be gained from the deeper strata of consciousness' (ibid.).

Unable to hypnotize her, Freud asked Elisabeth to tell him 'whatever appeared before her mind's eye or flashed through her memory' at the moment he pressed her head. She then reports the memory of an evening in which a young man accompanied her home from some social affair. Freud comments that 'with this first mention of the young man a new shaft was opened, the content of which I gradually brought out' (p. 104).

This content, as I have pointed out, is the aspect of her relation with her father which is unacceptable to her and which she will not admit to herself. What emerges from this is Freud's notion of the symptom as both a *substitute* for and also a *defence* against the longings and inclinations which enter into this aspect of her relationship with her father. He later talked of a neurotic symptom as a 'compromise formation' because it combined these two aspects in one. Here he talks of the 'motive of defence' (p. 119) and so describes the hysteria as a 'defence hysteria' (p. 120). So the symptom is not to be explained as a quasi-mechanistic conversion of the affect which belongs to a repressed idea, as Freud still tries to do here. Nor is it merely the patient's passive emotional response to a traumatic situation, a response that has been distorted because the emotion is inadmissable. It is in part an active attempt on the patient's part to defend herself against some affective longing which she finds unacceptable.

This not only complicates the idea of its *causation*, which Freud characterizes as 'overdetermined', but it gives it a new logical twist. Freud here talks of 'motive' and later in his discussion of the case of Paul Laurenz, who has come to be known as 'the Rat Man', he talks of 'cause' and 'motive' in one breath: 'the results of such an illness are never unintentional, what appears to be the *consequences* of the illness is in reality the *cause* or *motive* of falling ill' (1979, p. 79). Thus, while in the case of Miss Elisabeth's pain Freud emphasizes its defensive character, he is not very far from giving us a glimpse of its overdetermination: it enabled her to participate in her father's infirmity, to keep alive the memory of his swollen leg pressing against her thigh (symptom as 'substitute formation'), to admonish herself and pay for the pleasure she had felt when she went out with her 'boy-friend' and longed for her sister's husband (symptom as self-punishment).

2 FROM NEUROTIC SYMPTOMS TO THE PSYCHOLOGY OF NEUROSES

At this early stage in his career Freud concentrated on understanding the *causation* of neurotic symptoms and on their *removal* by psychological means. He focused on the symptom and located its cause in the repressed memory of a traumatic event in the recent history of the patient. He thought of a symptom on the model of symptoms of physical illnesses – for instance, an infection of the appendix causing the patient to feel sick, have high temperature, and so on. These are symptoms of appendicitis, and the illness, the infection, is what causes them. In the case of conversion hysteria such bodily afflictions as paralysis, contractures, pains, convulsions, insomnia, vomiting and other physical disturbances are the symptoms of the illness hysteria. The hysteria itself resides in the twists and turns of the patient's affective life. But if so, the relation between symptoms and illness cannot be the same in the two cases.

The symptoms, so-called, of hysteria are expressions of the patient's affective life – his emotions, longings, inner conflicts, and what he does in response to them. They are, for one who knows how to read them, the mirror of his soul. To take them away from him by hypnotic suggestion in the name of a cure, instead of making his inner conflicts accessible to consciousness and thus helping him to resolve them, is to deprive him of the only means of expression available to him at the time. The hysteria of which they are an expression is not something imposed on the patient's soul, it is an aspect of the particular life of that soul. As Freud himself remarked, in a paper entitled 'Types of Onset of Neurosis' (1912), neuroses are not due to the appearance of any extraneous 'cause of disease'. Thus, when Freud spoke of an hysterical paralysis as 'psychogenic' or 'ideogenic' he meant that it is an expression of the life of the soul or psyche, indeed an expression of the patient's *will*, determined by thoughts, fears and longings. That is why it is responsive to hypnotic suggestion. But the thoughts, fears and longings are at loggerheads with one another, and so the symptom gives expression to incompatible aspects of the patient's will. It serves the patient's various purposes, but it cannot serve any of them satisfactorily.

That is why 'abreacting' the 'strangulated' affects cannot resolve the patient's problems. If you look at it medically, or purely from the point of view of the patient's conscious personality, it would seem that the removal of the symptoms is what is called for in the treatment: they are encumbrances that damage the patient's interests, interfere with his life and stand in the way of his legitimate pursuits. But there is more to the patient, to his longings and interests, than meets the eye when one takes such a point of view, and much in it that he needs to sort out if he is to find his way in life, to form relationships in which he can both find and give fulfilment. To remove a symptom by suggestion, in response to the patient's wish for a cure, is to take his reasons for seeking a therapy at face value and to fail to respond to them.

It was Freud's appreciation of all this that turned him away from modes of psychotherapy that confine themselves to the removal of symptoms. He devoted his efforts to the development of a psychotherapy that aims to help the patient to understand himself, to see his conflicting aims and emotions in their full complexity, so that he can disentangle them and himself move towards actions and positions that satisfy him. As we have seen, even in Freud's first conception of them hysterical symptoms were not 'caused' by traumatic experiences as such, but by memories which the patient had himself repressed.

The popular view of what this comes to shows little appreciation of the character of the causality involved. It sees the trauma too much as the fire that makes the pot boil, and repression as a pressing down of the lid, thus causing the temperature to rise. It sees the symptom as a safety valve through which the steam escapes, preventing the pressure from reaching breaking-point. Therefore, remove the lid and you will have removed the need for the safety valve. This analogy ignores the inner conflict which, in Freud's view, is at the heart of neuroses and the extent to which the lifting of repression involves a reorganization of consciousness. Indeed, it was Freud's view that the inner conflict is preserved and perpetuated by being kept unconscious. The main objective of Freud's therapy was soon to become, and always remained, making the patient's inner conflicts accessible to him. Only then could the patient try to do something towards resolving them (see 1949b, pp. 363–6). Psycho-analytic therapy may involve abreaction and relief, but it involves much more than this, and above all what one may call 'inner work'. This engages the patient as an agent, but mainly at the level of his emotions.

The removal of symptoms which figured prominently in *Studies in Hysteria* soon ceased to be the objective of psycho-analytic therapy and came to be considered as a by-product, a bonus. Even there Freud viewed it as a limited objective and admitted that the loss of symptoms does not necessarily constitute a cure of the hysteria – not so long as the 'predisposition' remained unaffected (see p. 12). Besides, the fact that the patient wishes them to be removed does not mean that he is prepared to countenance changing and pay the price for giving them up. His understandable conscious desire to be without his symptoms may itself be an expression of a wish to have things made easy for him – a wish that he has to work against if he is to participate in the kind of therapy that psycho-analysis offers him.

Freud moved towards this conception of psycho-analytic therapy in stages, each stage anticipating the next. Though his contemporaries – Charcot, Janet, Breuer – sowed the seeds of his ideas, he differed from them from the start and grew these seeds very much in his own way. His 'dynamic conception of the mind', in which he differed from these contemporaries, placed inner conflict at the centre of the neuroses and was an expression of his interest in their *psychology*. The recent traumas to which at first he attached importance soon began to take second place. The predisposition to neurosis (e.g. to hysteria), which at first he treated as something unknown, was seen to lie very largely in the patient's *early experiences*. Indeed, it was these early experiences that predisposed him to the neurosis which his later traumatic experiences precipitated. Without them he would not have found the later experiences traumatic.

Thus, Freud's interest turned from the recent traumas to the patient's early history and childhood. At first he retained the ideas of a trauma and spoke of childhood traumas – attempts at seduction, threats of castration, and so on. He then shifted the emphasis from such 'traumatic' events in the patient's childhood to his *phantasies* at the time and the wishes and ideas which these involved. But one could hardly see these as traumata any longer since a trauma is a discrete event with a fairly definite temporal location. Yet what were in question were the patient's early childhood perceptions, thoughts, longings and experiences as these coloured his relations at the time.

When discussing the incidents which Dora had found 'traumatic', such as Herr K's attempts to seduce her, Freud comments that some of her symptoms, her nervous cough and loss of voice, had been produced by the patient's years before the time of the trauma: 'Their early appearances belong to her childhood.' He then goes on: 'If, therefore, the trauma theory is not to be abandoned, we must go back to her childhood and look about there for any influences and impressions which might have had an effect analogous to that of a trauma' (1977, p. 58). In his *Introductory Lectures*, delivered ten years later, Freud tells us that an experience is 'traumatic' when the emotions involved in it are too great to be assimilated by the person at the time (see 1949b, p. 232). Whether an experience is traumatic or not, in this sense, therefore, depends on the individual person and his particular mental condition at the time. It is clear, however, that what is of moment is no longer a particular incident or single experience, but the way a person interacts, as a child, with what he faces or cannot evade in the course of his relationships and chance contacts. It is his whole upbringing and interactions and the way he assimilated these that is in question. So the early idea of a trauma has by now dropped away all but in name.

Gradually, the name too is given up and the child's relationships, primarily within the family, his affective attitudes to members of his family, his ambivalence towards and conflicts with them, the way these conflicts are taken in and go into the shaping of the growing child's personality and character, so as to reappear in his later relationships outside the family, gain prominence. Traumata are what *some* individuals suffer, whereas these conflicts, of which Freud highlights the Oedipus conflicts, are what *everyone* faces. Indeed, Freud sees them as *unavoidable*: 'It seems to me that we concentrate too much upon symptoms and concern ourselves too little with their causes . . . I can imagine that it may have been to Hans' advantage to have produced this phobia. For it directed his parents' attention to the *unavoidable difficulties* by which a child is confronted when in the course of his cultural training he is called upon to overcome the innate instinctual components of his mind' (1977, p. 300, italics mine).

The idea of the preservation of what belongs to the past in the unconscious mind has always been important for Freud from the start. He gave early voice to it when he said that hysterical patients 'suffer from reminiscences'. In other words, they are haunted by something that happened to them in the past because they have not been able to face it, turned away from it, and so have not come to terms with it. Through repression the whole 'complex' has been put into cold storage, except that it continues to remain a 'burning issue' since in this state the affects involved cannot be defused. Freud did not give up this idea, but his interest widened to cover the whole *affective orientation* or 'structure' that is preserved in the unconscious.

In his discussion of the treatment of the Rat Man Freud uses the analogy of the antiques that got buried after the eruption of Vesuvius to explain how what is buried in the unconscious mind is preserved: 'I made some short observations . . . upon the fact that everything conscious was subject to a process of wearing-away, while what was unconscious was relatively unchangeable, and I illustrated my remarks by pointing to the antiques standing about in my room. They were, in fact, I said, only objects found in a tomb, and their burial had been their preservation: the destruction of Pompeii was only beginning now that it had been dug up' (1979, p. 57). That is why, of course, the lifting of repressions is given such pride of place in psycho-analytic therapy.

The 'affective structures' or 'orientations' preserved came to be seen as belonging to different stages of development. So the early interest in unconscious memories and amnesias shifted in the direction of *arrested development* ('fixations'). The 'abreaction' of affects dwindled in significance and Freud became more interested in making the patient aware of his resistances, helping him to overcome them so as to gain an awareness of early affective orientations preserved in the patient's present relationships and attitudes. As in abreaction, this awareness involves reliving them in the analysis ('transference') by going back in time to these earlier non-extinct modes of response ('regression'). Freud points out, however, that while reliving them is necessary to the awareness he was aiming to promote, it is not enough. Repetition, he said, has to be replaced by recollection (see 1949b, p. 371). The patient has to come to see what he is acting out for what it is, take responsibility for and recognize his part in it as belonging to the past, in contrast with blaming his present circumstances.

Indeed, Freud came to hold that the traumata whose memory he was trying to recover in the cases he presented in *Studies in Hysteria* had very little to do with the causation of neuroses since the neuroses pre-dated these. The traumata only 'precipitated' the neuroses which were already in existence – like a salt, invisible in solution, becoming visible by being precipitated by the addition of a precipitating agent to the solution. He went as far as claiming that we all go through some neurosis, mild or acute, in our childhood, and even though we may outlive it, we do not do so completely. He had said that 'the Oedipus complex is the kernel of the neuroses' (1949b, p. 283), and he claimed that the conflicts that go into it are never completely resolved. The childhood neurosis, therefore, does not completely disappear. Thus, where the aim of psychotherapy in Breuer's days had been the abreaction of affects, and so the reliving of traumatic experiences, now analysis came to be seen as involving the reliving of one's infantile neurosis – the reliving of it in the 'transference'.

Freud had begun with the idea of the psychological causation of the symptoms of hysteria. This was a striking revelation because the symptoms in question were largely somatic or physical. Because they were psychogenic they were removable by psychological means. But, as Freud developed his methods of treatment, his interest moved from the causation of the symptoms to the psychology of his patients. Indeed, he came to see that the patient's neurosis was a good part of this psychology and that it was this that the patient needed to understand and sort out. The objective of psycho-analysis thus became to help the patient to do so for himself. This was a long way from the conceptions that informed Freud's early forms of psychotherapy, yet continuous with them.

This broadening of the conception of psychotherapy opened psycho-analysis to a wider category of persons suffering from different kinds of trouble, and neurotic symptoms were no longer as much in prominence in the people who sought psycho-analytic therapy. Among them were people suffering from different forms of failure in relationships and dissatisfactions with themselves, those feeling a lack of direction and interest, and those unable to find much sense in the kind of life they led. To describe these as 'symptoms' is to strain the sense of the word. Lack of direction or meaning, for instance, or the inability to sustain relationships or find fulfilment in them, are not symptoms of something wrong in the life of the person, they are part of what is wrong there, a good part of it. Furthermore, the kind of problem or trouble in question is not medical in character. I would characterize it as 'moral' in a wide sense of the term. What an analysis can come to elucidate for the analysand here is how the way he is, his evasions, the fears behind these, his secret longings, the feelings of guilt attached to them, contribute to the state of affairs in question. There is not much room here for talking of 'symptoms and their causation', a phrase that is easy to misinterpret and misunderstand: 'the symptoms of physical diseases have physical causes and the symptoms of neuroses have psychological causes' – as if the two cases were logically parallel.

I have tried to point out how the lack of logical parallel gradually became more manifest in the course of the development of Freud's ideas on the nature and causation of neuroses. Different kinds of neurosis do not have different causes in the way that different physical illnesses do. The same basic emotional conflicts underlie the different kinds of neuroses. Their differences lie, it has been pointed out, not in their causes, but in the different ways in which different people deal with these conflicts (see Guntrip, 1970, p. 59). These inner conflicts pose the growing child serious emotional problems. Neuroses represent different ways of evading these, which preserve the conflict and create new problems. It is these which psycho-analysis aims to help the patient to face so that he can seek a way of resolving them. Thus, the shift is from 'symptoms to be removed' to 'problems to be resolved', the problems in question being problems *in* the patient.

3 HYSTERIA, REPRESSION AND THEIR MODERN COUNTERPART

I should like to take a brief break to reflect on a question raised for me by the dilemma over which the women in Freud's early case studies resorted to hysteria. I can easily imagine many young Western women today failing to understand the conflicts over sexual attraction that had exercised these patients of Freud. Like the Cockney boy who said 'When I itches I scratches' many of them would see no reason to hold back where mutual sexual desire exists. The 'philosophy' behind their conduct may be summed up as: 'What I do with my body is my business', 'We each have but one life on this earth', 'If what I do with my life upsets anyone else that is their tough luck; no one can be responsible for anyone else's hang-ups'. I can, therefore, see many of them acting out, without batting an eyelid, longings the mere having of which Freud's hysterical patients had paid for dearly with their hysteria. Maybe this is one reason why hysteria is not so common in the present day. Does that mean that we are more enlightened about these matters, that the insight Freud's patients fought hard to win in the course of their therapies has become a common possession?

I do not think so, and I do not believe that those women today who call themselves 'liberated' are necessarily liberated psychologically. They may be free from certain illusions cherished in the idealization of the opposite sex, but blind to other possibilities in the relationship of the sexes which Freud's hysterical patients showed an awareness of in their longings. Anyway, wisdom in relationships is something very different from Erica Jong's philosophy of 'how to save your own life'.

Certainly, the climate of opinion in which we live today is different from the one in which Freud's patients lived. No doubt this is to some extent a result of the popularization of Freud's ideas, though I doubt that it is one of which he would have approved. This difference is, not surprisingly, reflected in the psychological problems we 'moderns' are apt to face or evade in our lives.

It is also true that women today may not be subject to some of the social oppressions which affected the lives of Freud's women – at least not to the same extent. Although here we need to be careful in our judgements. For what *we* see as oppression may not have been seen as such by the women of Freud's Vienna. If we are inclined to say that they were duped ('false consciousness') we may be speaking from the standpoint of values which would have been foreign to them.

In any case, domination and oppression have always gone on between human beings and between the sexes, and will always do so. Cultural changes alter merely the form of the oppression, and each person, whether agent or victim, has still to come to terms with it in himself or herself.

What the women in Freud's case studies had to deal with, and failed to do so adequately, concerned not simply their attitude to sexual pleasure but questions of loyalty and betrayal of trust, debts of gratitude and obligations created by love, devotion and autonomy, selfishness and ambivalence towards loved ones, envy and generosity. These are a mixture of moral and psychological problems bound up with the give and take of human relationships. Many of the hysterical women whom Freud treated were intelligent and highly sensitive persons who took these matters seriously. But they had remained over-dependent on their parents and unconsciously resented their dependence. They were mixed up about their own sexuality and found if difficult to disentangle the different aspects of their longings and their own opposition to them. Furthermore, their responses to the situations created by these longings, whether submissive, guilt-ridden or rebellious, came from a self not commensurate with their age.

Freud often attributed their opposition to their own longings to their 'super-ego'. He regarded its demands as tyrannical and its punishments as 'archaic', and he clearly thought of a reduction of the power of the super-ego over the ego as a benefit and its achievement in analysis as a liberation. But this is not tantamount to a rejection of morality. What is in question is a transformation of the super-ego into a more genuine form of conscience. Certainly Freud did not see the aim of psycho-analytic therapy as the removal of 'moral' obstacles to the fulfilment of his hysterical patients' 'erotic' longings.

There was an inner conflict to be resolved and both sides to the conflict contained what represented genuine aspects of the patient's personality. The task of the therapy, as Freud saw it, was to disentangle the different elements on both siddes and help the patient to sift what was genuine among these from what was merely defensive, a reaction-formation, or a need for compensation. The patient could then gradually see his way to discarding the 'excess luggage' and reach a solution to his conflicts.

He did not take sides in the patient's inner conflict and would have said that anyone who does fails to appreciate the mixture of components that combine together to make up each side of the conflict. He certainly anticipated the kind of 'liberation philosophy' which others later were to derive from his thoughts and rejected it explicitly (see 1949b, p. 361). He would have said that love itself creates obligations and loyalties, which such a 'philosophy of life' disregards, and that human relationships which do not recognize them are shallow and unrewarding. He said that 'anyone who has successfully undergone the training of learning and recognizing the truth about himself is henceforth strengthened against the dangers of immorality, even if his standard of morality should in some respect deviate from the common one' (p. 363).

His reasons for thinking so are, I think, twofold. The first one is that such a person will be more genuine or authentic, and without being so he could not be moral. The second reason is that an analysis that has been successfully conducted will have opened up positive resources in the patient, rooted in love, out of which will grow respect for other human beings as individuals.

Freud never denied the existence of evil in human beings. In contrast to some other psycho-analytic writers, he did not think of evil as the result of either frustration or ignorance. He knew that what consitutes this evil – greed, envy, thirst for power or revenge, hatred – makes men selfish and ruthless towards others. He believed that this evil could be diminished in analysis if it is the result of deprivation, frustration and arrested development. Where it is not so and the patient lacks those inner resources that constitute the good in him analysis could do very little to help him. For he would not be able to form the kind of positive relation with the analyst to want to listen to, consider and respect the analyst and accept help from him. Where the evil in him is original and not the result of frustration, deprivation or humiliation, it can still be reduced provided the patient has sufficient love in him with which the analysis can bring it in contact. This is something that Melanie

Klein has worked out in her contribution to psycho-analytic therapy (see 1953 and 1957).

But let me return to those 'moderns' among us who believe in and practice what Freud calls 'free living'. Are those modern women who, at a young age, 'experiment with sex' instead of resorting to hysteria really more mature than Freud's early patients? Are they more 'healthy' or enlightened? Are those who break sexual relationships that have become 'boring', 'difficult', 'too demanding' or 'not worth the effort', without feelings of guilt, more liberated? It is dangerous to generalize. But may it not be that for some of them sex has come to be detached from their attachments, leaving their erotic relationships shallower? Freud had insisted that mature sexuality, that is, the sexuality of an emotionally mature person, has two aspects to it, namely sensuality and affection. He thought that it enriches an erotic relationship only when these two aspects form a whole: 'To ensure a fully normal attitude in love, two currents of feeling have to unite – we may describe them as the tender, affectionate feelings and the sensual feelings' (1949c., p. 174).

If the modern women in question are rebels then the likelihood is that they are reacting to something in themselves that they project onto others and do not recognize as part of themselves. They may suffer, for instance, from an inability to give themselves in relationships of intimacy, a fear of being possessed, a fear of their own deeply buried craving for dependency – what Ian D. Suttie called 'the taboo on tenderness' (see 1948, chapter 6). That is why they steer clear of all tenderness and show contempt for all forms of dependency. They develop a hard-boiled approach to erotic relationships. This is a reaction-formation to their own deep need for tenderness. They may not be rebels, on the other hand, and, sadly, be a little more than victims of a fad, itself made possible by the discredit into which such moral ideas as 'faith', 'loyalty' and 'obligation' have fallen. They may indeed not be 'repressed', but they may really not know anything better than what they seek. They may suffer from a shallowness of feeling which makes them ill-suited to sustain or find sustainment in relationships of sexual love.

Hysteria was a condition that crippled Freud's patients with inhibitions and disabilities which marred their lives and brought unhappiness to those who loved them. It seems to have been replaced by a condition which is as widespread today as hysteria was in Freud's days, namely rootlessness and listlessness, an inability to settle down and grow roots. Such people may not be repressed, but they are far from having found themselves.

Freud himself came to realize that there are other 'defence mechanisms' than repression, and many different forms of inauthenticity or being false. And when he talks of 'lifting repressions' as what is aimed at in psycho-analytic therapy more and more he has in mind helping the patient to find himself and be himself (see 1949b, p. 363). This is not merely a matter of helping the patient to come out into the open, though it involves that. It is also a matter of providing the kind of caring attention in which the patient feels accepted so that he can bring the conflicting aspects of himself together and grow in the process.

4 PSYCHO-ANALYSIS AS A FORM OF PSYCHOTHERAPY

I now turn to the development of Freud's conception of psychotherapy, its aims and methods. He came to psychotherapy from neurophysiology, a medical conception of illness and its treatment. Its first stage was the abandonment of suggestion and hypnosis. There were several reasons why Freud abandoned hypnotism. First, not all his patients were susceptible to it. Second, he came to realize that many of the beneficial effects of hypnotic suggestion were transitory. As he points out in *An Autobiographical Study*, 'even the most brilliant results were liable to be suddenly wiped away if my personal relation with the patient became disturbed. . . . They would be re-established if a reconciliation could be effected.' Reflection on this led him to conclude that 'the personal emotional relation between doctor and patient was after all stronger than the whole cathartic process' (1948, p. 47). The third reason why Freud decided to dispense with hypnosis is connected with his formulation of the idea of resistance. What the patient remembered and was able to tell Freud under hypnosis was painful in one way or another – alarming, disagreeable or shameful by standards of his personality (p. 50). The thought occurred to Freud that this was the reason why the patient had put it out of his conscious mind ('repression') and why he fought the therapist's efforts to make him think of it ('resistance'). This was surely as much a part of the patient, Freud reasoned, as what he found painful. Yet hypnosis completely by-passed it. Thus something, an understanding of which was equally important for the therapy, was prevented from coming into focus by the hypnosis. In short, while the hypnosis helped to reveal something, it equally helped to conceal something else. So Freud thought he would try to get to what the hypnosis helped to reveal without its help.

Freud then decided to question the patient directly on the origin of the symptoms, asking the patient to concentrate, to try to remember. He first used this method – 'concentration technique' – in the case of Miss Elisabeth von R (see Freud and Breuer, 1950, pp. 103, 200). On an earlier occasion, another patient, Mrs Emmy von N, reproved Freud for interrupting her flow of thought by his questions. Ernest Jones tells us that Freud 'took the hint and thus made another step towards free-association' (1954, p. 268).

The kind of therapy he practised was still Breuer's cathartic method which he had modified in the ways I have indicated. The two principal innovations to it were the importance of understanding the patient's role in resisting an awareness of those emotions and inclinations which the treatment aimed at uncovering and the significance of the patient's relationship to the therapist for the progress of the treatment. In cathartic therapy the emphasis was on the purgation of strangulated emotions. Freud shifted this emphasis towards the *understanding* of these emotions and the patient's opposition to them. The resolution of inner conflict gradually came to occupy the centre of the stage and the reliving of repressed emotions came to be seen, as a consequence, as part of what the patient has to go through in the course of the treatment, of benefit in the context of what he needs to assimilate, come to terms with and work through.

'Chimney-sweeping', or recollection, whether or not under hypnosis, had been the main instrument of cathartic treatment, the means to the abreaction of affects. *Free-association* became the means to an enlargement of consciousness and self-understanding, and the therapist's contribution to this enlargement was through the *interpretations* with which he responded. Obviously, what Freud made of these ideas guided the way his practice evolved, so that a discussion of the philosophical questions they raise is not only of academic interest. Suffice it to note at this stage that he regarded free-association as the best way to the patient's unconscious mind. What came out in the patient's associations was a tangled skein and the therapist's interpretations were seen by Freud as the untangling of it: 'When the riddle they [psycho-neuroses] hold is solved and the solution accepted by the sufferers these diseases will no longer be able to exist' (1950, vol. ii, p. 292). He saw himself in his capacity as interpreter as telling the patient some *truth* about himself as revealed in his associations.

It is the patient's appreciation of this truth, his making it his own, part of his consciousness, that enables him to sort out his inner conflicts, to make his own aspects of himself that he has been running away from, to integrate them, bring them into connection with the rest of himself. Freud often thought of this as bringing them under control.

This emphasis on 'getting the patient to see and accept the truth about himself' was made by Freud into the hallmark of psycho-analysis. With this exclusive interest in 'getting at the truth' or 'insight into oneself' on the part of the patient, 'psycho-analysis' became equivalent to 'insight therapy', and as such to be distinguished from all other forms of psychotherapy. Naturally, the early interest in the removal of symptoms faded into the background.

Freud says: 'The analyst respects the patient's individuality and does not seek to remould him in accordance with his own – that is, according to the physician's – personal ideals; he is glad to avoid giving advice and instead to arouse the patient's power of initiative' (1950, vol. v, pp. 126–7). The idea is that the patient must be allowed to find his own solutions and be himself. If the patient must be allowed to find his own solutions to his problems and to be himself, he must equally be allowed to see the truth for himself, and even to find it for himself. Thus, Freud insists, not only does he avoid providing the patient with reassurance, but he is also not interested in convincing him of anything. His point is that the truth must not be imposed on the patient. As he puts it in connection with his discussion with Paul Laurenz, the Rat Man, of his ambivalence towards and death-wish for his father: 'It is never the aim of discussions like this to create conviction. They are only intended to bring the repressed complexes into consciousness . . . and to facilitate the emergence of new material from the unconscious. A sense of conviction is only attained after the patient has himself worked over the reclaimed material' (1979, p. 62 fn). The Rat Man does later reach such a sense of conviction by reliving the truth in question within the transference. Thus the patient must not be forced to accept a truth even by cogent argument, for this will at best produce a theoretical or intellectual conviction: 'Psycho-analysis is not an impartial scientific investigation, but a therapeutic measure. Its essence is not to prove anything, but merely to alter something' (1977, p. 263).

When Freud here says that the aim of psycho-analysis is to alter something, he means 'alter the patient's consciousness and understanding': 'make what is unconscious conscious'. But this has to be done by helping the patient to dispense with his resistances. That is how the patient is enlightened; not by means of persuasion. Interpretations must only articulate what he has already come to of his own accord.

As for the emotional content of the patient's relation to the therapist, the so-called transference, the analyst does not use it to persuade the patient to accept an interpretation. That would be a form of manipulation. He only analyses it, thus allowing the patient to live his problems in the analysis and see what he is like in the living of them. Thus the analyst allows the patient to come out of his shell, to enter into relationship with him, without either encouraging it, or himself entering into the relationship except as someone interested in helping the patient to find himself. He does so in the belief that this is in the patient's best interest, even when it hurts the patient at the time.

The analyst avoids all falsity and deception in the analysis: in the way he *is* with the patient as well as in what he *tells* him. He never leads the patient away from the truth, but neither does he impose it on him. Nor does he try to persuade him to change either, to impose his own wishes or values on him. He avoids all forms of manipulation. Thus Freud warns the analyst against the zeal to reform the patient: 'So far as possible we refrain from playing the part of mentor, we want nothing better than that the patient should find his own solutions for himself.' 'We are not reformers' (1949b, p. 362).

Against those who object that analysis is not enough since it does not provide any directions to help the patient to come together, Freud writes: 'Pyscho-synthesis is achieved during analytic treatment without our intervention . . . We have created the conditions for it by dissolving the symptoms into their elements and by removing the resistances' (1950, vol. ii, p. 395). What he means is that at this level analysis will have freed resources in the patient which will enable him to come together.[3] This is what, I think,

[3] What such resources might be will be considered in chapter 9.

makes Freud often speak of his neurotic patients as being fundamentally healthy. But he knows, of course, that there is no guarantee that analysis will reveal such resources in the patient, or indeed, that the patient does have them in his make up.

Certainly, Freud did not think that every patient could benefit from a psycho-analysis, and in the essay 'Analysis Terminable and Interminable', written two years before his death, he expresses some cautious doubts as to whether analytic therapy can accomplish anything which does not occur spontaneously under favourable normal conditions. He is inclined to think that what it does is to create conditions approximating those by removing encumbrances. The rest is up to the patient, to what he is like underneath, to the inner resources he possesses. The analysis cannot create these in him. But Freud is not sure: 'our experience . . . is not yet wide enough to enable us to come to a definite decision' (1950, vol. v, p. 329).

In any case, as Freud said long before then, the patient's external circumstances may be such that for him his neurosis may represent the most favourable adaptation to these circumstances, it may represent the lesser of the evils that face him: 'It is not for the physician to confine himself in all situations in life to the part of the fanatic about health; he knows that there is *other* misery in the world besides neurotic misery – real unavoidable suffering' (1949b, pp. 319–20).

Optimism or pessimism on one side, there is a philosophical point with which every non-causal therapy needs to come to terms. It concerns the logical limits to what another person can do for one. I discussed this question in a different context elsewhere (see Dilman, 1986, pp. 96–8, 105–6). As I put it: 'You can give me not only advice, but sympathy and support, put yourself out for me, you may even hold me together when I am falling apart. But you cannot make me whole. My wholeness, like my convictions, has to come from me.' These are things to which I am *internally* related. With things to which I am externally related it is otherwise. Thus you can leave me money in your will and make me rich; a physician can cure me of an incapacitating physical disease and make me healthy again. Indeed, he can remove a malignant tumour and thus change my life, whether I will it or not. What he cannot do is make me grateful if I am riddled with envy, or happy if I am unwilling to be satisfied with what I have.

The point in question is expressed in the old saying that 'you can lead a horse to water but cannot make it drink'. It is not enough that the horse should need the water in order to survive, he should himself want to drink it. In psycho-analytic therapy the problem is that even when the patient does want to get better and has an incentive to put himself out and work for it, he may also and at the same time get something out of remaining as he is and be unwilling to face what it would take for him to change. Reviewing, as he puts it, 'the play of forces brought into action by the treatment', Freud writes: 'The primary motive-power used in therapy is the patient's suffering and the wish to be cured which arises from it. The volume of this motive-force is diminished in various ways, discoverable only in the course of the analysis, above all by what we call the "episonic gain" [secondary gain or advantage gained by illness]; the motive-power itself must be maintained until the end of the treatment; every improvement effects a diminution of it' (1950, vol. ii, p. 364).

In short, the patient must want to 'get well', to be different, he must be prepared to give up something for it – something which protects him from pain, or compensates for some lack, or simply points him in the opposite direction. He must be prepared to put himself out, to face risk, to work, and he must have the inner resources to allocate to such work. What analysis does is to make such resources as he has accessible to him. It may even 'hold' the patient together in the course of bad patches in the treatment by means of its caring interest in his problems. But it cannot pull a psychological switch and make him better, take away his problems, in the way that physical, causal therapies do. As Harry and Bonaro Overstreet put it: 'Because of what they cannot do for the patient . . . most therapists . . . are reluctant to use the word *cure*. It seems to promise too much. They have no magic way of giving the individual what he can only give to himself' (1954, p. 64).

The point is a *logical* one. If psychotherapy could work as a causal therapy it would have to work by magic, for it would have to by-pass the patient. But even hypnotherapy engages the patient, if only unconsciously. Thus, as Freud puts it in *An Autobiographical Study*: 'there was something positively seductive in working with hypnotism . . . and it was highly flattering to enjoy the reputation of being a miracle-worker' (1948, p. 29). But he soon came to recognize that in order to work hypnosis had to enlist the patient's will and that hypnotic suggestion could not be very effective, certainly not of lasting benefit, where the patient's troubles are rooted in inner conflict. He denied that psycho-analysis, which deals with such conflicts, is 'a kind of magic' in the practice of which 'the patient's malady is blown away' (1947, p. 6). He denied that it is 'a causal therapy in the literal sense' (1949b, p. 364; see also Freud and Breuer, 1950, p. 196).

An instance of causal therapy in the psychological sphere is where a drug is given to the patient to clear or remove his depression. Presumably there is a physical condition here which distorts or colours his affective vision of the world. He sees everything in blue as it were. The drug acts on this condition causally, dissolves the blue film, and restores his affective vision to normality. Here the patient's depressive view of the world is a distortion of his normal affective vision caused by something external, such as a hormonal imbalance in his body. Its treatment is a means to an independent end, namely the alteration or removal of the condition causally responsible for the patient's trouble. The treatment is thus the exercise of a means to an end which does not engage the patient, except in so far as he may have to agree to it, obey instructions, submit to certain operations. But he could be treated against his will in the way that someone on hunger strike can be force-fed.

There are some psychotherapies which are causal in character in this way. They confine themselves to the removal of symptoms such as phobias, though they deny that these are symptoms of anything, seeing them as bad habits, the effects of past conditioning. They by-pass the patient, treating him as an 'object'. Behavioural therapies are instances of such psychotherapies. But then these are psychotherapies in only an attenuated sense of the term. Persuasive therapies are not forms of causal therapy, they work through the patient. But they manipulate him through the will. Psycho-analysis is not the only form of psychotherapy which does not do so, or at least purports not to. For there are forms of support and work therapies which are not manipulative. But psycho-analysis is unique in being an insight-therapy, in placing the enlightenment of the patient at the centre of its concern – enlightenment in contrast to persuasion.

Its avoidance of manipulation is part of this concern for truth which is central to psycho-analytic therapy. For to manipulate the patient is to make him false, to deny him the opportunity to find himself. His troubles and problems are bound up with his evasions, with his difficulties in being true to himself. Therefore, if he must change, he must himself want to change, and change because he wants to. So the analyst must not try to change him; he must confine himself to the work of interpretation.

Concern for truth, in the broad sense indicated, that is, authenticity of the patient, includes respect for his individuality and separateness. To manipulate him is to fail him in this respect. Indeed, for the analyst to *accept* the patient he must respect the latter's individuality, which does not mean that he has to like the patient. He must be honest about what he does not like in the patient and still not reject it, making the patient feel he must change to be acceptable. Whether or not he changes is up to the patient. The analyst must not deny his separateness and his right to be what he wants to be. In any case what the patient becomes as a result of manipulation remains *external* to him. That is why those beneficial changes in him that come about in the course of the therapy must come from him. As I said, there are logical limits to what the therapist, as another person, can do for the patient. In a book entitled *Psycho-analysis and Zen Buddhism* Erich Fromm puts this point as follows:

> Neither the analyst nor any man can 'save' another human being. He can act as guide, or as a midwife . . . but he can never do for the patient what only the patient can do for himself. He must make this perfectly clear to the patient, not only in words, but by his whole attitude. (p. 67)
>
> His relation must be free from any interference of the analyst in the life of the patient, not even that of the demand that the patient gets well. If the patient wants to get well and to change, that is fine, and the analyst is willing to help him. (1960, p. 87)

Keith Oatley makes the same point in words which may at first sound paradoxical:

> The relationship of therapy is simply itself. An end in itself, not something with some other end. It is simply a matter of being present, participating in what one is doing, although it often takes a long time to reach this, working through projections, resistances, and transferences. But in the end, participating in the relationships is what there is. The doing of therapy is not a means to an end of getting better (though one does get better). It is the end in itself. The taking part in it is the 'I' that I am seeking. (1984, pp. 153–4)

Oatley is not denying that if the patient is to get well he must want to do so and be prepared to work for it. His point is that the patient must not make this into an end to the attainment of which he subordinates the therapeutic relationship. He must bring himself into and live the relationship. It is in the living of it that he becomes himself, for it involves being made aware of what is false in him as well as what he, himself, finds objectionable, shedding it, and growing in the kind of acceptance that the analysis provides. He must not treat the relationship as an instrument of therapy. If he were overconcerned to achieve a therapeutic goal he could not give himself to the relationship and, therefore, to the treatment itself. In this analysis differs from all forms of causal and manipulative therapy.

The analyst too, while obviously concerned with the treatment of the patient, must not treat the relationship as an instrument, the patient as a means. He must genuinely care for him in the context of the therapy; the therapy itself must be a form of caring for the patient.

5 CONCLUSION AND FURTHER QUESTIONS

Freud started by developing a psychotherapeutic method for the removal of psycho-neurotic symptoms. In the evolution of his method and ideas symptoms dropped into the background, and more and more the enlightenment of the patient came into the foreground and gained importance. Freud came to realize that this enlightenment and the therapeutic relationship belong together and provide the opportunity for the development of self-knowledge and the growth of the self which is part of that development.

This is the direction in which I see Freud to have been moving from the start. But how is self-knowledge and the growth of the self connected? In what way is relationship with another person crucial to such growth? How do the interpretative enlightenment of the patient and the analytic relationship belong together? Why is it that coming to greater self-understanding requires a relationship with someone else, or at least the response to one of another person? What role does the other play in this process of coming to greater self-knowledge? What kind of relationship does the psycho-analyst offer the patient? These are some of the questions that need discussion if we are to appreciate the nature of psycho-analytic therapy, the connection between insight and change, and the ideas in terms of which Freud developed and expressed his psychotherapeutic aims and methods.

5

Communication and Self-disclosure in Psycho-analysis

We have seen that psycho-analytic therapy is based on communication and contact between patient and therapist. The term 'talking cure', while in one way perfectly accurate, is a misnomer. For it disguises how much more than 'mere talk' goes on in the verbal interchanges between the patient and the analyst. In this chapter I shall concentrate on the patient's contribution to the *verbal dialogue* that takes place in the therapy between him and the analyst. The next chapter will consider the analyst's contribution to this dialogue, and in chapter 7 I shall turn to the *relationship* that develops through this dialogue between patient and analyst and the *contact* they make in the course of its development. It is through this contact that the patient changes in himself and moves towards greater self-knowledge and autonomy.

1 FREE-ASSOCIATION

The verbal utterances by means of which the patient expresses himself, and through which he progressively comes out into the open in the analysis, are usually referred to as his 'associations'. This term bears the imprint of its historical ancestry and is burdened by philosophical presuppositions which belong to this ancestry – presuppositions which need criticism.

What are called associations comprise absolutely everything that the patient says during the analytic sessions. If, for instance, he starts by asking the analyst to change the time for his next session, this request is usually treated in two different ways: as an ordinary request and as an association. In so far as the analyst sees some special significance in the fact that the patient starts the session with such a request he is treating it as an association. He is always alert to just this kind of significance in anything that the patient says.

Compare this with an ordinary conversation. We all know that a great deal goes on in a conversation: humour, irony, manipulation, expression of concern, reassurance, sympathy, hostility, boasting, self-gratification, placation, one-upmanship. The personalities of the participants come into play and engage each other for good or ill in what is said on an endless variety of topics. In some cases the particular topic may be mostly a vehicle for this kind of interchange and engagement. The personalities of the speakers and the particular relationships they establish with one another are, therefore, at least just as relevant to what goes on in the conversation as what is actually said. Indeed, what is *said* cannot be entirely divorced from all this, as these different undercurrents of the conversation contribute to, and even make up, the subtle nuances of meaning that belong to speech. Novelists and playwrights know how to tap these resources in bringing to life a dialogue or conversation between their characters. The way a good analyst listens for his patient's 'unconscious communications' in his 'associations' is continuous with all this.

The history of the term 'association' goes back to the associationist school of psychology. In an early paper, 'Psycho-analysis and the Ascertaining of Truth in Courts of Law' (1906), Freud traces the ancestry of the idea of 'free-association' to the 'associationist tests' first introduced by the Wundt School and later developed in Zurich by Jung (see Freud, 1950, vol. ii).

One could think up a great many different kinds of word-game. These can be used to test the players' knowledge. For instance, one is given the name of a country and is asked to give the name of its capital in response. The person playing the game has to observe the rules of the game, apply the appropriate criteria.

A so-called association game, in contrast, is one in which the only rule is that one should utter the first word that comes to one's mind in response to the stimulus-word. The response-word is not selected in accordance with any criterion. Since in other word-games the response-word is selected in accordance with certain criteria, so long as the players possess the relevant knowledge, their response-word will not vary from one player to another when they get it right. As Simone Weil would say, if a player utters the right word 'his personality does not enter into it at all'; if he does not 'the mistake bears the stamp of his personality' (1962, p. 14). In the association game every word would bear the stamp of the player's personality. For there is nothing outside the player to which his utterance is responsible. That is what is meant when his association is characterized as 'free'.

Still, this use of the word 'free' is misleading. It does not really mean 'spontaneous' or 'unhindered'. For words that are governed by criteria can be thought of spontaneously, and the criteria do not constitute a hindrance. Conversely, a person may fail to be spontaneous with his 'free-associations'. He may be bashful, or ill at ease in the company of those with whom he is playing the game.

Freud made use of this idea of saying the first thing that comes into one's head in analysis. His rationale was that such thoughts and words would bear the stamp of the speaker's personality and reveal something about his preoccupations, fears, phantasies and longings. We find an early form of this idea in Jung's notion of a complex. Freud acknowledges his debt to Jung's idea 'that the connection between the stimulus-word and the reaction-word . . . must be determined by a pre-existing group of ideas (a complex) in the mind of the person reacting' (1950, vol. ii, p. 14). He compares the way in which this complex comes to be revealed in the response-words or associations of the subject with the way in which a suspected criminal may give himself away in what he says. He suggests that a method based on this analogy, could be devised by means of which the suspect can be made to betray his secret, confess his crime, and supply the missing 'objective' evidence which supports his confession. I can think of no better example of what Freud had in mind here than the one provided by Dostoyevsky in Porfiry's interviews with Raskolnikov.

In *Crime and Punishment* Raskolnikov has managed to commit the so-called 'perfect crime'. He has left no material evidence to link him with the crime. However, the crime weighs on his conscience and leaves him no peace of mind. That this condition (the depression, ravings, deliriums, etc.) is due to the crime he has committed can at best be an hypothesis to someone who does not know that he is the criminal. No one in the book knows this for a long time. They put forward different explanatory hypotheses. Porfiry, the investigating magistrate, is the first person in the book to suspect Raskolnikov, the first one to hit on the right hypothesis. To his experienced eye the hints dropped by Raskolnikov on different occasions, the scraps of behaviour that he comes to hear of, all point in one direction and support the same hypothesis. His problem is to find further support for his hypothesis, to test it, and in the end to extract a confession from Raskolnikov. His method, characterized by Raskolnikov as 'psychological', consists of talking to Raskolnikov, trying to catch him off his guard, to take him by surprise, and finally to trust that part of him that is ready to co-operate with Porfiry. He succeeds because his initial hypothesis is correct and he uses this method with sensitivity and understanding, making contact with the part of Raskolnikov that wants to confess and expiate the crime.

There is certainly some parallel between Porfiry's 'pyschological' method of investigation and Freud's method of investigating the unconscious mind. Both rely largely on the patient's or suspect's utterances, try to makes sense of these, and both count on some co-operation from the patient or suspect, despite his unwillingness to give away some secret of his soul. But there is one big difference. Porfiry wants to ascertain that it was Raskolnikov who killed the pawnbroker and her sister. He feels quite certain, and with good reason. But he needs Raskolnikov's confession and the objects he has stolen from the pawnbroker and hidden. What Porfiry wants to make sure of is that Raskolnikov has committed a known crime. He resorts to his 'pyschological methods' because Raskolnikov has left no material evidence to link him with the crime. But he could have left such evidence, or it could have come to light later. The police could have found the objects stolen, and were the crime committed today they could have found on them Raskolnikov's fingerprints. They could have found his blood-stained socks which they could have tested for the blood group. My point is that Porfiry's 'pyscho-logical methods' give us an *indirect* way of establishing what can be established directly. In themselves they could not provide conclusive evidence. Even a confession from Raskolnikov would not, in itself, be enough to establish, to a court's satisfaction, that he did really commit the crime.

In contrast, there is no other way of establishing the kind of thing that Freud is concerned to investigate, and the methods he uses are not indirect or a second-best. For Freud is not concerned to establish that the patient *did* something, or that something *happened* to him, but that he *thought, wished, imagined,* or *experienced* something, and also perhaps that he still does so. And this cannot be established in the same way. Here the connection between what the analyst bases his interpretation on and what he claims is not purely contingent.

The patient's associations are not, in this sense, merely *associated* with what they reveal in him.

Imagine a man separated from his wife but still in love with her, though he will not admit this even to himself. A sympathetic friend may know it from the way the man talks or avoids talking about his wife, the way he fills his days, his listlessness, and so on. What kind of connection is there between this kind of evidence, imponderable as it is, and the belief of the man's friend that he has not forgotten his wife?

Certainly, his still being in love with his wife, though he denies it, is something over and above the expression this finds in the man's words and behaviour. But it is not something behind or alongside these, something that can be inferred from them in the way that a detective may infer that the suspect was at the scene of the crime from the fingerprints he has left on the furniture. It is something over and above any particular expression it finds in the man's thoughts, speech and behaviour in the sense that it cannot be identified with any stretch of these. All the same, if he is still in love then this is something that characterizes his present life, his attitude to life, the tenor of his thoughts. It is in these that the friend sees the state of soul the man is in, in which, indeed, he finds it disclosed, despite the man's attempt to hide it.

Thus there is an important difference between Porfiry's 'psychological' method of investigation and Freud's method of investigating the unconscious mind. The connection between the free-associations on which Freud based his interpretations and the connection between the suspect's speech, when off his guard, and the crime that he refrains from admitting to are different. That the latter has committed the crime in question, that the patient as a child pushed his baby sister out of her pram, that the seduction scenes he relates to his analyst did in fact occur – these are different kinds of hypotheses from the analyst's suspicion, or even near certainty, that he still resents his sister's success in life though he will not admit it to himself, or that he had had death-wishes for his father and phantasies of having his mother all to himself as a child. The final confirmation of these latter hypotheses or interpretations is not the discovery of hidden evidence, eye-witness reports, the memories of a childhood nanny; but rather the full-blown expression of the feelings in question in the transference and the patient's own admission to them.

A good example of this is to be found in Freud's report on the analysis of the Rat Man. During the early sessions Paul Laurenz reports some thoughts that lead Freud to suggest that Laurenz had wished his father's death. Freud makes certain connections between the thoughts reported by Laurenz and gives some explanations. After his initial denials Laurenz 'admitted that all this sounded quite plausible, but he was naturally not in the very least convinced by it' (1979, pp. 61–2; see also pp. 59–62). Later on in the analysis, after having talked about the emergence of the patient's masturbatory practices after his father's death (pp. 82 – 5), Freud 'ventured to put forward a construction to the effect that when he was a child of under six he [the patient] had been guilty of some sexual mis-demeanour connected with masturbation and had been soundly castigated for it by his father' and that 'it had left behind it an ineradicable grudge against his father and had established him for all time in his role as an interferer with the patient's sexual enjoyment'. Freud describes this as 'an hypothesis'. At that stage that is all it was.

To Freud's 'great astonishment' it elicits from the patient a story about himself he had heard from his mother but which meant nothing more to him; he could not himself remember what the story related about him: 'When he was very small . . . he had done something naughty, for which his father had given him a beating. The little boy had flown into a terrible rage and had hurled abuse at his father even while he was under his blows . . . His father, shaken by such an outburst of elemental fury, had stopped beating him' (pp. 85 – 6). His father never beat him again and, as for himself, a change came over his own character: 'from that time forward he was a coward – out of fear of the violence of his own rage'.

The patient subsequently questioned his mother who confirmed the story and added some further details. But, Freud comments, 'he [the patient] kept urging against the evidential value of the story the fact that he himself could not remember the scene'. He adds: 'it was only along the painful road of transference that he was able to reach a conviction that his relation to his father really necessitated the postulation of this unconscious complement. Things soon reached a point at which, in his dreams, his waking phantasies, and his associations, he began heaping the grossest and filthiest abuse upon me and my family, though in his deliberate actions he never treated me with anything but the greatest respect. His demeanour as he repeated these insults to me was that of a man in despair' (p. 89). Freud then goes on to describe the patient's behaviour and his own explanations of it and concludes: 'Thus, little by little, in this school of suffering, the patient won the sense of conviction which he had lacked – though to any disinterested mind the truth would have been almost self-evident' (p. 90).

It is important to note the contrast between the patient's 'associations', as Freud speaks of one part of his behaviour, and his 'deliberate actions'. In these associations we find the child in his mother's story, alien to his conscious thoughts, come out of the character he had developed subsequent to the incident related in the story, the character behind which he had gone into hiding. What the analyst interprets thus becomes a living reality for the patient as he, himself, turns into the little boy, with murder in his heart for his father. He comes to see that he had never given up his grudge, but had only covered it up. He later sees that this is not all there is to him, that he had loved his father and did not stop doing so after the beating which turned him against his father.

The relation between the earlier associations, on which Freud had based his construction, and the later ones, which provided its confirmation, is this. In the earlier ones the patient gives Freud disorderly glimpses of his soul. As they accumulate Freud pieces them together and begins to build a picture of the patient's soul. In the later ones the patient comes out into the open, he shows a face of his soul which he had concealed.

Raskolnikov too finally confesses his crime to Porfiry. But the crime is not something he cannot admit to himself, and it is the kind of thing whose reality can be conclusively established independently of Raskolnikov's admission. Whereas, in contrast, until the patient comes out into the open the analyst cannot be completely certain that the picture he has built of the patient's soul is accurate. If Porfiry needs Raskolnikov's confession, this is because Raskolnikov has committed a 'perfect crime' – if only partly by 'luck'. Thus the difference between the use of free-association in the investigation of the unconscious mind and its use for the ascertaining of truth in courts of law.

There are, on the other hand, also many differences between free-association and the association tests and games mentioned by Freud in his 1906 paper. One could hardly describe a man taking part in such a game as talking, whereas a patient who 'free-associates' in analysis is certainly *talking* to his analyst. Why then did

Freud describe his utterances as associations? Because of his idea that when a person can suspend his 'conscious control' over what he says his unconscious mind will 'take over' and his talk will be 'directed' by its peculiar logic. Freud identified this 'logic' with the associationist psychologists' 'laws of association'.

This idea is by now well discredited philosophically. All the same, behind its philosophical façade lies the truth that a man reveals what is innermost to him in his most unguarded moments. What Freud was asking his patients to do was to drop their guards. They were supposed to move in that direction by suspending the kinds of criticism people normally exercise in talking – consideration of other people's feelings, realizing a particular purpose, expediency, evidence, keeping to the point, consistency, etc. The feature Freud wanted to highlight was the *undisciplined* character of such talk.

But what connection is there between dropping one's guard in one's speech and suspending the forms of criticism that one normally exercises in what one says? Do not those forms of criticism belong to speech? Can one speak at all without exercising some judgement or criticism? If one is to speak sense at all need one not take some trouble to be coherent? Doesn't speech inevitably involve some responsibility to what one is saying?

2   FREE-ASSOCIATION AND LOGIC

Freud spoke of free-associating as following 'the fundamental rule' of psycho-analysis: the patient must say anything and everything that from moment to moment comes into his head, without any restraint or reservation. All right. But even if a rule is not a restraint, following a rule is submission to a discipline. Yet is that not too what the patient is being asked to avoid? There is no short description of what the patient is being asked to do when he is told to free-associate.

He is being asked to be honest, to be himself, and as part of that to talk freely and without any reservation. But you cannot instruct a person in how to do that, and normally there is no need to do so. Indeed, there is no rule to follow here: one cannot be honest by following a rule. At best the analyst can indicate, in general terms, some fairly common things which the patient may be tempted or inclined to do which he must avoid doing. But he cannot list them all, for such a list is open-ended.

Freud said: 'the patient . . . must restrain all the logical and affective objections which would urge him to select' (1950, vol. ii, p. 328). That is, he must not leave out something that occurs to him because it is irrelevant, or inconsistent with what he has already said, or because he feels ashamed. So, he must not worry about keeping to the point, or to the same subject, or contradicting himself. If he suppresses a thought that occurs to him because it contradicts something else he has said he may leave out an important clue about the way he feels about something. In his case studies Freud often uses such thoughts, which the patient is inclined to dismiss as of no significance, to lead him to something important, though at first unacceptable. So the patient is not to concern himself with whether what occurs to him is important or trivial; it is the analyst who is to be the judge of that. Indeed, he is to speak, as the French say, *à bâton rompu*. But does that mean that he must not worry about speaking coherently or responsibly?

To begin with, certainly one can speak perfectly coherently without worrying about it. Indeed, normally one does not worry. If a patient in analysis does so, this is usually a sign that he is anxious about what he might give away if he is not careful. A patient whose sentences are too well arranged, too impeccably ordered, is usually one who keeps his emotions under control. What is in question is a 'character defence'. But, in any case, there are times when normal coherence is not a consideration, for a person can speak quite incoherently and yet express what is close to his heart. Thus extreme anger or grief which finds direct expression in a person's speech may make him speak incoherently. He may say one thing and then immediately something quite different, even contradictory. He may rant and rave, threaten, moan or complain, without being consistent in what he says, or scrupulous about the facts of the case – the offence, the injury, the injustice, etc. Yet his response is direct, the emotion he communicates is clear.

On the occasion when Paul Laurenz as a little boy hurled abuse at his father, he knew no bad language. So he called his father all the common objects he could think of, screaming: 'You lamp! You towel! You plate!' and so on. Yet what was being expressed was clear enough to shake his father and stop him on his tracks. He declared: 'The child will be either a great man or a great criminal' (1979, p. 86).

Indeed, if one tries to speak responsibly, is concerned to be fair, if one is scrupulous in the way one blames the other person, then one is restraining one's anger. For anger and rage exclude such concerns and desires, while conversely the persistence of such concerns is a restraint on one's anger. They can block its expression, and even one's awareness of its presence in one. That is why Freud asked his patients to put aside such scruples while speaking to the analyst.

This does not mean, however, that the language of emotions excludes such moral and logical scruples and concerns. It does not. But unless a person can face emotions in him which have not become part of his language and personality they will not have a coherent expression in his language. The case of repressed or rejcted emotions and desires provides one context in which logical and moral scruples may be at loggerheads with the urge to give free reign to their expression in words. There are, of course, other paradigms of free-association where considerations or consistency, fairness to facts, other people's feelings or expediency would constitute a hindrance – paradigms to which we can find approximations outside analysis. But it does not follow from any of this that free-association is not governed by logic, only by laws of association, or laws that govern products of the unconscious mind – like dreams.

To describe what the patient says as 'his associations' is to characterize the way his utterances are treated or taken by the analyst in the analysis. To describe them as 'free-associations' is to say that the patient does manage, at least to some extent, to suspend some of his everyday scruples and considerations and to give expression to thoughts and feelings that he restrains in much of the normal course of his daily life. But many of these thoughts, reminiscences and feelings are themselves expressible in perfectly coherent speech which has its own logic. The patient's utterances would not make sense if this were otherwise.

The way the analyst treats the patient's utterances in taking them as associations does not mean that the patient and analyst are not *talking* to each other. A dialogue is certainly established between them, a dialogue in which the patient is the centre of attention for the duration of the analytic session. But, of course, the character of that attention depends on the continuity between the sessions and the dialogue cutting across them. The patient's talk, treated as his associations, includes a wide variety of forms of discourse: telling the analyst or talking about different things, including his own thoughts and feelings about a variety of things, reporting conversations, describing situations, passing judgements, praising, blaming, criticizing, justifying his actions, expressing his longings, enthusiasms, discouragements, anger, disappointments, pleasure, grief, indignation, making demands, pleading, complaining, making fun, laughing, crying, etc. These are the patient's way of being himself in analysis, of responding to the analyst's presence as the analyst becomes a familiar figure with whom he forms a relation. In these responses he discloses himself more and more, and in these disclosures he gradually recovers himself – aspects of himself from which he has turned away and which he has put out of his conscious mind.

I quoted Freud's words to the effect that the patient must restrain the logical and affective objections which would urge him to be selective in what he says. This is connected with the idea we find in Freud that the language of the unconscious is illogical, as exemplified by dreams, and that we gag the unconscious mind by our attachment to logic. I have tried to convey the truth there is in this idea, but suggested that it oversimplifies the relation between those concerns of a person's 'conscious personality' which make up his logical scruples and the ways of thinking which characterize aspects of his personality he has not made his own.

Yet many other analysts go in for such an oversimplification in characterizing what constitutes a free-association. For instance, Professor Kubie writes: 'In analysis the free-associations are provided by the patient, the logical scrutiny by the analyst.' And again: 'Ordinary conversational speech, logical and chronological thinking, and asking and answering of questions, arguments and expositions, are the product of a continuous automatic screening of the pyschological process. The screening selects certain ideas for attention because of their logical and chronological relationships, rejecting others as irrelevant . . . The product of this selective process is . . . a weighed sample of our psychological processes' (1950, p. 46). And Marion Milner writes that 'blind thinking completely ignores the laws of logic' (1952, p. 125).

Indeed, reason and logic can be used to build obstinate character defences against emotions that are felt to make a person vulnerable. Thus there are highly articulate people whose very rationality has flushed out much of their emotions from their speech, from their responses to others and attitudes to life. The above remarks may fit in the case of such people, but as general theoretical statements they misrepresent the relation between logic and speech. For they speak as if logic were external to and superimposed on our talk and thought

– characterized as 'secondary processes'. Whereas, on the contrary, without it we do not have anything we could call talking or thinking. All forms of thought and speech are governed by logical criteria. But these are not on a par with the psychologist's 'laws of association', or any other 'laws of nature', and the sense in which our thinking is 'governed' by logic is very different from the sense in which the words a man associates with a given idea are 'governed' by any laws of association. Indeed, I have argued that very few of the patient's associations in analysis are 'associations' in this sense.

What is wrong with the way psycho-analysts so often represent the relation between logic and free-association is sometimes seized on by patients to caricature what they are supposed to do in analysis: in the name of free-association they speak nonsense and try to defeat the analysis by adhering to their analyst's demand to suspend all logical scrutiny. The analyst may then point out to the patient that he is adhering to the letter of the fundamental rule of psycho-analysis while mocking the spirit in which it is meant. But what is the spirit in which it is meant? That is what I am trying to clarify. On the other hand, psycho-analysts cannot disclaim all responsibility for the letter of the fundamental rule. Our philosophical problems lie in understanding the connection between the letter and the spirit of the fundamental rule of psycho-analysis.

3 FREEDOM AND FREE-ASSOCIATION

I argued earlier that the term 'free', used in connection with the patient's utterances treated as 'associations', indicates that the patient is at least trying to suspend many of the conscious considerations that govern or enter into his speech in most situations in his day-to-day life – 'conscious' in the sense that he can articulate them, or at least recognize them as operative if articulated for him by someone else. But that his utterances are 'free-associations' in this sense, that is, genuinue associations and not, for instance, a speech he has rehearsed, does not make them 'free' in the sense of being spontaneous and unhindered. To the extent to which the patient is divided in his wish to change and recover from the condition for which he has sought help, ambivalent in his attitude towards the analyst, and so resists the treatment, his co-operation will be qualified and his associations will not be 'free' in this second sense.

Let me illustrate the sense in question with an example from outside analysis. A prejudiced judge who gives a verdict on the case before him, we could say, has not been able to consider it freely. In so far as he is unaware of his prejudices and has not been able to discount them, they will have influenced his judgement, interfered with his verdict. Since justice is what he is aiming at in the considerations in which he engages as a judge, his prejudices will thwart him in that particular activity – an activity with which he identifies himself and which he does not carry out cynically. They will impede the realization of goals that are *his* in his capacity as judge or magistrate. That is why we say that he has been unable to weigh the pros and cons of the case freely.

The use of the epithets 'free' and 'unfree' in these connections has reference to the goals people pursue in the activities in which they engage. When we say of someone that he did not act, decide or judge freely we are thinking of something that holds him back or deflects him from the realization of goals built into the activity in which he engages. But, as I said before, the rules, standards and criteria internal to that activity cannot be said to restrict, impede or constrain him in so far as he is wholeheartedly engaged in that activity. They may do so in so far as he engages in other activities and pursues other goals, while continuing to adhere to them exclusively. But if he cannot let go of them in other contexts it may be that they have got under his skin, a case of '*déformation professionelle*'. A psycho-analyst would look for something more in it than that. He may, for instance, be a barrister and winning arguments his trade. Yet his single-minded devotion to winning arguments may impede his consideration of other people's feelings, something for which he may pay dearly in his private life. What has got under this person's skin is deeper than his skin; deeper, that is, than well-established habits. It goes into his character. If he were to enter analysis he would find that what hampers him in his private life hampers him in his ability to free-associate.

Associations in analysis are taken as expressions of the patient's unconscious mind and personality. Hence standards of directness and straightforwardness, of what counts as an unreserved expression and truthful utterance, are what is relevant to the analyst's estimate of how free the patient's associations are. When considering association games I said that an association is called a 'free-association' in the sense that the word uttered by the player is not chosen in accordance with any criterion and is genuinely the first word that comes to his head. But this does not guarantee that it is spontaneous or unhindered. The same applies to what is meant by a free-association in analysis. To free-associate means for the patient to tell the analyst whatever comes into his head. If the patient consciously censures what he tells the analyst he is breaking the fundamental rule of psycho-analysis. This would be interpreted by the analyst as a resistance to being analysed. On the other hand, not all resistances constitute a breaking of the fundamental rule. Thus a patient's utterance may be a free-association, that is, a genuine association, and yet more than anything the analyst may see in it an expression of the patient's resistance to being analysed – an expression of his fear of relaxing in the presence of the analyst, his anxieties with regard to talking about himself.

Hence, I think, we should distinguish between *speaking whatever comes into one's head*, which is all that the patient has to do to comply with the fundamental rule of psycho-analysis, and *speaking freely* and being oneself in what one says. Yet psycho-analysts often run these two ideas together in their notion of 'free-association'. Thus, while they are sometimes inclined to say that everything that a patient says in analysis is a free-association (see Glover, 1955, p. 300), they are also inclined to say that nothing that the patient says is a free-association, or hardly ever. So Glover writes that 'from the moment the fundamental rule has been expounded to the patient and has been ostensibly accepted by him, a large part of the analyst's work will up to the last moment consist in an endeavour to circumvent its evasion' (p. 27). Certainly, the patient will, without recognizing this himself, try to evade self-disclosure. But this is not to say that he will constantly break the rule of free-association.

Let me return to the question of the freedom of free-association and of the obstacles which impede this freedom. Take the case of a person who wants to tell someone, a friend or colleague, what he thinks of him. When would we say that he spoke freely? If he were afraid of hurting the other's feelings, for instance, or if he were concerned with the effect of his words, or if he were overcome by scruples about whether he was right or wrong, fair or unfair, then we would say that he had been unable to speak his mind freely. His scruples may actually change what he thinks about his friend or colleague, what he thinks may lose its definiteness or sense of conviction. But it is equally possible that they drive what he thinks underground so that he can no longer express it directly. Even when this does not happen, if his scruples lead him to give his friend or colleague his considered opinion, he would be defeating his purpose. I do not mean to say that what he thinks of his friend in the first place may not be his considered opinion. But if he is convinced and does want to give his friend a piece of his mind, not necessarily in an unfriendly spirit, then he would have no scruples about whether or not he is right or fair. Such scruples are incompatible with the desire to give someone a piece of one's mind. In this sort of situation diffidence and overscruplousness will result in evasion. Here the paradigm of the person who speaks his mind freely is one who speaks without fear and with genuine conviction and feeling.

It is what is external to his aims and purposes that curtails a person's freedom in what he says, such as when he means to speak his mind on some matter in which he is personally involved. The more he is divided in himself, in conflict about what to say, the more anxious he is, or the more he expects things for himself and calculates the consequences of his action, the less freely will he be able to speak his mind.

Obviously, it is only if one knows one's mind that one can speak it. The notion suggests a specific objective – for instance, to get something off one's chest. But this does not mean that one has worked it out beforehand. If one has done so, this usually suggests that one has other concerns, that one is worried about the consequences of being direct. Thus, if I feel strongly enough about telling you what I think, I shall do so in a first-hand way. In analysis the patient's talk sometimes approximates to this.

If one does not know one's mind, if, for instance, one does not know what to think about a particular matter which affects one, one cannot speak it. One may not know one's mind because one has not made it up. In such a case, clearly, one needs to make up one's mind before one can speak it. But one may equally not know one's mind because one is afraid of the commitments one would have to face in acknowledging what one thinks and feels about something or someone. In that case one way to find out is to suspend a deliberate search and simply let it become accessible in one's unguarded, free-wheeling musings. This is one paradigm of free-association. Thus, in analysis the patient may come to a session with nothing specific to tell his analyst. He is then expected to say the first thing that occurs to him. If he searches his mind for something to say, instead of just waiting, he will have transgressed the fundamental rule. If he is not too anxious he will be silent or say that at the moment he does not have anything to say. Often such silence is an expression of anxiety and the analyst may respond by saying: 'There is something you don't want me to know.'

4 LEARNING TO FREE-ASSOCIATE

I distinguished between not associating freely and not free-associating at all. The line between these is not, of course, a sharp one.

I also said that you cannot tell a person how to do something freely, any more than you can tell him how to speak frankly or how to be sincere. You can only warn him of the obstacles and sometimes instruct him in how to avoid some of these. In the case of free-association the patient is briefly instructed in what he is to do. That is, he is told what it means to free-associate. He is thus told to tell his analyst whatever occurs to him without omission, to talk about whatever happens to interest, concern or bother him at the time, not to be bound by any overall purpose, not to be afraid to express his feelings openly, and always to speak truthfully.

Almost every patient, however, will find it very difficult, especially at first, to do what is required. This idea of what is required will itself have a self-stultifying effect. If he is anxious to please or to do what is expected of him, to comply with what he takes as a demand of the analyst, if he is anxious to do the right thing – and this may well be part of his character – what he will do will be contrary to what he was told to do. As René Laforgue puts it: 'An analysand who tries too hard to say everything that he is thinking ends by becoming a slave to this obligation and is no longer in a state of mind favourable to the unfolding of his thoughts, for he is preoccupied with the desire to catch on the wing every idea which comes into his mind' (1937, p. 35).

So in most cases the patient will at first find it very hard to know what is being asked of him. His mental habits will constantly get in the way. He will learn that a certain relaxation of discipline, a certain disinterestedness and abandon, which Freud describes as 'passivity' (1950, vol. ii, p. 18), is needed before he can free-associate. This may not come easily to him. Some patients, on the other hand, will literally talk nonsense in the name of free-association (see Ferenczi, 1950). So Freud says that 'although we have impressed upon the patient the rule to communicate all his thoughts, he does not seem to be able to keep it' (1950, vol. ii, p. 19).

I think that in the first stages of analysis there is a sense in which the patient is not clear what he is supposed to do. He will have to be 'educated' to analysis. In his book *Character Analysis* Wilhelm Reich explains that this is best achieved by analysis. He calls it 'education to analysis by analysis'. But this does not consist of teaching the patient anything new. For what he has to learn is to be 'conversationally open' in a new sort of situation, and this belongs to learning to talk. Only one who can speak openly and truthfully can resort to lying and artifice. So the patient has to *unlearn* certain habits which prevent him from being conversationally open with his analyst. But the trouble goes deeper, for the habits in question are habits of evasion, and that is why Reich speaks of 'education by analysis'.

Once the analysis has begun to move and the patient's relationship with his analyst develops there will be a great deal he will wish to communicate to him. He will find, however, that all sorts of reservations, fears, anxieties, aims and desires interfere with his freedom to communicate, that is, with his ability to talk openly and without reserve. There will even come a time when the very intensity of his feelings will stand in the way of his talking about them, articulating his responses. He will, instead, act them out, and it will take some analytic work before he can begin to talk about what is in question, to reminisce around these subjects about which he feels so heated.

Experiencing these difficulties in free-associating is part of the process of coming to know oneself. As the difficulties diminish and the patient is able to free-associate more freely, that is, speak more directly, put more of himself into what he is saying, he will gradually learn to be himself and in doing so come to know himself. He will meet himself in what he is saying. Once he knows how to be open with another person, once he has regained this ability which he may have lost early in childhood, once he is able to trust himself with others, he can use his discretion in the future: he will be able to form relations of trust in which he can open up to others, but he will also know how to keep to himself and where to be reserved. He will have lost his inability to open up, and he will open up only when and where he, himself, wants to do so.

5   A MISCONCEPTION

There are, then, many obstacles to the patient's talking and expressing his thoughts and feelings freely; his resistances to analysis take many forms. Hence analysts are hardly ever satisfied with their patients' free-associations, these are hardly ever sufficiently free for their liking. I have argued that this does not mean, as many analysts have thought, that patients constantly evade the fundamental rule of psycho-analysis.

Neither can it be taken to support mental determinism. The idea that associations are never free because they are always determined, because 'determinism in the psychic realm is . . . carried out uninterruptedly' (1954, p. 212), is a confused one. Freud said: 'It will not surprise us to find that not only numbers but also mental occurrences of different kinds of words regularly prove on analytic investigation to be well determined' (p. 204). And again: 'For some time I have been aware that it is impossible to think of a number, or even a name, of one's own free will' (p. 193). As I have argued elsewhere (Dilman, 1984a, chapter 9, section 3), the point Freud is trying to make, however confusedly, is not the previous one that free-associations in analysis are hardly ever completely free, since they are partly in the service of the patient's resistances to analysis, but that whatever the patient says contains some expression, however indirect, of his thoughts and feelings, of his desires and fears.

Freud believed that any utterance whatever, to some extent, bears the stamp of the speaker's personality and, therefore, reveals something of his preoccupations, the way he thinks, the way he deals with certain situations, and so on. To look in it for what it reveals about the speaker's mind and personality is precisely what is meant by treating it as an association. Thus, when Freud said that 'it is impossible to compose nonsense intentionally and arbitrarily' he meant, I think, that as an association any utterance necessarily has some significance. But to see it one has to be perceptive, know something about the person in question, and pay attention to the context in which he speaks. Freud believed further, as we have seen, that the less guarded the person is, the more free and spontaneous will his utterances be, and therefore also the more revealing about him. This is the rationale of the use of free-association in analysis and of the priority analysts give to the interpretation of their patients' resistances with a view to reducing them. This work is aimed at enabling the patient to associate more freely and thus to disclose more of himself, or disclose himself to a greater extent.

6 PHILOSOPHICAL CONCLUSIONS

My main contention has been that free-association in psycho-analysis takes many different forms and has more affinity to a conversation than the ideas from which it has developed would lead us to suppose. An association is not an utterance governed by any law of association, but one in which the patient's thoughts and feelings find expression. It is an utterance in which the analyst looks for the workings of the patient's unconscious mind.

This search involves a flair which is akin to an aesthetic flair. I contrasted the substantiation of the conclusion towards which it leads the analyst with the substantiation of a conclusion similarly arrived at about some *deed* of a person which he refuses to admit – to wit, Porfiry's 'psychological method' in *Crime and Punishment*. The question of the substantiation of a psycho-analytic interpretation based on the patient's free-associations will be discussed further in the next chapter.

Third, I argued that the word 'free' in the expression 'free-association' is meant to refer to the undisciplined character of the verbal communication in question. But a free-association may be in the service of the patient's resistances and so may not be free. In this sense its freedom admits of degrees. So I distinguished between speaking whatever comes into one's head, which in analysis constitutes the patient's free-association, and speaking freely, of which speaking freely whatever comes into one's head is a sub-species.

Freud believed that the less guarded, the more off his guard a person is, and the less preoccupied with getting something across, and so the less concerned to meet standards and requirements, the more will he reveal himself in what he says. This is the rationale of the use of the method of free-association in psycho-analysis.

6

Interpretation and the Enlightenment of the Patient

1 WHAT IS A PSYCHO-ANALYTIC INTERPRETATION?

In the last chapter we saw that associations are the patient's contribution to the analytic dialogue. In these the patient does not describe but *discloses* himself. Indeed, in them he moves towards being himself. Interpretations are the analyst's contributions to this dialogue. In them he does not merely make statements about the patient's unconscious mind, tell him what he does not recognize about himself. He tries to *make* conscious the patient's unconscious, to make him see and face what he turns away from in himself. Yet the analyst seeks to get the patient to do this for himself and of his own free volition. He makes no attempt at convincing the patient. In thus confining himself to giving interpretations he avoids exerting any pressure on the patient. In other words, interpretations are aimed at making conscious the unconscious and yet they leave the patient to turn away from self-deception to authenticity of his own accord. There is nothing paradoxical about this claim.

The dialogue, of which the patient's associations and the analyst's interpretations are the two complementary parts, has a *consciously* agreed common purpose: jointly to explore the patient's personality so that he can come to a deeper understanding of himself, become less blind to what he is up to in the activities he pursues and the relationships in which he engages, and so to the patterns into which he constantly forces these, and thereby come to have the option to modify these patterns in those respects which bring him trouble, frustration and pain. The patterns are, of course, expressions of his personality, what he brings into and so reaps from the activities and relationships in which he engages, in short, the way his personality shapes these. But this conscious purpose which the patient shares with his analyst is constantly subverted by him in the course of the analysis. The patient does so through other purposes he brings into and pursues in his analysis, with the same blindness to them as outside, purposes which belong to those very patterns about which the analyst, in accordance with the agreed joint purpose of the treatment, seeks to enlighten him.

To seek to enlighten the patient about these patterns, as he seeks to establish them in the analysis, is, for the analyst, to refuse to go along with the patient in his attempts to do so. It is for the analyst to desist from entering into them. And this is already more than just telling the patient something about himself. It is *responding* to his attempt to manipulate the analysis. The patient is likely to invest this response with a significance it does not have and to react to it on that basis. Instead of reacting back to this the analyst tries to point out that the significance which the patient attributed to his, the analyst's interpretation comes out of the patient's own very special repertoire, distinctive of his personality. He reminds the patient of other instances of it in his life, related on previous occasions in the analysis. But, once more, doing so is also *responding* to the patient's reaction to the analyst, a reaction which may be provocative or placatory, seductive or insulting. For, in sticking to the analysis of the patient's response, the analyst refuses to take the bait thus put in his way. Given his genuine concern to help the patient by analysis, in thus resisting manipulation the analyst preserves his integrity.

In this way a relationship develops between the patient and analyst in which the patient constantly pulls at the seams of the analysis and the analyst remains vigilant and true to it – vigilent about the patient's aims and intentions as well as about his own motives and reactions, but not self-consciously so. In this relationship the patient reveals himself and in doing so changes in so far as he is unable to elicit from the analyst the kind of response which suits his unconscious schemes. He reveals himself equally in so far as he finds in the analytic relationship some genuine caring attention which renders some of his habitual defences redundant so that he can discard them. This caring attention finds expression in the way the analyst listens to the patient, is patient with his repetitive return to the same patterns, avoids being provoked, and is able to attend to the pain the patient brings to the analysis with sympathy and without pretending that it is something less than what it is.

The interpretations are certainly attempts on the analyst's part to *say* something to the patient, to point something out to him for his benefit. But they are also expressions of compassionate attention – a compassion that necessarily involves sympathy for the patient's plight and respect for his being a separate fellow human being: no more and no less. This is what they are in a positive sense. Negatively they are what they are in not being those responses which the patient tries to elicit from the analyst in the pursuit of his unconscious aims. I mean that interpretations also often represent the analyst's refusal to go along with the patient and provide him with the kind of response he unconsciously seeks. All these different aspects play a role in the way they work to enlarge the patient's consciousness of himself. The authenticity of the analyst, in the way he avoids pressurizing the patient or enticing him to come out into the open and in resisting being himself manipulated by the patient, contributes to the realization of this therapeutic aim. So also does his readiness to accept the patient and respect his separateness. All this is part of the analyst's confining himself to interpretation work. It is by giving interpretations with a view to conveying his perceptions to the patient that the analyst speaks the truth, as he sees it, and is himself truthful – that is, does not pretend about the patient's condition, as he sees it, and is genuine in his responses to it.

If the analyst had something to hide or something to gain for himself his interpretations would not be honest or truthful. They would not help to build up trust in the analysis, and so they would discourage the patient from being himself and disclosing his secret thoughts and feelings. But let me repeat that there is a big difference between being genuinely truthful and being 'truthful' for a purpose, however laudable. The latter would be bogus truthfulness and a way of manipulating the patient. It is when the patient realizes that the analyst is genuinely truthful that he comes to trust him and so is able to be honest and more open in himself. For in analysis, as elsewhere, it takes two to have a relationship of honesty, and psycho-analysis is a psychotherapy based on honesty and truthfulness. Since interpretations are responses in which the analyst confines himself to conveying his perceptions to the patient their truth combines these two aspects. As such, the analyst differs from a mere observer reflecting the truth as he sees it. For in the interpretations he gives truth is offered to the patient in the hope of both enlightening him and of making him more truthful.

The process of 'making conscious the unconscious' combines these two features which are the two sides of the same coin. The patient's greater truthfulness or authenticity, thus achieved, in turn serves the analyst to take the analysis further forward. Let me re-emphasize: enlightenment or insight into oneself and authenticity are logically interrelated, they form part of the same whole.

If analysis is not a moulding of the patient in the image of the analyst's perceptions of him ('suggestion'), neither is it a stripping off of masks which the patient uses to hide behind. This would be a form of psychological violation. It is a careful nurturing of greater truthfulness in the patient. As a result the patient gives up, of his own free will, defences he has kept up and self-deceptions he has maintained. He gives them up, bit by bit, as they become redundant in the analysis as a result of the way he is accepted and his anxieties diminish. These defences, which become a way of resisting analysis, are the pursuit of schemes and solutions adopted in the past. The patient is also able to discard them as he finds new fulfilments and loses the need to compensate for old inadequacies which he could not accept. In this way he moves towards greater insight and authenticity himself, and the analyst's role in the process is a benign one. It does not infringe upon the patient's autonomy.

We see that interpretations are a special vehicle of communication which takes place in the course of interpersonal contact. Their ability to enlarge the patient's consciousness turns on the analyst's use of them to respond to the patient's unconscious mind as this is revealed in the way it comes to be engaged in the analytic relationship. For the analyst to confine himself to interpreting what thus surfaces in the analysis is for him to refrain from entering into the patient's unconscious schemes, to refuse to be drawn into them.

In this respect Freud has compared him to a mirror: 'The physician should be impenetrable to the patient, and, like a mirror, reflect nothing but what is shown to him' (1950, vol. ii, p. 331). In other words, in what the analyst says to him the patient should be able not to see the analyst's soul, but his own. The analyst, that is, should not reveal himself by either reacting to the patient or engaging with his unconscious strategies. But this must not be a way of hiding from the patient: he must not reveal himself not because he has something to hide, but because he thinks of the patient. Instead of engaging with the patient's unconscious strategies he must only convey his perception of them.

This makes the analytic relationship asymmetrical, but not one-sided. For the analyst does participate in the relationship in the way he works for the patient's welfare. The fact that he refrains from serving the patient's unconscious strategies, from colluding with him in furthering them, does not mean that he is concerned to protect himself. He does so to help the patient; part of the analyst's way of helping the patient is to make him consider things about himself that he resists looking at. Far from retreating from him, the analyst gives something of himself to the patient in the way he listens to him, exercises patience, puts up with provocation, obstinacy and determined attempts to subvert his therapeutic objective, bears the patient's pain, and gives him understanding. But this compassion for the patient, of which respect for his autonomy is one aspect, is *impersonal*: it does not do anything for the analyst personally and it is something he is prepared to give to any patient he believes he can help without personal preference.

One should not, however, confuse this impersonality with the kind of detachment and objectivity that the mirror analogy may wrongly suggest. A mirror cannot care one way or the other for what it reflects; whereas the analyst participates in the relationship within which he works for the patient's welfare. What Freud wished to convey is that he is completely transparent or selfless in the way he attends to the patient, or at any rate aims to be. This means that in his analytic contact with the patient his concern for him leaves no room for the analyst's own wishes and anxieties about himself to intrude into what he says. Or, to put it another way, he has sufficient mastery over these to be free to attend to the patient selflessly. This mastery itself is nourished by his concern for others, his ability to respond to their needs. Indeed, it is an aspect of a personality that is orientated towards others.

The analyst thus exercises reserve about himself for the sake of the patient because the kind of treatment that psycho-analysis is demands it from him. When Freud says that the analyst should be like a mirror he is emphasizing how much this exercise of reserve is part of interpreting, of reflecting his unconscious to the patient. If the patient and the analyst are to see what the patient is like when he gives expression to his unconscious in the analytic relationship, the patterns that emerge there must, as much as possible, be the patient's contribution. They must not be shaped by what the analyst brings to the relationship. Thus the analyst must do nothing other than help the patient towards greater self-understanding and authenticity. He must not try to win the patient's conviction, he must leave him to come to see the truth in what he, the analyst, says for himself and to accept it for that reason only. This is what is meant by a purely interpretative therapy.

In such a therapy not only does the analyst leave it to the patient himself to reach the insight that the analyst communicates to him, without being pushed or bribed, to make it his own, he also leaves it to the patient to take on board what he comes to see, and to find his own solutions to his problems. Thus the analyst's 'passivity' and 'neutrality' make room for the patient's engagement in the therapy, they make room for his autonomy to grow. But, once more, this does not mean that the analyst does not participate in the therapeutic work. His passivity and neutrality characterize his participation, they are the form which this participation takes.

There is no incompatibility, of course, between interpretations being *verbal communications* to the patient about his unconscious self and their being *responses* to him – responses to something in him operative in his associations and in the 'transference' at the time, aiming to draw it out into the open. Thus, to take a common example, when you praise someone you tell him how well he has done and express your admiration or encourage him to continue. This is not to do two different things, of course, for one cannot do one without doing the other – not under normal circumstances. To praise someone is to do these two things in one.

To think of psycho-analytic interpretations as 'descriptive statements' or 'explanatory hypotheses' is both to ignore the personal dimension and therapeutic objective of the psycho-analytic dialogue and to fail to appreciate the way they address the patient. They are not meant to prove something which he doubts, to inform him of something he ignores, to explain something he does not understand. This is to confine the communication in question to the sphere of the intellect and to misrepresent what goes on in analysis. Although interpretations are formulated in a language the patient is able to understand, they are not addressed to his intellect – not primarily at any rate. And even when they are understood and accepted intellectually the patient may continue to remain impermeable to what they say to him.

When an interpretation gets across, when the patient is touched by its truth, it makes a difference to him, even though intellectually he may continue to reject it. For him to become convinced of its truth, to accept it and be able to articulate it, this impact has to reach his consciousness. This means that it has to work its way 'from inside out' rather than the other way around as the rationalist model suggests.

Plato's distinction between knowledge and opinion may throw some light on what is in question here, despite its rationalist overtones (see Dilman, 1979, chapter 3). Plato had insisted that one who has knowledge is one who is able to give reasons for what he believes and that it is these reasons that make the truth of what he believes incontrovertible, thus changing opinion to knowledge. Where self-knowledge is concerned, however, reasons alone cannot carry the self to the truth, leaving the belief they engender as something external to the self. The real distinction Plato wanted is between what is first-hand, that is, what one has arrived at oneself or made one's own, and what is only second-hand. This is crucial for understanding the difference between genuine self-knowledge and some other person's *borrowed* perceptions of oneself, however well he may know one. The latter cannot amount to knowledge in the person concerned both because they are not his own perceptions and because they have not been taken into the self. To be taken into the self that self would have to change. Whereas in contrast, although for one's perceptions of *another* person to amount to knowledge they equally have to be first-hand, coming to such knowledge does not have to involve any change in oneself: it is sufficient that one's vision or understanding of him changes.

For these reasons seeing the truth of an interpretation in analysis is not like seeing the truth of any other statement. For the interpretation speaks to the person in analysis about himself, and seeing its truth is very different from coming to see an 'objective' truth, one to which he is not related differently from anyone else. That is why insight into oneself involves a change in the person who comes to it – a change from naïvety to maturity, from self-deception to authenticity. This is a change in the self, not merely in the person's understanding of himself.

An interpretation, furthermore, does not merely say something about the patient that anyone can consider, it is addressed to him and engages him personally. Therefore, it cannot be treated as a biographical remark. It has its life in the particular analysis, it is a move within the analytic dialogue. It derives its *raison d'être* from the psycho-analytic relationship in the context of which it is given with the specific aim of enlightening the patient about himself and keeping the analysis moving. Separated from this context it would lose its character as a response to the patient's associations and turn into a mere biographical statement or explanation.

I am not suggesting that a third person cannot appreciate the truth of a psycho-analytic interpretation. Indeed he can, as the analyst himself does. But this is only achieved through a long period of contact with the person in question, in the course of which another person may come to know him. Or, if he already knows the person well, he can say: 'This is indeed something I have myself seen about Fred. I can see what his analyst means, what he is referring to when he says that Fred feels empty and is greedy for what would fill the void in him, but that he is unable to be nourished by what others have to offer him since in his envy he destroys it before he can incorporate it.' In either case the knowledge needed in order to appreciate the truth of the interpretation is not acquired by means of observation or 'objective scrutiny' (see Dilman, 1986, chapter 9).

Even then there is a difference between the case of this third person and the psycho-analyst. For the analyst does not simply come to see something about the patient which the patient himself does not recognize. He sees the patient coming to recognize it, witnesses the change in him involved in coming to it, a change in the coming about of which he, the analyst, has himself played a role. This, as we shall see, is precisely what constitutes the confirmation of the interpretation.

2 INTERVENTION AND ENLIGHTENMENT

If interpretations aim at and play a role in bringing about such a change how can they avoid being a form of interference? How can the analyst claim that his therapeutic role is a purely passive one, that he nurtures and does not infringe upon the patient's autonomy?

The answer to this question is two-fold, comprising both the change in a person which is part of his coming to realize something about himself he has thus far avoided recognizing, and the change he undergoes in taking this realization on board and responding to life on that basis. We have already seen that Freud explicitly said that what the patient does with what he has come to see about himself, indeed what he does with his life now that he can allow himself to be himself in this respect, is up to him. It is not the business of the analyst to give him any direction here.

The former kind of change, however, is one in which the analyst has played a role in realizing by means of his interpretations. In that sense the interpretations are interventions, they impinge on the patient's behaviour in analysis, they make a difference to it. How can the conduct of any therapy avoid being that? But here a distinction needs to be made between using persuasion and making it possible for the patient himself to come to the realization of whatever truth the interpretation points out. Only in the latter case will the change be authentic and the insight something that the patient will have made his own. Even when the insight is formulated in the first place by another person in the process of making it his own the patient comes to see the truth is what he is told for himself.

Here, to borrow a simile from Socrates, the analyst acts as a midwife: the insight delivered is that of the patient. The analyst merely recovers it and makes it available to the patient. He helps the patient to see something for himself, to find his own truth in himself. Thus the change involved is not one that has been imposed from outside, and the patient's autonomy remains intact. Indeed, it has been nurtured.

In the development of his ideas and methods of therapy Freud came to realize that the analyst's role should be to help the patient to let the insight aimed at to emerge from within. Thus he points out in his *Introductory Lectures*:

> At one time we thought that [to bring what is unconscious in the patient into his consciousness] would be very simple; all we need to do would be to identify this unconscious matter and then tell the patient what it was. However, we know already that that was a short-sighted mistake. Our knowledge of what is unconscious in him is not equivalent to his knowledge of it; when we tell him what we know he does not assimilate it *in place of* his own unconscious thoughts, but *alongside* of them, and very little has been changed. (1949b, p. 364)

In other words, what is at best in the patient's understanding remains dissociated from what he is and continues to be like in himself. So the role of the analyst should not be to verbalize this insight before the patient is able to take it in (what Wilhelm Reich called 'direct interpretation', 1950, p. 10) but to prepare him for it and help him to come to it himself in the movement of the analysis. This movement, Freud points out, is maintained by the elimination of the patient's resistances (1949b, p. 365). But then the question arises: is it not the insight that moves the analysis? If insight is merely the result of the movement, how can psycho-analysis be an insight-therapy?

It is sometimes said that Freud came to realize that 'filling in the hysterical patient's amenesias' is not what brings about the cure. The recovery of these memories is a symptom of progress in the hysterical patient's therapy, it does not bring it about: the replacement of unconscious reminiscences by conscious memories is, as it were, a therapeutic epiphenomenon. This is an ambiguous statement in which truth and falsity are intermingled. It is misleading in so far as it makes it seem that Freud's early belief in the liberating power of truth (insight, authenticity) was a mistake and that Freud, himself, went back on it. This is not so. What was a mistake was Freud's naïve view of what constitutes such insight and how it is to be achieved. Freud came to see that such insight cannot be imparted by 'just telling the patient' and that even when achieved it has to be 'integrated', the patient has to make it part of his life. It is the latter integration that did not happen when, in Freud's earlier days, the patient recalled a traumatic experience while in an hypnotic trance.

The insight which psycho-analysis aims to promote involves an affective reordering or reorganization of the self. It both liberates resources that are deployed in maintaining the old order, 'defensive' in character, and gives the person a better basis for self-understanding. These resources enrich his new life and the self-understanding makes his wiser, helping him to avoid earlier mistakes.

Freud always believed that the order which allows greater autonomy is the one which involves greater authenticity and, therefore, self-knowledge. It is such an order which the psycho-analyst aims to promote, which makes psycho-analysis an insight-therapy. For to promote an order or regime of the self which involves greater authenticity *is* to promote insight into the self.

It is true that insight arises as a result of the movement in the patient's analysis, but that movement itself is the result of previous insight which the patient has acquired in the analysis. The movement is never initiated by anything other than the patient being helped to come to a new piece of insight. What starts the analysis moving in the first place is the desire of the patient to come out of his 'conscious self' with which he feels dissatisfied and the permissiveness of the method of free-association. Where this leads to the 'transference' the analysis is moving satisfactorily.

Freud believed that even though everyone is afraid of the truth, i.e. that there is *some* truth about each person of which he is afraid and about which he deceives himself, in most people there is a deep-seated desire for authenticity: a desire to be what they are and to be accepted as such. In our very desire to do what we wish, to give to and serve others, to improve our relationships with those whom we work and those for whom we care we crave for greater authenticity. We feel ashamed of and diminished by everything that tempts us to turn away from it. We feel that our calculation of gains is something foolish, something that impoverishes our life. Freud believed that this feeling and this craving exists in many of us. It is precisely this desire with which the psycho-analytic therapist sides against the patient's resistances.

But does this not mean that, contrary to what Freud said explicitly (see 1949b, p. 361), he does take sides in the patient's conflicts? The short answer is that, after allowing for special circumstances (see 1949b, pp. 319 – 20), he is on the side of everything in the patient that turns him towards greater authenticity. After all, progress in psycho-analytic therapy turns on the patient overcoming his resistances and giving up his defences in analysis. However, with most inner conflicts which a psycho-analysis reopens, liberation and authenticity do not lie entirely on one side or the other. That is why Freud says the analyst should refrain from taking sides and should allow the patient to find his own solution (see 1949b, p. 366).

All right. But in so far as he does take sides against the patient's resistances and defences in analysis, can he still be said to be 'neutral' and 'passive', to leave everything to the patient? In a sense he cannot, of course. But this is the sense in which 'neutrality' becomes indifference and 'passivity' becomes irresponsibility. In *that* sense, if the analyst were to be 'neutral' and 'passive' he could not treat the patient at all. What we should remember, however, is that, unless the patient has sought analysis wholly at someone else's initiative, it is for a reason of his own that he has come to analysis. This could be one or more of many different reasons to be explored in the analysis. For the analyst to agree to treat him is not for him to give the patient a blank cheque for the duration of the treatment, to agree to support him whatever his reasons for wanting to stay in analysis.

Unless the patient shows a genuine desire to search for greater authenticity the analyst cannot support him in his desire to achieve whatever it is he desires to achieve through what the analyst provides. The analyst tries to wean him from such a desire by taking sides with his desire for greater authenticity. Where this is absent it is doubtful that the patient can move towards a genuine relationship with the analyst. Freud pointed out that this is so in some extreme cases of 'narcissistic disorder' (see 1949b, p. 353). Here the therapist cannot help the patient by means of analysis.

I come back to the fact that psycho-analysis is based on honesty, and in those rare cases where a patient is incapable or unwilling to be honest the treatment cannot proceed. Unless there is *some* will to be honest, however much it may be overgrown with habits of dishonesty and deception, the analysis cannot get going. So a patient must be prepared to be honest if he is at all serious in his desire for analytic treatment, his desire to come to grips with his problems. Therefore, demanding honesty from him, supporting his desire for greater authenticity as against what constitutes his resistances to analysis, is not to interfrere with him. It is not to show disrespect for his separateness and potential autonomy. Thus, while interpretations are interventions, in giving them the analyst does not make the patient do anything against his will. He does not persuade him to accept a particular view of himself, or entice him to move in this or that direction.

I said earlier that psycho-analysis is an insight therapy and works on the principle that insight liberates. But while intepretations are the sole vehicle for the communication of this insight, certain conditions are necessary for the communication to take place. Such communication does not consist of just telling the patient what one sees about him. It is essential that the person addressed is able to receive and consider what is said to him. It should come to him as something live and strike him with genuine immediacy. It has to be something he cannot ignore, something to which he must respond. It has to be something a response to which stretches him. It must challenge his established ways of dealing with what is new without frightening him so that he withdraws into himself or otherwise evades its impact.

Certainly, it is essential that the communication comes to him from another person and is directed to him. It must not be something he reads in a book or something that is passed on to him second-hand by someone who acts as a go-between. Otherwise it will not be something to which he has to respond, and which will, in turn, elicit a response from another person. This is the cut and thrust which breathes life into the communication. It is a logical requirement, and the analytic setting obviously satisfies it.

But it is also important that the interlocuter sees that the person addressing him is genuine and cannot be twisted or manipulated. This will encourage seriousness and discourage evasion. It is also important that he can be trusted: trusted to speak the truth as he sees it and to respect others. These are obviously moral qualities necessary in the other person for the insight he communicates to get across.

It still remains true, of course, that the interlocuter has to see the truth in what he is told for himself and in himself. This may be immediate or it may take time and inner work for this truth to sink in. In analysis the analyst's tolerant acceptance of the patient makes this possible.

So, while the patient must come to the insight he acquires in analysis himself, the presence of another person is crucial. The patient, like anyone else, needs another person's response in order to come out of himself and see what he is like. The kind of sustained work which analysis consists of further necessitates that he engage with this other person, the analyst. The analyst's role in this position is a complex one. He at once challenges the patient with what he shows him about himself, the patient, and he accepts him. He makes the patient's defences in analysis inoperative or redundant and he holds him together. He gives the patient benevolent attention and also refuses to take responsibility for the patient's responses to him. He does not take on the role of a parent despite the patient's efforts to make him do so.

The analysis moves largely as a result of the analyst's success in getting the patient to drop his defences and come out into the open. This process involves the patient, returning to the past, becoming as he was when a child: this is 'regression'. In this way he meets his childish self and faces, in adulthood, the conflicts and problems that he failed to come to terms with then. The way he dealt with them, his particular 'solutions' of that time, come up for revision. Thus, analysis works by removing those layers of defence which hide the way the patient has remained since losing his naïve authenticity. But this descent of the patient into himself through the past is only half of his journey. He will have to ascend to an authenticity that is commensurate with his age and station in life (see Dilman, 1984a, pp. 128–9). Again, analysis helps the patient to do this by removing obstacles, leaving him to learn from new experiences that are opened up to him.

3 TRUTH AND CONFIRMATION

Psycho-analytic interpretations, we have seen, refer to the patient's unconscious, that is, to what he is deceived about in himself in acting the way he does, and they aim to make it conscious, that is, to make him conscious of it so that it becomes part of what comes under the domain of his will. What is crucial for understanding their mode of confirmation is that: (i) they are about *another person*, the patient; (ii) they speak *to him* directly; (iii) they refer to what is *hidden from him*. Therefore, their confirmation inevitably involves: (i) the other person's assent to what they claim; (ii) his response to what they say to him; (iii) this confirmation inevitably awaits a time in the future, however near the present it may be, when what is hidden from the patient is revealed to him. Where such confirmation is obtained we say that the analyst was right, that the interpretation was true or correct.

The fact that their confirmation lies in the future should not in itself present us with a problem since this is a feature in the confirmation of many other statements, and certainly of all hypotheses. But what does present a problem is the fact that psycho-analytic interpretations seek to realise the state of affairs which constitutes their confirmation. In that case is not the confirmation obtained worthless? For surely what the analyst takes as confirmation must obtain independently of his agency, independently of the utterance of the interpretation, if it is to be confirmation.

The point is that the patient's subsequent behaviour must be genuine, something that comes from him now in identity with the way he was *before* he heard the interpretation. It must not be something engineered by the analyst. Let us be clear about this distinction. On the one hand, the way the patient was before he heard the interpretation is something of which he was not himself aware at the time. On the other hand, his subsequent behaviour is something that has been 'brought about' by interpretation work. It is true, the psycho-analyst could have kept his perceptions to himself, withheld the interpretation, and the patient could have changed his behaviour in the way in question without interpretation work. But in that case we would not have had a psycho-analytic therapy, only clinical observation as part of an experiment.

Even as such, however, it would have been a poor sort of experiment, since a normal experiment attempts to bring about a result that confirms an hypothesis under investigation by producing the conditions that the hypothesis states to be its cause. If the result obtains then the hypothesis is confirmed, otherwise it is not. It would be unrealistic, in any case, to wait for the analyst's hunches to come true independently of psycho-analytic work. If there had been much probability of this taking place there would have been little need for psycho-analytic therapy.

What we need to understand is the difference between the case where the behaviour that is taken as confirming an interpretation is 'engineered' by the analyst, whether intentionally or not, and the case where an interpretation 'works' because it is true and 'gets across' to the patient. Here we should remember that what is 'engineered', that is brought about by means of suggestion or manipulation, is human behaviour, the behaviour of the patient. Even if we deny that such behaviour 'comes from him' in a particular instance, the fact remains that it still 'comes through him', it is still 'his' behaviour in the ordinary sense of that personal pronoun. What forms part of his personality and character enters into it, e.g. his desire to please, his fear of being rejected. In such a case, even if only unintentionally, the analyst, through what he says, manipulates the patient's behaviour through his, the patient's will. He does so by finding there something responsive. Here the interpretation 'works' by means of 'suggestion' or some other similar means.

When, in contrast, it 'works' because it is true, and so 'makes conscious what is unconscious', the patient's response, his behaviour, comes from a different part of him, a part that has so far been hidden. Consequently, it has a different character, which any perceptive person in touch with the patient over a period of time can detect. It is spontaneous, overwhelming to the patient, fresh, not made to measure, and how he goes on from it in subsequent sessions is different from how he has proceeded thus far. Similarly, the content and character of his associations and dreams changes. In them the patient brings 'new material' which can be seen to be connected with what the interpretation says and the analysis begins to 'move' instead of 'marking time'.

My point is that there is a difference between such behaviour of the patient which confirms an interpretation and behaviour which seems to confirm it by imitating the former. There is nothing recondite about this difference; we constantly use this kind of distinction in our day-to-day judgements: does he really feel what he says he feels? Is what he shows authentic or is it merely the way he is when he is with me? Am I making him unable to be himself? Do I inspire him with genuine enthusiasm or does he paint in order to please me? Is he interested in painting or in pleasing me? Where he is interested in painting what he paints comes from him, where he is interested in pleasing me it comes from his idea of what would please me. It is my standards, my taste that shape what he paints, as he knows them, and not his own requirements, not his own judgement of what the particular painting requires.

So when an interpretation 'works' because it is true, when it 'gets across', when it engages with what it is directed at, it brings it into the open: the patient reveals what he has contained and concealed from himself, what he has evaded acknowledging as his. Therefore, when its truth is confirmed what appears is something that has been *hidden* from the patient, through his own agency,[1] and seen by the analyst as such at the time he gave the interpretation. Hence, if what the patient subsequently reports and the way he then behaves is to be a confirmation of the interpretation it must be judged by the analyst to be continuous and identical in character with what made him give the interpretation in the first place. Unless this is so the behaviour elicited in analysis would be like a rabbit the analyst had pulled out of his hat. In other words, it would be the result of suggestion, something put into or imposed on the patient, however much he may have colluded with the analyst, for his own reasons. It would not be the expression of something that had been there all along, unconscious, repressed, and now released.

This difference is crucial to the possibility of thinking of an interpretation as having been true at the time it was given and as having made the patient see something about himself that he had so far evaded recognizing. My point is that it is a real difference and one which the analyst has the opportunity to detect. I stress again the fact that psycho-analytic interpretations speak directly to the patient

---

[1] As a result of the exercise of his own will, whether with the object of concealment or some other aim which the patient was unconsciously determined to pursue.

and their confirmation belongs to the communication that takes place between patient and analyst. This confirmation is part of the movement of the analytic dialogue and interaction.

Because the patient and analyst are distinct and separate beings,[2] and the patient has a special relation to what the analyst interprets which no one else can have without being him, and because the patient is a language user, an articulate being, capable of lying and deception, his assent to the interpretation is an important part of its confirmation. The interpretation may well be true, of course, before the patient assents to it. Indeed, this is inevitably the case with interpretations that are true since, being about the unconscious, when they are true the patient cannot assent to their truth at first. He may agree or say 'yes', but this is only a sign that the interpretation has not touched him; it is not real assent. Until the patient genuinely assents to it, that is, sees it to be true, the analyst, however justifiably confident about its truth, cannot be as certain of it as it is possible for him to be. He does not have as much justification for being certain of its truth as it is possible for him to have.

It is important to be clear that what is concealed from the patient in his own breast may be recognizable to the analyst with various degrees of clearness. It may be so clear that it could be said of him that he sees what the patient is blind to in himself. Still, as long as the patient is blind, or deceives himself, it will not be something that finds a completely *direct* expression in his behaviour. So even when the analyst is confident about what he sees in his patient's behaviour, his view of it will still not be the best view *he* can have. This will be obtained only when the patient himself comes out into the open, recognizes and acknowledges what is in question.

He can, of course, come out into the open and still not recognize it for what it is, acknowledge or own it. He may, for instance, act it out but not remember what it is he is acting out, and where it is something bad blame his external circumstances. In that case more analytic work will have to be done. When, on the other hand, he does acknowledge it and assents to the interpretation, its truth will be finally confirmed for the analyst.

Obviously, the analyst will have to use his judgement in the light of his knowledge of the patient in taking this to be the case, i.e. in

---

[2] What we have is not self-analysis and the analyst does not lend himself to being treated as a narcissistic extension of the patient.

taking it that the patient has finally won the battle against his resistances and acknowledged the truth of the interpretation. These different aspects of the patient's behaviour hang together and are seen in each other's light when they are taken by the analyst to constitute a confirmation of his interpretation. This is as it should be since what is in question is the assessment of what is true about another human being – and here I would put the emphasis on 'human being' as much as on 'another'.

Yet it has troubled critics of psycho-analysis, philosophical critics as well as others, and seemed to undermine the only kind of confirmation that is possible here. This whole method of confirmation has seemed arbitrary when measured by criteria of scientific accuracy and objectivity. The criticism, or part of it at any rate, is that the observations necessary to the confirmation of psycho-analytic interpretations are themselves subject to interpretation, and those in turn to be confirmed by observations which are themselves subject to interpretation – endlessly and viciously. Freud himself gave words to this criticism in the mouth of an imaginary critic:

> Interpret! An ugly word. I don't like to hear it, for it destroys all certainty. If everything is to depend on my interpretation, who is to say whether I interpret correctly? Everything is left to my arbitrary notions. (1947, p. 44)

There are, of course, genuine difficulties and uncertainties here, and what the psycho-analyst is dealing with is not something that is amenable to experimental confirmation. The question is whether this justifies the kind of scepticism that critics level at the mode of confirmation of psycho-analytic interpretations. Whether or not we wish to talk of interpretations being confirmed by further interpretations, one thing is clear, namely that this is not an endless process. The different aspects of what transpires in the course of a developing analysis give each other mutual support. That is, the different ways in which each could be taken in relative isolation from each other narrow down as each throws light on the other.

It is true that inevitably the analyst has to use his judgement – a judgement acquired in his analytic experience of *other* cases, a variety of cases, and informed by his knowledge of the patient acquired in the course of contact with him in *this* analysis. Such judgement is not substitutable or exchangeable, and in that sense it is personal, and though it can be taught, it takes a certain kind of apprenticeship to acquire it, which is to be contrasted with the impersonal training of scientists. It is, therefore, perhaps worth highlighting this logical feature by talking of the *art* of interpretation. For what is in question is much more of an art than a science.

Wittgenstein, who discusses this question briefly in *Philosophical Investigations*, talks of those whose judgement is 'better' and those whose judgement is 'worse'. He says that 'correcter prognoses will generally issue from the judgements of those with better knowledge of mankind'. This knowledge can be learned, 'not, however, by taking a course in it, but through "experience"'. Those who have it do not stand to the rest as 'experts' in a special field (see 1963, p. 227).

The main reasons for this are the following. First, this knowledge ('knowledge of mankind') cannot be acquired in a detached sort of way – 'objectively'. It is the kind of knowledge that shows in one's responses to others and in one's judgements in one's dealings with others. The learning of it goes through one and is at one and the same time the learning of self-knowledge. This is what Wittgenstein means by 'experience' and why he uses inverted commas around the word. Second, experts are those with special skills, whereas the kind of judgement in which we are interested is shared by all mankind, even though some people have better judgement than others. Furthermore, what we have here is not a special field of interest; dealing with human beings, judging their motives and character, is part and parcel of human life. Psycho-analysts are not experts in human relations. There is no such thing, and to think of oneself as an expert here would be an arrogant piece of self-deception. All human beings are subject to blindness and self-deception, and no one is immune from making a mess of his relationships. One who is not alive to this in himself would have neither the sympathy nor the understanding to be able to help others who are in such a mess.

Third, experts are those who, by and large, agree in their judgements, at least after they have conducted the proper methods of testing or investigation appropriate to their field. Whereas, in contrast, as Wittgenstein points out, 'there is in general no such agreement over whether an expression of feeling is genuine or not', for instance, or let me add, whether a person's assent to what is said to him is an expression of genuine agreement or merely an attempt to pacify the other. As Wittgenstein points out, the judgement of such matters is not a technique which can be applied by anyone, leaving no room for disagreement.

4 THEORY AND PRACTICE

Freud does not agree with Wittgenstein's view. He thinks of the psycho-analyst as an expert whose judgements are the result of the application of a scientific theory which he, Freud, has inaugurated, a theory about man and the workings of his mind:

> If an assertion about psychology is made, everyone feels entitled to express an opinion or to contradict. Seemingly, there is no specialist knowledge in this field. Everyone has his own psychical life and everyone regards himself accordingly as a psychologist. But this does not seem to me sufficient title. (1947, p. 11)

Certainly it is not. Not everyone is a psychologist. But what they lack is not expertise; it is insight, judgement, depth. Dostoyevsky, I have argued elsewhere (Dilman, 1986, chapter 10), as have others, was a great pyschologist and much of his insight coincided with Freud's. But he had no theory of human nature.

What Freud represents to himself as a theory is the special *perspective* he developed and formulated almost single-handedly, a perspective the main features of which I tried to highlight in my earlier two books on Freud. Freud was ready to acknowledge how much this perspective is to be found in many great novelists' presentation of character.

Freud is also right in thinking that most of us, in many of our judgements of motive and character, take a view of people that is two-dimensional: we take what they show to us at face-value, allow moments of people's lives to stand in isolation from each other, think of them as able to change easily, consider their motivation as fairly rational, do not make room in our assessments of them for ambivalence and a mixture of opposites, and we do not show sufficient appreciation of the forces that rule their lives – forces which are part of their own will and personality, forces which rule them blindly because they themselves are blind to these forces. When Freud says that most of us are not psychologists this is the truth in what he says. He misrepresents what it is we lack.

Of course, psycho-analytic interpretations come from such a perspective. But the perspective is broad enough to include many differences, these being differences in emphasis, differences in presentation and, sometimes, philosophical differences. Many of the psycho-dynamic schools of pyschotherapy share such a broad perspective and are off-shoots of Freudian psycho-analysis. In their different emphases and concepts they vary in what they highlight and what they disregard. Therefore, what one illuminates another will obscure, and vice versa. So while it may matter vitally in the case of one patient what school of therapy his therapist belongs to, in the case of another it may make little difference.

These differences within the Freudian, psycho-dynamic perspective in the broad sense are at one with the differences in judgement, the lack of general agreement which Wittgenstein was speaking of, differences which he took to characterize what he called 'knowledge of mankind'. Having such knowledge is much more important in a psycho-analytically orientated psychotherapist than where he stands with regard to such differences, that is, what particular school he belongs to.

After all, as we have seen, the therapist is largely passive and does not steer the patient in this or that direction, but rather interprets what comes near the surface and is near the patient's grasp. It is the relationship, the analyst's authenticity, his capacity to accept the patient, his perceptive vigilance, and the way he allows the patient to talk and to move towards being himself in what he says that play such a crucial role in the way the patient drops his habitual defences and comes out into the open. In this 'undoing' which brings insight, the differences between the different schools play relatively little role. In so far as the different schools are concerned I take a good therapist to be one who keeps an open mind to the emphases which vary from one school to another, one who can see the relevance of their different insights in particular cases, and who is neither dogmatic nor doctrinaire.

7

The Analytic Relationship

1 PROFESSIONAL OR PERSONAL RELATIONSHIP?

Psycho-analysis, we have seen, is a therapy which engages the patient. It does not 'treat' a condition external to the patient while by-passing him as a person, as an agent responsible for what he takes on in life and what he contributes to his relationships, shaping them for good or ill in ways that make a deep difference to him. It engages the patient, however, without manipulating him. This means that the analyst himself enters the process of therapy as a person. He does not simply deploy certain professional skills to change the patient or draw him in, prompt, prod or persuade him to move in a particular direction.

He enters the process of therapy as himself. That is, he avoids any form of pretence, he does not take refuge behind his profession, hide behind attitudes that pertain to it. He tries to remain himself in his responses to the patient. Yet he does not meet or see the patient for personal reasons, because he likes him, for instance, or enjoys his company. He is not a friend, nor does he make friends with the patient, which would be detrimental to the purposes of the therapy. In short, he is engaged in giving personal help to the patient, but he does so on a professional basis and charges a fee for his services.

His motives thus are not friendship, since he does not even know the patient when he agrees to give him help. Nor are they charity, as he makes his living from the help he gives. In any case, if he can be said to come to know the patient, it is not in the same way that a worker comes to know a colleague, an employer his employee, or even a doctor his patient, that is, through complementary interaction shaped by the context of the work in which they are engaged. I say this because, while even a doctor may show his pleasure, for instance, at the way his patient co-operates and benefits from the treatment, and indeed show his own personality in the way he responds to his patient, the psycho-analyst reserves himself on this personal plane: he keeps the analytic incognito. I have argued that this does not make the analytic relationship one-sided, or wholly one-sided at any rate, since the analyst does respond to the patient affectively, and does put himself out for him, giving something of himself in the process. But it makes the relationship asymmetrical.

He does respond affectively, but his feelings, his motives for helping the patient (I have argued) are *impersonal*. He feels compassion for the patient in his suffering, yet he is not the agent of a charitable institution. He is the member of a profession, working much like a physician, a solicitor, an accountant or a financial adviser in this respect: making a living in a profession for which he has been trained and which involves giving a certain kind of help to people who ask for it in return for a fee.

Yet the help he offers differs from these other kinds of help in one important respect: it is *personal* help, help for *personal* problems, problems not just of the patient, but *in* him. They involve his strengths and weaknesses, failures and longings, regrets and feelings of guilt and shame, pleasure and pain. There is, therefore, no aspect of his life the patient can keep from the person he asks for help. Professional help, normally, restricts itself to a particular field. This is a charted territory over which the member of the particular profession has been trained to proceed with certain aims and goals in view. While it is true that the analyst also restricts himself in the help he offers, in so far as it falls outside his brief to give legal, financial or medical advice or help, the personal help which he offers itself admits of no restriction save, paradoxically, in one fundamental respect: that ultimately no one can help the patient in his problems and difficulties except himself.

To bring this home to the patient and to enable him to take responsibility for his problems there is nothing the patient brings to analysis from which the analyst can turn away or exempt from analysis. He cannot say, 'This does not concern me as an analyst' or 'This is irrelevant to your problems'. He treats it as an association and looks in it for reflections of the patient's personality in relation to the problems under consideration.

Thus, the analytic relationship, unlike any other professional relationship, is an *open* one. The patient is free to bring to it, by way of claims, expectations and responses, anything and everything, genuine as well as inauthentic, which he would bring into any intimate personal relationship. The patient's freedom in this respect is complemented by the anyalst's acceptance of him as he unfolds himself in the course of the analysis. While this acceptance makes the analyst personally vulnerable to the various temptations, these are temptations which he must recognize in himself and resist for the sake of the patient as well as for his integrity as an analyst – professional and personal integrity at one and the same time. To accept the patient is not the same thing as indulging him, of course, nor does it involve the analyst in compromising his own standards or putting them aside.

This fundamental feature of psycho-analytic therapy has the consequence that the patient himself refuses to acknowledge any restriction in the help he seeks in analysis, or if he does at the outset, the analyst leaves him free to move in the direction in which he gradually loses his sense of such limits, expecting, demanding that the analyst gives him his 'all'. He has to learn the existence of these limits through his experience of the temptation to disregard them. He learns this as he learns affectively that the analyst's life and his own have their separate courses and are part of different networks of relationships, having only crossed each other in a special sort of way, limited by specific objectives and the duration of the treatment.

What the patient thus learns in the analytic relationship he can 'apply to' or 'practise in' his personal relationships outside the analysis – his friendships, his marriage, his relationships with his children and with his colleagues. Yet the fact remains that this relationship in which he learns to be himself and to recognize the separateness of others, however much he may need them, is distinctly different from all these other relationships. For although it is a 'personal' relationship, it has been brought into existence in the first place by a restricted request on the part of the patient and agreement on the part of the analyst; both parties share a mutual agreement to end it when its objective has been reached, within the limits of what has proved possible in this particular case. And this is the hallmark of all professional, contractual relationships.

Yet, in contrast to all such other relationships, the analyst's motives in offering help to the patient make a difference to the outcome of what he works for. There is an internal relation between what he works for and his motives for working for it. In the case of a lawyer or a physician what counts is his competence and, at most, his tact in the way he works with his clients. Other than that his soul and personality are his own and make little difference, save accidentally, to what he can do for his clients.

This is not so in the case of the analyst. For if, for instance, his motive in helping the patient were financial remuneration or personal prestige, he could not inspire the confidence in the patient to lay bare his soul to him, the analyst, by admitting it openly. Nor could he do so by hiding his real motives from his patient, pretending a concern that he does not feel. There is no substitute for actually having the concern, the vocation. This is one respect in which the relationship makes a *personal* demand on the analyst, so that what he is like as a person makes a difference to his therapeutic achievements.

We have already seen that psycho-analysis demands authenticity from the analyst: it matters to the treatment whether or not he is himself in the course of it. It also demands an interest in the patient's welfare, a concern for him as a person. Thus, when, as early as in *Studies in Hysteria*, Freud wrote,

> I could not imagine myself entering deeply into the psychic mechanism of an hysteria in a person who would impress me as common and disagreeable, and who would not, on closer acquaintanceship, be able to awaken in me human sympathy; whereas I can treat a tabetic or a rheumatic patient regardless of such personal interest (Freud and Breuer, 1950, p. 198)

he was not merely expressing a personal predilection, something accidental to his capabilities. He was making the point that the kind of psychotherapy he practised demands something *personal* not only from the patient but also from the therapist. It is the therapist's response to *this* demand that makes the analytic relationship a personal one, even though his interest in the patient may, for reasons I have given before, be characterized as 'impersonal'. There is no contradiction here.

But though personal in this sense, the relationship, as we have just seen, bears many of the hallmarks of a professional, contractual relationship. And the question is: how is this possible? How can a relationship be both personal and professional at the same time? The first thing I want to say in answer to this question is that there are genuine *tensions* in what the psycho-analyst is engaged in and attempts to do, namely helping people, as individuals, with their personal problems on a professional basis. These are tensions between aspects of the particular kind of relationship into which he enters. These aspects can be represented as forming two antithetical poles, the personal and the professional poles of the relationship.

I am sure that the analyst has to face these tensions as an individual and try to come to terms with them in himself. That is, he has to sort out his relationship to the work he is doing and his priorities. Unless he does so he will not be able to develop clear attitudes towards his patients so as to be able to help them effectively. Secondly, these same tensions are what turns the characterization we are attempting to give of the analytic relationship into descriptions that are paradoxical. Philosophers and other interested parties, in their attempt to appreciate more clearly what the analytic therapist is engaged in, have to face these paradoxes. But obviously the philosopher, as an observer, is differently related to what he faces in these paradoxes from what the analyst, as a practicioner, is related to what he faces in the tensions between different aspects of his work.

Certainly, the analyst is not the patient's friend, nor is he a parent to him or a spouse. If he were, he could not help the patient in the way he means to help him. He needs to maintain a certain distance while continuing to care for the patient. He may find that the way he comes to care for the patient, the sympathy he feels, makes it difficult for him to keep this distance. But this is a tension he has to resolve *in himself*. There is nothing intrinsically incompatible between caring for someone and maintaining such a distance.

All of us, to some extent, in our desire to give help and support to another person want to be a parent to him, a mother, a father, or both, understanding what this amounts to on the model of our own parents. In doing so we run the risk of wanting to make the person who asks our help into a child, even wanting to realize our own dreams in him or her. This is a risk, since it interferes with our ability to help. Parents themselves have to beware of this tendency in themselves. But more than this, a parental relationship inevitably has built into it certain expectations and obligations, as well as a particular past or history, which set limits to the relationship and to what a parent can do for his or her child by way of helping him. This may be an asset. But it may also be a liability, so that what the person needs may be a *stranger*, someone who is not involved with him, someone he cannot fail, hurt or disappoint in the way one can fail, hurt or disappoint a parent, a friend, a spouse.

To be able to help, the analyst must remain such a stranger to his patient. But a stranger does not have to be someone who does not care, nor is he someone with whom one cannot be oneself. He is someone with whom one does not have a common past, a past in which one's life has got entangled with his. For him to remain a stranger, to keep his distance, is for him to steer clear of such an entanglement.

For the analyst to manage to do so while caring for the patient in the particular way under consideration is for him to confine himself to the caring, to expect nothing for himself in doing so, and to take on the relationship in the clear realization that it has no future. It has no future in the sense that it is to be terminated when the patient is 'well' enough to manage without the analyst's help. In some ways this is like a parent letting a child grow up and have a life and a family of his own, though there is a difference: however separate a life the child builds when he grows up he does not usually break his ties with his parents. But in the patient–analyst relationship there are no such ties. None have been fostered, except perhaps ties of gratitude which carry no obligations.

In this respect the analytic relationship can be regarded as a 'transitional relationship'. It has its own kind of reality while it is nurtured by the analytic intercourse, but it is meant to lead to other relationships, including the renewal of old relationships in the light of what the patient 'learns' about himself in analysis. The analyst works for this and is happy to fade out of the patient's life, to become no more than a memory in it. This is made possible by the fact that he does not engage in the patient's life, confining his contacts with the patient to the analytic room, these contacts themselves never going beyond the enlightenment of the patient.

As for the analyst's charging fees for the help he offers, we must remember that he is neither giving charity nor being a parent to the patient. It is particularly important that the patient should come to recognize this if he is to learn to stand on his own feet and assume responsibility for his own life. It is true that in the way the analyst keeps his distance and maintains the analytic incognito he tends to become a somewhat shadowy figure, suited to act as a foil for the patient's transference. Nevertheless, it is equally important for him to be a real person to the patient, someone the patient has to consider and take account of. Otherwise the patient would not learn from the analyst and the relationship he has with him. The analyst's restricted time and set fee help to bring this home to him.

The fact that the analyst charges a fee need not debase the help he offers. He does not treat his patients because he feels sorry for them, even though at times he may feel so. He treats them because they have asked for the help he is qualified to give. He has undergone a rigorous training to obtain this qualification and he, like everyone else, has to make a living if he is to be useful to others, to serve them in his own way. But he does not treat them simply to earn a living. His work is not merely a means of making money; each of the therapeutic relationships into which he enters absorbs and challenges him on its own account. He does become genuinely interested in the welfare of his patients. What would debase the help he offers is if he were to subordinate the consideration of his patients' welfare to considerations of money. Obviously, friendship that is given in return for money is no friendship: friendship (one can say) cannot be bought or sold. But this does not apply to services or help, even where we are concerned with help in the sphere of the personal, provided there is (i) no pretence or deception and (ii) no exploitation.

Is there not still something one-sided, a certain asymmetry, about the psycho-analytic relationship? The analyst does engage with the patient in the way we have considered, but he does not bring the patient into his life, nor does he himself enter the patient's life. He restricts his contacts with him to the analytic room, and keeps the relationship on a 'business' footing.

Second, the analyst gives help, puts himself out for the patient, and the patient receives this help. The analyst is in a position of strength relative to the patient. This is the pattern characteristic of helping: one person gives and the other receives, the giving being unconditional when it is genuine. Certainly, the analyst does not help the patient *in order* to be remunerated. But this complementarity, which is part of what it means to help, does not exclude reciprocity of a different kind. Even to receive what one is given is a form of return, a giving back, though obviously this depends on the spirit in which the person receives what he is given. In any case, the analyst is not the only person who puts himself out. The patient does so too. He does so for the analysis and not for the analyst, since the analyst does not want anything for himself from the analysis. All the same, the analysis is something the analyst works for and wishes to succeed. So in putting himself out for the analysis the patient is giving something of himself to the analyst. The real asymmetry here lies in the fact that the patient is asking something for himself from the analyst, and the analyst is not asking anything for himself from the patient.

Third, the patient lays bare his soul before the analyst, whereas the analyst keeps his reserve. This means that the analyst comes to know the patient while himself remaining a stranger to him. We have seen that this is a condition necessary to the kind of help he offers and why it is so. If we ask how it is that a personal relationship can be one-sided in *this* way, the answer briefly is as follows. To help someone on a personal plane one has to know his problem or difficulty. Since the problem is one that is in him, a consideration of the problem is a consideration of him and calls for his co-operation and openness. On the other hand, what is required of the helper is that he gives help. The spirit in which he does so is what is crucial, but for the person receiving the help to appreciate this spirit and respond to it, is not for him to come to know his helper in any other respect.

So the spirit in which he is offered help and his recognition of and response to it is a form of give and take; it may well create a bond between the helper and the helped. One can have this kind of personal bond with a stranger who has come out of the unknown to help one, but more is needed for him to cease being a stranger to one, for one to come to know him. This is what the analyst avoids in the analytic relationship.

2   IS THE RELATIONSHIP REAL OR ONLY A TRANSFERENCE ONE?

One sometimes talks of a 'real' relationship by way of making a contrast with a relationship in which one or both of the parties does not allow himself to recognize what the other is like, or does not permit him to be himself. Each, then, is having a relationship with an imaginary person, that is, a person as he is imagined to be, or with someone false, and in that sense someone who does not exist. A real relationship, by contrast, is one which admits of mutual contact between the parties and in which each person comes to know the other.

The patterns that characterize a relationship at the personal level are shaped by the contribution which each person makes to it in response to the other person and his contribution. Each person's response to the other is thus shaped both by what the other person is like, at least as he perceives him to be, and by what he is like himself. The more he can allow the other person to be himself in the relationship and remain in touch with him, and, correspondingly, the more the other person allows him to be himself, the more will he be himself in his responses to the other person and the more will those responses be directed to the other person as he really is. Genuine deception and honest mistakes apart, a person cannot be himself in his responses to another person if he does not allow that person to be himself, or if he does not allow himself to see that person as he really is.

Thus, when a person is manipulative he is not being himself. Someone may object: he may be a manipulative person and so in being manipulative be himself. Why not? There is, of course, no doubt that that may be his character. But in being true to one's character a person is not necessarily being himself. Whether or not he is depends on what kind of character the person has. After all, falsity and insincerity may be part of a person's character. A manipulative person is someone who feels that he cannot get what he wants from people if he is himself and that, therefore, he must exert himself, try to please others, bribe them or twist their arm. Intent on what he feels he must achieve or maintain he cannot be himself. In pleasing others, for instance, he has ulterior motives. He is not doing what he wants, but what he feels he must do. He cannot get away from it because his reasons for wanting to please people are invariably operative in all his relations and casual contacts, they apply irrespective of what the other person is like. Indeed, he is not himself clear what these reasons are and why they hold for him – what it is in his mode of existence that gives him such reasons for wanting to please people. Given his tunnel vision of himself, he either feels he cannot have what he wants any other way or fears that if he were to cease to exert himself in keeping people pleased things would turn out badly for him. He is thus driven to do what has become second-nature to him, part of his character, so that he feels he is behind it. But this is an illusion. Perhaps he even rationalizes what is in question, thinking, 'I am friendly, I like people', and thus avoiding a recognition of the extent to which he tries to manipulate

people. Part of the truth which he will not recognize is that he cannot
be at rest with others, be himself with them, and let them in turn be
what they are and who they are.

What we have here are two sides of the same coin: if one cannot be
oneself with others they cannot be themselves with one, and if one
cannot let them be themselves, if one has to have them a certain way
and so tries to manipulate them to this end, then one cannot be
oneself with them. One is taken up too much by seeing to it that
things are as one is anxious they should be to be oneself with others.
This is the inevitable price of manipulating them. It goes without
saying that if one is to be oneself with another person he, equally,
has to make this possible by letting one be oneself. It takes two to
make a real, authentic relationship.

Just as in one's relationships one can manipulate the other person,
one can also manipulate one's perception of him, thus deceiving
oneself about him. Both manipulation of the other and self-
deception make for an unreal relationship. Obviously, it is the fears
and defensive strivings that one imports into it which prevent it from
being real. One has acquired these fears, developed these strivings,
learned these tactics in earlier relationships at a time when one was
weak relative to the other person, when one's abilities to fend for
oneself were limited, and when one's sense of proportion was
precarious, one's longings and fears more apt to undermine one's
contact with reality. This importation is what Freud called 'transference'.

The idea is that what is in question is not a response to what is
there in the relationship, namely to the other person's response, but
rather is scripted, predetermined and, therefore, blind. It is 'scripted' in the sense that the person cannot get out of the grooves within
which he moves without letting go of something to which he clings
and so without being prepared to change. He is unwilling to pay the
price for doing so. If it is 'predetermined', it is nevertheless
determined by the person himself, though as fixed by a past which
does not let him live entirely in the present. The response is 'blind'
in the sense that the person's reasons are invariant in the way I have
pointed out and rooted in what he is blind to. But, though blind, a
'transference response' is often touched off by what is there and,
when it is not, it seeks a foothold on which to stand.

The point is that it 'pre-exists' the occasion which evokes it. Being
scripted it is not really a response to it. The occasion is an occasion

for re-enacting something, and the response is largely a repetition, something from which the person cannot get away. He cannot get away from it because certain models from the past colour his vision, interfere with his perception of people and their responses to him, come between him and them. They do not let him see the other person as he is in certain respects and they do not let him be himself. They mould his responses in the image of the past.

But, let me ask again, is that not precisely what he is like? Why am I saying that in these responses he is not himself? The answer is, because he is not free to respond to the other person as he, the other person, really is – assuming that he is himself – or if the other person is not himself, then to take this into account in his response to that person. True, he does put himself into his response. The anger he feels, for instance, may be real. But it is not in touch with the reality of the occasion that has evoked it, and so he is not in touch with that reality in feeling angry. Therefore, in the face of what provokes this reaction, he is not himself, that is, as he would be were he in touch with the other person and his circumstances.

Now psycho-analysis, we have seen, aims to help the patient to be himself. For this to be possible the patient has to drop his defences and disguises. As he does so more and more in his associations and in what he brings to the analytic relationship, he does not at once become authentic – himself. On the contrary, different aspects of the personality and character in which he is trapped make their appearance and become operative. This is the transference which is to be analysed and which he should himself 'correct' in the light of the present as his eyes begin to open.

The analyst makes himself as 'invisible' as possible to allow the transference to become visible. The patient begins to treat the analyst as a good parent and as a bad one alternately, expecting to be spoon-fed, to be taken care of, to be reassured, to be healed by magic, and also fearing to be exploited, frustrated, persecuted. He regresses, that is, into a state of dependency, complaining about the analyst's meanness, attempting to fight being exploited, trying to please, bribe, and in other ways manipulate him. But the analyst is none of these things in the analysis and he does not respond to the patient on the basis of his complaints, accusations, provocations and bribes; he remains vigilant and does not allow himself to be sucked into the patient's transference. If he did, he would reduplicate the early situation in the patient's life in which the patient 'learned' these responses in the first place, thus fuelling them and perpetuating their repetition. Instead he tries to wean the patient off them by analysis, that is, by enlightening the patient about what he is up to and promoting a perception of the contrast between the time when the patient first resorted to these patterns and the present.

Does the fact that, at the peak of the analysis, so much of the patient's contribution to the analytic relationship has this transference character make the relationship unreal? Just as it takes two to make a relationship real so, equally, it takes two to make it unreal. The relationship in analysis is, ideally at least, constantly changing. The analyst, if he has resolved his inner conflicts and transferences in his own analysis, will be awake to the patient's transference and will not respond to it, except with an interpretation. In this way he will leave it one-sided and provide the patient with the opportunity to 'correct' the transference, that is, free himself from the pattern of responses in which he has so far remained entrenched and thus respond with greater insight into the object of his response and in a manner more commensurate with his age.

So the analyst's restraint in the face of the patient's attempts to draw him out does not, as we might think at first, make the realationship unreal. On the contrary, in resisting being drawn into the patient's transference the analyst resists the patient's efforts to turn the relationship into something unreal, something that has little to do with the reality of the analytic situation. On the other hand, until he succeeds in weaning the patient off the transference, the relationship will not be a real one. It thus remains between these two poles, pulled in opposite directions, for the duration of the analysis. When it has every prospect of becoming real it is broken off and the patient can continue with a life and relationships in which he can be himself to a degree he has not achieved previously.

It is true that if a person were to act in his life as the analyst does during analytic sessions he would not be able to make relationships with people, not real ones at any rate. People would not be able to find much substance in his responses and they would find their contacts with him frustrating, and even alienating. An analyst, himself, does not act this way with people in his own life, outside analysis. So does this not say something about the character of the analytic relationship which we have been at pains to assess? If, when transplanted outside the analysis, it makes an unreal relationship, how can it be real in the analysis?

In responding to this question we must remember the difference which the context of a relationship makes to its character. In analysis we have two people engaged in a very special kind of work of a personal nature. Even when the analyst is being reserved he is still doing domething for the patient and so the two are in constant interaction with each other. Not all interaction involves contact, of course, but the analyst is constantly trying to make contact with the patient and, when he succeeds, the patient's response is directed at him, the analyst. So the relationship encourages and obtains some mutual contact, and it is one between two people engaged in a real piece of work.

It goes without saying that personal relationships outside analysis are not relationships between people engaged in such work. Therefore, the fact that the analyst's attitude within the analysis would be alienating outside it does not make the analytic relationship itself an unreal one. After all, if a teacher were to treat his wife, or even his children, as he treats his pupils at school this would introduce an element of unreality into his relationships with them. They would find it difficult to be themselves with him and to treat him as someone who is himself. But this does not mean that his relationship with his pupils is unreal or artificial – unless he takes it to an extreme where he is no longer fully in touch with his pupils as individuals and becomes a caricature of himself as a teacher.

This is just as true of the psycho-analyst. What he can bring into his everyday relationships outside analysis with benefit is not his analytic practice but his insight into human beings and into himself. However, we must not forget that he has no monopoly over such insight.

3 A RELATIONSHIP OF ACCEPTANCE

We have seen that the analyst's chief concern is to reflect what he sees as the patient discloses himself in his associations. This he does in the interpretations he gives to the patient. His role is to act as a foil to the patient's transference. In the previous section this raised the question of whether the patient's relationship with the analyst is real or only imaginary. Like the mirror analogy, the foil analogy too needs to be balanced dialectically.

Of course, the analyst comes through to the patient as a real person. His reality is just as important for the analysis as his reserve. There is no contradiction here. He should keep his feelings to himself, not reveal his soul to the patient, but he should be *there*: the patient should not be allowed to forget that he is in the presence of *another* person, someone with a mind and a life of his own, someone who is not there to please him. We have seen that *in addition* he must have certain qualities: he must be truthful and trustworthy, and he must be capable of respect for others as persons and have compassion for them in their personal failures. I characterized these as *impersonal* qualities, in the sense that they are not selective and are unconditional, and that he has no personal interest invested in those to whom the attitudes in which these qualities find expression are directed. These are personal qualities, in the sense of being qualities of the person, and he develops them in the course of his own analysis, given his desire to help others.

It is these qualities which enable him to accept the patient so that the patient can come forward, feel progressively that he can be himself and find healing in the relationship. I mean healing or restoration of the self in the person who finds acceptance. To be ourselves we each need to have been accepted when it counted most and to have made that part of ourselves. At the root of our self-acceptance lies the confirmation we receive from someone who is important to us – our parents in the first place. Thus, our own acceptability to ourselves comes to us originally from outside. Where our self-acceptance is well established we can survive rejection and humiliation. But, however well established it may be, it is sustained and replenished by relationships in which we find acceptance, by works in which we make ourselves useful to others and find respect, and by the fulfilment of standards which we share with them. There are many ways in which our sense of our own acceptability can be undermined: by our violating those standards, by failing others, but also by our failure to find love and respect, and even as a result of being unfairly rejected or unjustly accused. I would go as far as to say that even the strongest among us needs justice, love and the respect of others.

In George Eliot's novel *Middlemarch*, Lydgate, an idealistic doctor, fails to realize his ideals largely on account of external circumstances and a bad marrige into which he enters of his own volition. His wife, Rosamond, is utterly narcissistic and a headstrong, spoilt creature who thinks of no one but herself. His relationship with her is almost completely one-sided: what he gives her is never considered enough by her and so gives her no satisfaction, and he receives no consideration from her. In the midst of a financial crisis and involved in a public disgrace, when he is completely innocent, he goes to speak to Dorothea. As he speaks to her 'he is feeling the ache of despair as to his being able to carry out any purpose that Rosamond had set her mind against'. The way Dorothea listens to him, the way she enables him to talk, restores him spiritually. In her attention he finds all that he has lost. As he put it: 'Everything seems more bearable since I have talked to you' (p. 563).

In a similar way a patient can find sufficient restoration in the way his analyst listens to him to enable him to openly be himself in the analysis. Many patients feel a sense of isolation in their struggle with personal problems and often a sense of unworthiness too in the way they may have failed in their personal relationships. The acceptance they find in analysis does not signal that all is well with them. If it did, it would not help them. No, it gives them hope by demonstrating that they can be accepted *despite* their faults and failures, that these can be forgiven, and that as individuals, they are not wholly to be identified with these. It is in this hope that they will find the will to change and the courage to bear what cannot be changed.

Acceptance is not the same thing as approval. Therefore, it is compatible with criticism. The analyst is critical in the sense that he does not accept everything his patient tells him at face value. Nor does he go along with the patient's requests, reassure him, fall in with his unconscious strategies, facilitate his schemes. In accepting him the analyst is responding with compassion to what is real in the patient, something with which the patient himself may be in touch only erratically. It is not the frustrations that the patient suffers in making his way in life as someone false which inspires compassion in the analyst, but what it is that makes him resort to such an inauthentic existence. It is the frailty and vulnerability of human beings which lead them to be false, to deceive themselves, and it is this that touches him in his patients. It is the particular form that this takes in each of his patients that makes him willing to help them. He accepts each one as the person he really is, frail and inauthentic, yet struggling for a more authentic existence.

We have seen what part the analyst plays in this struggle and on which side he stands in the help that he offers. He is experienced by the patient resisting the analysis, and seeking his habitual compensations, as standing in his way and making things difficult for him instead of helping him. But that is only because of the side he takes in these struggles. To help and support the patient in his desire for a more authentic existence is neither to pander to his every wish and need, nor to make things easy for him. Just as accepting him is not confirming him in his inauthenticity.

8

Insight and Change

1 TAKING STOCK AND LOOKING FORWARD

We started this inquiry by considering what it is that makes people turn to psycho-analysis and what kind of therapeutic help they can find in it. This led to a consideration of the differences between psycho-neuroses and physical illness and between psycho-analytic therapy and medical treatment. The very notions of 'mental illness', 'neurosis', 'the causation of neuroses', 'being a psycho-analytic patient' and 'psycho-analytic therapy' raise deep philosophical questions, some aspects of which the early chapters of the book discuss.

On these questions Freud was pulled in opposite directions. Nevertheless, the direction in which he developed his ideas on neuroses and their treatment led him away from his early medical framework for these.

Having considered this development from the point of view of the philosophical questions raised by Freud's ideas I turned to the psycho-analytic dialogue through which the treatment takes place. I concentrated on the roles played in it by the patient's self-disclosures, the analyst's interpretations and the analytic relationship which feeds this dialogue. I was concerned to correct certain natural misapprehensions and to examine some paradoxes. This, one could say, is an examination of the *talking* involved in what has been called a 'talking cure' – one short-hand description of psycho-analytic therapy.

Another description, 'insight therapy', highlights the notion of *insight* which we are now ready to consider: what kind of change does it involve and in what sense does it involve change? Once we are clear about this we shall consider whether these changes are all that the analyst attempts to promote and how others, if there are any, are connected with them. Freud talked of the initiation of the changes involved in acquiring insight into oneself in analysis as 'making conscious the unconscious'. But he also said that what the analyst aims to achieve can be captured in the formula: 'where id is there ego shall be'. I have added to this: 'where super-ego is, there ego shall be'. This is not merely an enlargement of consciousness, but an enlargement of the self.

In his *Introductory Lectures on Psycho-analysis* Freud talked of this change as the patient 'becoming his best self: what he would have been under the most favourable conditions' (1949b, p. 364). This, he said, is what 'the recovery of a nervous person', 'the cure of a neurotic' amounts to. Colloquially, we sometimes speak of this as a person 'finding himself'. Well, what does this amount to? How is it achieved by 'making conscious the unconscious, removing repressions, filling in the gaps in [the patient's] memory'? That is, how does insight bring about this latter kind of change? And why is it identified with 'recovery from a neurosis'?

When these questions are 'answered' through a philosophical clarification of the concepts involved, I want to highlight the variety to be found in the changes, differing from person to person, in the move towards greater personal authenticity and autonomy, and bring out the sense in which they are 'restorative of the self', 'healing', 'liberating', to show how they bring the self greater unity, enhance its life, turn the person outward. This will be the topic of chapter 9. But how can personal autonomy and mastery of the self be achieved by the removal of repression? What would hold the self together then and give it a sense of direction? Would it not leave the person exposed to the tyranny of impulse? This will be the topic of chapter 10.

The final chapter will be concerned with the relationship between psycho-analytic therapy and moral values, from the point of view both of the notion of cure, that is, of a change towards greater personal well-being, and also of the possibility of the patient himself being able to will such a change. I shall there attempt to spell out the values implicit in psycho-analytic therapy. Jung criticized Freudian therapy for its scepticism towards morality, claiming that it has no moral values to offer the patient and that it tends to undermine those which the patient already has. Some more recent psycho-analysts have defended psycho-analytic therapy against such a charge and suggested that, on the contrary, it promotes a certain set of values in the patient, characterized as 'humanistic'. Where does the truth lie between these two opposite reactions to psycho-analysis? This question will be examined in chapter 11.

We have then, broadly, three further stages to our inquiry: (i) How does insight promote change? (ii) In what way is such change restorative of the self and its autonomy? (iii) How does its achievement involve a change in the relation of the self to certain moral values and in what relation does psycho-analysis itself stand to these values? I return now to the preliminaries of the first stage: the sense of the term 'consciousness' in Freud's phrase 'making conscious the unconscious'.

2   CONSCIOUSNESS AND THE UNCONSCIOUS: A BRIEF NOTE

Freud talks of feelings, thoughts and desires as conscious and as unconscious, and he also talks of the person as being unconscious or as becoming conscious of them. When the feelings are unconscious they are *hidden* from the person who has them, when they are conscious he can own and articulate them.

Now, whether or not an object is hidden from us – as, say, a cat behind a curtain – makes no difference to what the object is like. So to say that it is hidden is not to describe the object, but only to speak of its relation to possible observers. The relation in question is an 'external' one in the sense that it does not enter into the identity of the object in question.

This is not true of the distinction 'conscious – unconscious' as it applies to feelings, thoughts and desires. These things are not 'objects' and there is a difference between a man's anger, fear or anxiety when it is conscious and when it is unconscious (see Dilman, 1984a, chapter 4, section 4). This is the justification for applying the terms 'conscious' and 'unconscious' to feelings, thoughts and desires as well as to the person who has them. Hence Freud's phrase 'making conscious the unconscious' – for instance, making conscious the unconscious anger in a person.

When that happens the person himself becomes 'conscious of' the anger in him. This is a way of talking that is more familiar to us. Here the distinction is between a person who apprehends something and one who does not, perhaps avoiding doing so. In the case of 'unconscious anger or fear' what he does not apprehend or denies the existence or reality of, is *his own* anger or fear. That is, of course, what makes *it* 'unconscious'.

Normally, we do not characterize a person's fears, let us say, as 'conscious'. We take consciousness in this sense to be the norm and make sense of the unconsciousness of unconscious fear in relation to it, by way of contrast. The sense of the term 'unconscious' in this connection takes for granted the sense of the term 'conscious' and our understanding of it. What make it true that a person is afraid are not, of course, his sensations of the moment, those that characterize his consciousness severed from the before and the after. That is the Cartesian conception, or, I should say, misconception, and Freud goes along with it when he thinks of 'consciousness' and 'unconsciousness' as 'qualities of mental states' (see 1949e, chapter 4). But fear characterizes a person's consciousness in an altogether different way. The consciousness that it characterizes is the person's consciousness of what it is he responds to in his fear of it. If, for instance, he really fears an imminent confrontation, then his fear is the form which his consciousness, or anticipation, of that confrontation takes, the terms in which he thinks of it, his affective response to it.

The state of consciousness which takes this form is directed to the object of his thoughts and responses, namely the dreaded confrontation. What gives it the particular character it has, the one we designate as 'fear', is not a matter of what goes on in him at the time. At least this is relevant only in the light of the significance it assumes in its relation to what took place before it and what will come after. It is his relation to the imminent confrontation, together with the circumstances that surround his present thoughts, sensations and inclinations, that constitute his fear, characterize his state of mind – his consciousness of the imminent confrontation. If he is afraid, he must not only see that confrontation in a certain way, think of it in certain terms, but his vision and these thoughts must enter his responses, affect his behaviour in a certain way. In certain cases it must affect the very rhythm of his physical life.

Now this, namely how he is related to the imminent confrontation, what he makes of it, how he responds to it, is *itself* a possible object of reflection, and the way *it* figures in his consciousness may be quite different from the way he anticipates the confrontation in reality. The content of his consciousness and what he really feels need not coincide. It may seem to him that he is confident and without fear when in fact the opposite is the case.

It is the idea both of consciousness and of what is mental that we misapprehend, in the way Descartes did, when we identify the two and think of an unconscious emotion or inclination as a contradiction in terms. Consciousness is not the stuff that constitutes what is mental, but rather the person's apprehension of what concerns or affects him. It may be explicit in his thoughts or implicit in his responses.

Equally, and in the same way, a person's own responses, his emotions and inclination, can be the object of his consciousness. Here, too, his consciousness of them may be reflective. He may apprehend them correctly without ever spelling them out for himself, or he may misapprehend them. In the latter case they take a distorted form in his consciousness, they take on an appearance there which makes them seem different from what they really are. In cases where the discrepancy between appearance and reality is great we could rightly say that the person has no consciousness of what he feels. In other words, his feelings do not figure in his consciousness, or what figures there has little to do with what he really feels. He actively avoids taking cognisance of what he feels. This is where Freud speaks of the feelings in question as unconscious.

So much for consciousness. As for its object, the feelings and emotions in question, their reality or existence is, as I have said, a matter of the person's relation to their objects, the significance these have for him, the way they touch or affect him. The latter embraces his thoughts, the actions he takes, the responses he controls or contains, and also the bodily, somatic reactions or reflexes that he experiences as sensations and bodily feelings. It is these things, taken as a whole, that John Wisdom once referred to as 'patterns in time'. Obviously, what patterns they constitute depend on the particular circumstances of the person's life which surround them. These patterns may be hard to take in at a glance and so offer scope for error and misapprehension from which the person himself is not immune. Indeed, it may suit him to avoid recognizing them for what they are and he may actively pursue such self-deception.

3   BECOMING CONSCIOUS OF WHAT IS UNCONSCIOUS: ENLARGEMENT OF CONSCIOUSNESS

Given that a person can feel angry, anxious, afraid or depressed without being conscious of it, what does his becoming conscious of what he feels amount to or involve? Certainly it involves a change in aspect, but it goes beyond that. When Wisdom spoke of 'patterns in time that are hard to take in at a glance' the patterns to which he was referring are the aspects or 'gestalts' which our actions and reactions, together with what these are directed towards, constitute in our apprehension or consciousness. Indeed, the particular aspect *is* our consciousness of what is in question.

In our example of the person who is afraid of an imminent confrontation what constitutes the temporal pattern in question is what he himself feels. *He* is not related to it *externally,* as a third person would be. It is he who feels the fear, he who responds to what he anticipates with fear. The things in which this fear finds expression, those in which he is or becomes conscious of it, are his own actions and reactions, his own movements, gestures, quivers and heartbeats. Some of these, at any rate, are subject to his will. It is he who gives in to the fear, he who gives expression to it, contains or controls it. In the case where he has avoided admitting his fear to himself and then becomes aware of it, it is not simply that the aspect under which he sees what is in question changes, he *also* gives up his control, he enters into what he feels, even allows himself to be taken over by it. This means that his very way of responding to what inspires fear or anxiety in him *changes*, but without losing its identity with his original mode of response. He does not *become* afraid, for he *was* afraid before this change: his fear was unconscious. Now he givers *more direct expression* to the fear he continues to feel. He no longer hides it from himself, no longer disguises it from his own consciousness: his fear has become conscious.

It is clear that the change in question is more than a change in aspect, though it involves that. The following analogy will throw some light on this matter. A piece of music played on the piano could be recorded so that one could listen to its performance again and again. Yet, as one does so, the way one hears the music may change. One may hear sadness there, for instance, which one had not heard before. This is a change in aspect, the aspect under which one hears the music. Suppose now that someone plays it on the piano and changes the emphasis given to certain notes. He may play it more brightly, so that the sadness one came to hear in the melody diminishes and, perhaps, altogether disappears. Here, in this new rendering, one hears the same melody, but now it contains or expresses something different; indeed, one hears it differently.

However, this is because it is performed differently. It is not only one's hearing of it that has changed, that is, the aspect, but also the performance – performance of the same piece.

But how is the piece to be played? Is it a bright piece or a sad one? How should one hear it? Without going into the character of these questions I will simply say that these are normative, aesthetic questions. We are all related to what they are asking us to settle *in the same way*, including, I would argue, the composer himself – even though each one of us has a unique relation to the norms and taste that enter our judgements: they are the person's own norms and taste. This is not so in the case of those 'patterns in time' that constitute a person's feelings – his fear, in our example. We can, however, make our analogy come a bit nearer to it if we roll into one the player and the listener and direct our question to the perform-ance. Here the player, in his performance, gives expression to something he *discovers* in the music, something which he comes to see as being in the melody in the sense of coming to think that the way of playing it which brings it out is the *right* way to play it. Previously it was not in his rendering of it, but it was still then (he would now say) the right way to play it. He missed this right way to play it then (he would now say) and so in playing it wrongly he missed an appreciation of the music and of what was in it.

In the case of the person who comes to see how angry he has been all along, though he thought otherwise, the claim that there was anger in his heart is different, of course, from the claim made by the musical peformer that the piece he is playing is a melancholy melody though he had not realized this until now. For the anger the person now comes to see he was feeling earlier is *his* anger and he feels that anger *now*, he becomes conscious of it in giving it direct expression, in ceasing to repress it. In giving it expression and becoming aware of it while doing so he is *like* the musical performer. But in that what he gives expression to is *his*, something to which he is internally related, he is *unlike* the musical performer. He is 'internally related' to it in the sense that its identity involves his identity.

I said that the change in those 'patterns in time' that takes place in his becoming conscious of the anger in him, in the unconscious anger becoming conscious, goes beyond a change of aspect. I referred to the change in the musical performer's *performance* to bring this out. But I emphasized that this change, that goes beyond a change of aspect, is yet not a change in the identity of these patterns in time that constitute his anger. That maintenance of identity through time is essential to our claim that he feels now consciously what he has been feeling in the past unconsciously; in other words, that he has *become conscious* of his anger, and not that he has *become angry*.

But although what he *feels* does not change when he becomes conscious of the anger, there is a respect in which *he* changes. It is as a less repressed, more open, less afraid or anxious person, and even perhaps as a braver one, that he feels angry. He is no longer afraid to feel the anger he felt before sneakily, to come out into the open with it, and so to face the question of what he is going to do about it. This is a step in the direction of greater freedom. Previously, he had devoted much energy to keeping himself from becoming what he has now become in admitting and owning his anger. So not only can he face the question of what to do about it but there is more of him to devote to the task.

Let me emphasize that this is the *first* step in the process of psycho-analytic therapy, the *first* of those changes in the patient that constitute his 'cure' in the sense that he is restored to a greater degree of wholeness and autonomy. In his *Introductory Lectures* Freud wrote:

> The aim of our efforts may be expressed in various formulae – making conscious the unconscious, removing the repressions, filling in the gaps in memory; they all amount to the same thing. But perhaps you are dissatisfied with this declaration; you imagined . . . that after he [a nervous person] had been subjected to the laborious process of psycho-analysis he would emerge a different person altogether, and then you hear that the whole thing only amounts to his having a little less that is unconscious and a little more that is conscious in him than before. Well, you probably do not appreciate the importance of an inner change of this kind. (1949b, p. 363)

It is precisely what such an inner change amounts to that concerns us in this chapter and the sense in which it is a *sine qua non* of insight into oneself. But I wish to emphasize that it is not the only inner change that takes place in the therapy, that it is the first of those changes and the only one that is directly aimed at in the analytic work of interpretation. As we have seen, Freud himself has said, 'we want nothing better than that the patient should find his own solutions for himself' (p. 362) and that 'psycho-synthesis [that is, the healing of the splits within the self, its integration] is achieved without our intervention' (1950, vol. ii, p. 395).

These further inner changes could be described as constituting an 'enlargement of the self' in contrast to the 'enlargement of consciousness' that I have been discussing – even though, of course, an 'enlargement of consciousness' also involves some change in the patient. In Freudian terminology what *follows* such an enlargement of consciousness may be summed up by saying that parts of the id and of the super-ego become part of the ego. This, in turn, changes the ego's relation to other people and its outer circumstances. These changes involve an increase in the patient's autonomy. What we need to understand is how these further inner changes arise out of the enlargement of the patient's consciousness and the crucial role of the patient in bringing them about.

4 INSIGHT INTO ONESELF AND INNER CHANGE

I had insisted earlier that the insight, which the analyst attempts to convey to the patient, is itself a change in him. We have now seen that what Freud described as 'what is unconscious becoming conscious' is an inner change, a change that the person undergoes in coming to such insight. It should be clear that 'what is unconscious beoming conscious' and 'the person becoming conscious of something in himself which he has so far avoided recognizing' are two aspects of the enlargement of consciousness, related to each other like the two aspects of the Jastrow figure, the duck and the rabbit.

In becoming conscious of something he has felt all along the person in question *sees* something new about himself. He thus acquires *insight* into certain aspects of his behaviour. For instance, he sees why he has consistently failed to respond warmly to certain kinds of friendly overture made to him, why he has consistently withdrawn from certain opportunities, suffered various setbacks. His whole way of understanding this pattern of failure and loneliness collapses; his new insight takes the wind out of its sails. He acknowledges his own role in the series of setbacks for which he had always blamed other people and circumstances. All this stems from what he has come to see about himself. That is what makes the seeing a piece of insight.

Yet this kind of seeing in question is not just a recognition of what is the case. It is the living of it, experiencing it in oneself, becoming it. For what one comes to see is a part of oneself, so far denied. That means that up to now one has dissociated oneself from it. In becoming conscious of it one allows it to become part of oneself in one's conscious ego. Becoming conscious of it one becomes conscious of it as part of oneself, one admits it into the fold of the ego, one owns it. When I speak of 'owning' it I mean the opposite of dissociating oneself from it.

It is, of course, possible to see it as one sees it in someone else and so continue to remain dissociated from it, not experience it oneself. Th ; is the kind of second-hand knowledge which Freud warned us against: 'There is knowing and knowing,' he said, 'they are not always the same thing', and 'psychologically [they] are not by any means of equal value' (1949b, p. 237). And again: 'There is more than one kind of ignorance' (p. 238). The kind of knowledge through which, in analysis, the recovery of the patient is sought, Freud said, 'must be founded upon an inner change in the patient which can only come about by a mental operation directed to that end' (ibid.). What is in question is the patient giving up his defences, ceasing to repress his feelings, allowing them to find direct expression in his responses and enter into his consciousness, thus changing his view of things.

At the opposite extreme it is possible to live or act out certain feelings and phantasies without seeing them for what they are and accepting responsibility for them. In analysis this is equally a form of resistance – a 'resistance of the id'. For while one acts them out one is denying their roots in the past, seeing them in terms of current concerns and blaming them on one's present circumstances. Here, as Freud puts it,

> the unconscious feelings strive to avoid the recognition which the cure demands; they seek instead for reproduction, with all the power of hallucination and the inappreciation of time characteristic of the unconscious. The patient ascribes, just as in dreams, currency and reality to what results from the awakening of his unconscious feelings, he seeks to discharge his emotions, regardless of the reality of the situation. (1950, vol. ii, pp. 321–2)

'The patient ascribes . . . reality to what results from the awakening of his unconscious feelings'. I would prefer to say that, for the time being at any rate, the perspective of his unconscious feelings becomes his perspective and so changes his consciousness of the different things with which he is in immediate interaction, including, of course, the analyst.

This reliving of the past, this stepping back into one's childhood shoes, retreating into one's childhood self, is not what constitutes insight into oneself either. To have such insight one needs to return to or regain one's present, adult, informed or enlightened mode of judgement. That is, one has to revisit the past without losing one's foothold in the present. So, as Freud puts it, 'we require him [the patient] to transform his *repetition* into *recolleciton*' (1949b, p. 371). The repetition (Proust would say) is one way of remembering. But it is only in retrospect that it can bring insight, that is, when the person retains the memory but regains his present self. For it is only as his present self, living in the present and equipped with what he has acquired through learning, that he can come to insight into himself. True, this self can be an obstacle to progress in analysis and insight, and often it has to be lost before it is found again. But without it insight is impossible.

Insight, then, combines the direct experience, or recovery in consciousness, of aspects of oneself, so far denied, with a perspective in the light of which their role in one's patterns of behaviour and their consequences for one are understood. Neither one without the other amounts to insight. But though this insight involves an inner change in which dissociated aspects of oneself are recovered, this is not the same thing as what is meant by 'finding oneself'. From the one inner change to the other there is much inner work to be done. Indeed, there is a difference in logic between what is meant by 'recovery' in the first case and 'finding' in the second. It is to the second that I now turn.

5 FINDING ONESELF: ENLARGEMENT OF THE SELF

It is what comes under 'finding oneself' that constitutes the 'cure' or 'recovery' of the patient. This covers many different changes, to be considered in the next chapter, and which vary from patient to patient depending on what each is suffering from. At present I am only interested in its own particular logic and the way it goes beyond coming to insight into oneself, while requiring that insight and growing out of it.

In the passage in his *Introductory Lectures* from which I quoted earlier Freud says:

> A neurotic who has been cured has really become a different person, although at bottom of course he remains the same – that is, he has become his best self, what he would have been under the most favourable conditions. (1949b, pp. 363–4)

Let me elucidate. The neurotic – and this, to some extent, applies to everyone – has reached certain solutions to his inner conflicts in early childhood. These solutions involve splitting off and denying certain aspects of himself, devoting some of his energies to maintaining this state of affairs. Consequently, he has confined himself to certain modes of response and closed himself to certain forms of interaction and experience. What he has thus become excludes what he could have been had he not rushed into these solutions and been able to tolerate pain, anxiety and uncertainty a little more than he was able to. What he has missed in the process is 'his best self', namely, 'what he would have been under the most favourable conditions'. Missing it implies a degree of inauthenticity and some curtailment of personal autonomy.

But what he has missed is not something that exists, albeit hidden or unconscious. The patient's 'best self', in the sense Freud means it here, is not his unconscious self. Finding it is not finding something ready-made awaiting discovery. 'Finding' here is used as in 'finding one's style'. It means making, shaping, learning, growing into. When Leonardo da Vinci spoke of the sculptor *finding* the sculpture he was creating in the block of marble on which he was working, getting to it by removing parts of the block which hid it, he was underplaying the part played by the artist's creative vision in this process. His reason, I imagine, was to emphasize how much the artist's creative vision is responsible to something outside him, something that exists independently of him, namely an artistic tradition and its standards. The possibilities that shape his conception of what he sets off to create or realize come from that tradition, and he sees these possibilities in the material on which he works, limited by its relevant characteristics – the size, shape and texture of the marble block. It is only in this sense that he *finds* the sculpture, the statue, in the block, only in this sense that the statue exists within it in advance.

It is in some ways the same with 'finding oneself'. What corresponds to the block in this case are, on the one hand, one's past experiences and, on the other hand, those aspects of one's character which make up one's inauthenticity. What emerges *ultimately*, as one chips away the protective, defensive aspects of one's character, giving up the pursuit of certain ambitions which one comes to see undermine what one cherishes, coming to terms with old injuries and forgiving those whom one held responsible for them, etc., has a great deal to do with values and loyalties that are rooted in one's past, the life and culture to which one belongs and the interests made possible by it which absorb one.

But for anyone whose growth has in some way been stunted to 'find' or 'grow into' himself, his 'best self', he has to stop deceiving himself, face aspects of himself he has denied, feel the pain he has avoided in avoiding facing these, regain the resources he has deployed in keeping them at bay, and so find greater openness to new experiences. This is the part of the process which Freud used Leonardo da Vinci's metaphor *per via di levare* to highlight. However, he missed emphasizing the patient's further positive contribution to it which is 'creative' in character, and the part played in this by what comes to the patient from *outside* as he becomes more open and less rigid in himself.

Let me re-emphasize, this 'best self' that a person grows or would grow into, given the right circumstances, is not something predetermined – as in the case of a chrysalis which grows into a butterfly. On the contrary, what gives a person a 'fixed' character, so that what he comes to is to some extent predetermined, is what makes him as it were a 'closed system'. Such a person being closed to the outside, nothing new can enter into his life from that direction and change him. In finding himself a person loses this 'fixity'; he opens up, while at the same time finding a new stability. How he grows then depends on what he encounters in life, and this is not something fixed in advance.

This is not to say, of course, that he is shaped by outside circumstances. That would mean that he had no personality of his own. Indeed, the opposite is the case: he makes his own life and he develops through it. Although he is open in his emotions and in his mind, he has his own values and loyalties and he knows his own mind. In other words, he knows where he stands, what he wants and where he is going. Finding oneself is the process of coming to this knowledge. The point is that a person who has this knowledge, and so has found himself, is open in his interactions with other people and the culture of the society in which he lives, but he interacts with them as himself, rooted in a past which nourishes him without holding him back.

Psycho-analysis, one could say, enables the patient to find the conditions necessary for his arrested growth to pick up again by removing obstacles, by helping him to dispense with defences and to turn back from the road of repression. This can only be achieved with the patient's collaboration. For the rest the analyst leaves the patient on his own, refusing to guide or direct him. It is true, of course, that the patient finds someting of *what he is like* when he stops repressing those thoughts, inclinations and feelings which he has so far repressed. But 'finding out what he is like' is not the same thing as 'finding himself'. The way from the former to the latter is paved with integration and reconstruction.

Psycho-analysis then reopens inner conflicts which the patient has buried, exposes old psychic wounds which have not been allowed to heal. It thus provides the patient with the opportunity to reconsider his old solutions in the light of his present knowledge of himself and to modify these with the help of his present resources. The idea that it aims to free the unconscious self or id (not the same thing) for it to take over so that the patient can find happiness in this new liberty is a popular misconception. Freud himself made this clear in his *Introductory Lectures*. A conflict in the patient between a repressive 'moral' attitude (super-ego) and repressed desires (id), he says,

> is not resolved by helping one side to win a victory over the other. It is true we see that in neurotics asceticism has gained the day; the result of which is that the suppressed sexual impluses have found a vent for themselves in the symptoms. If we were to make victory possible to the sexual side instead, the disregarded forces repressing sexuality would have to indemnify themselves by symptoms. Neither of these measures will succeed in ending the inner conflict; one side in either event will remain unsatisfied. (1949b, p. 361)

Thus where the repressive 'moral attitude' has triumphed we have one kind of neurotic unhappiness and inauthenticity, well illustrated by the character of Mrs Solness in Ibsen's play *The Master Builder* (see Dilman, 1984a, chapter 11). Where the scales are tipped the other way and the 'moral attitude'[1] is given up in favour of 'licence', on the other hand, the person becomes the plaything of impulses which destroy the possibility of his finding cohesion in himself. Such a person is as far from autonomy as the first. He may, further, develop symptoms in which he satisfies his desire to punish himself for what he feels he disregards, violates and destroys in the way he gives in to his impulses and in them pursues old scores.

Compulsiveness and impulsiveness, repression and licence, the super-ego and the id: these are the two poles between which the ego has to negotiate in the course of the person's struggles to find himself. This negotiation is 'dialectical' in character. I am using this term as a metaphor here. Analysis is not on the side of the super-ego and it uncovers repressions dictated by it in the hope that the patient will be able to dispense with these as he finds greater self-confidence. But it does not do so to enable the patient to give free reign to his impulses. That would be a different form of slavery. As Freud puts it: 'the task of therapy . . . [is] to uncover repressions and replace them by acts of judgement which might result either in the acceptance or in the rejection of what had formerly been repudiated' (1948, p. 53). This, however, is not a simple choice between two immediate alternatives. The patient has to learn to tolerate inner conflict as it is opened up in analysis and stay still rather than jump one way or the other. For, as the analysis progresses, the alternatives will continue to change their aspect. This is the direct consequence of the patient's 'descent' from current conflicts to earlier ones, the current conflicts being the result of his earlier 'solutions'. It is these early solutions which, Freud tells us, 'come up for revision again' as the old conflicts are opened up in analysis (1949b, p. 366).

This 'revision' of old solutions, which the lifting of repressions makes possible, is a change in the self. It is made possible by the insight brought about by the lifting of repressions. Yet it goes beyond the inner change which belongs to such insight. It can be represented as the healing of splits between the ego on the one hand and the id or the super-ego on the other. As aspects of the id and the super-ego are transformed into parts of the patient's ego, they change character and come under the domain of the patient's will. Impulses he had repressed, compulsions that had ruled his life, now

---

[1] The inverted commas are essential here, since the attitude in question is not a genuine moral attitude, but is in the service of the person's defences and bad feelings.

become inclinations that no longer overwhelm him. He can repudiate or endorse them, give them up or act on them in particular circumstances. When he gives them up they stop plaguing him, and when he acts on them he is behind his actions.

This is only a broad, abstract characterization of what I called 'enlargement of the self' and its transformation. In the next chapter we shall examine some of the forms it takes and thus consider some concrete instances of it. These are changes in the self towards greater unity and autonomy, changes which liberate resources deployed to maintain divisions within the self, and they open the way to renewed contact with the outside world through which the self finds new growth. That is why they constitute a 'healing of the self'. They coincide with Freud's therapeutic ideal: 'where id and super-ego were, there ego shall be'.

6   INSIGHT AND SELF-KNOWLEDGE

We saw earlier that insight into the self is that inner change wherein what was unconscious becomes conscious. I shall argue now that self-knowledge is that inner change or transformation of the self wherein a person finds himself.

This self that one finds or comes to, we have seen, does not pre-exist its discovery, nor is it a predetermined destination towards which one moves in the changes one undergoes. Rather, it is what one comes to in an open or free development in the course of one's interactions with the 'outside world'. But in that case, how can it be said to have been *found* or *discovered*, and how can one speak of the coming to it as coming to a *knowledge of the self*?

I have already touched on this when commenting on the use of the word 'finding' or 'discovery' in connection with art. Thus, to take the example from music, the composer may 'discover' a sequence of notes that are just right in the piece he is composing, or the performer may similarly 'discover' a way of playing a piece that he would say is the right one. It is the possibility of distinguishing between what is right and what is not that enables us to talk of finding or discovering something, although it did not exist before and is, in that sense, something that the composer or performer has 'created'. One could say that it existed as a 'possibility', shaped by a particular tradition and its standards.

Similarly, the self that one comes to, though it does not pre-exist one's coming to it, is not just any self. It is the self that makes one an authentic person. What one discovers, if I may put it like this, is the way for one to be authentic. It is in this discovery that one finds oneself, or, in other words, finding oneself is making just this discovery. And the question is, that being so, why is this to be described as 'coming to know oneself'? If that seems to be wrong, the reason for it is that we are still thinking of 'coming to know oneself' as 'coming to know what one is like', 'acquiring true beliefs about oneself', that is, beliefs which correspond to what one is actually like.

But let us remind ourselves that self-knowledge has many anti-theses. One of these is self-deception, which has many different forms (see Dilman and Phillips, 1971), another is innocence, yet another is naïvety. Here a person is not innocent about or of something; innocence in one case, naïvety in another characterize the person himself, his mode of being. It is in himself that the person is innocent, that is, untouched by the knowledge of good and evil as these find expression in human lives. It is in himself, in another case, that he is naïve or sentimental, and similarly in many cases of self-deception it is in himself that he is deceived. He can, of course, be deceived *about* himself. He may, for instance, hide his weaknesses from himself. But he can also be deceived *in* himself. That is he can be *false* or inauthentic.[2] When this is so, the change in him from falsity to greater truth is a change from self-deception to self-knowledge. Thus, the person who has self-knowledge or 'knows himself' is a person who is no longer deceived *in* himself – 'in' as opposed to 'about' himself.

What does he know then? Himself. What does he know about himself? This second question misunderstands the logic of the term 'know' used here. Thus contrast 'he knows *himself*' with 'he knows *something* about himself he does not like'. Self-knowledge is *not* the sum total of what on knows about oneself, although the latter is the basis from which one moves to self-knowledge.

'He knows himself' is in some ways like 'He knows such-and-such a person well, or intimately'. This does not mean that he knows a

---

[2] Professor D.Z. Phillips and I have argued this in *Sense and Delusion* but, by and large, what we said seems to have remained unheard in contemporary discussions of self-deception.

great deal about him. It would be surprising if he didn't, but that is not what is being claimed. For he could come to know a great deal about this person without ever meeting him and so coming to know him. I have discussed elsewhere what it means to know a person, someone other than oneself. The knowing here involves making contact with the other person through mutual responses in which each person discloses something of himself to the other. I argued that it is crucial that each person is himself in his responses to the other, whether these responses are friendly or hostile (see Dilman, 1986, chapter 9). What is involved here are disclosure and contact.

Similarly, what is involved in self-knowledge is self-disclosure and coming to oneself. As one drops one's pretences, ceases to deceive oneself, or perhaps loses one's innocence, one moves towards greater 'truth' or authenticity. The term 'truth' here does not characterize one's *beliefs* about oneself, but oneself (one's *self*). It is in coming to be true to oneself that one comes to be oneself. What is in question is how one stands with regard to oneself. This is not a relation of oneself as subject to a pre-existing or fixed object-self: an external relation. No, what we have here is the 'inner organization', the 'cohesiveness' of the self as this finds expression in the person's actions, in the character of his interests, in his responses and orientation to other people. It is here that the truth or authenticity that characterizes *him* as a person shows itself. His having self-knowledge *is* his possession of such truth *in himself*.

There is some logical parallel between this knowledge of oneself and what Socrates called 'moral knowledge' or 'knowlege of good and evil' and identified with virtue (see Dilman, 1979, chapters 3 and 9). Many philosophers have found this identification difficult to stomach because they have thought of the knowledge in question as being a matter of the truth of the person's *beliefs about* someting or other. This Platonic paradox raises other difficulties; but this one is removed by coming to a proper logical appreciation of the way the term 'knowledge' is being used here. It is in just this respect that it throws light on the notion of self-knowledge under discussion. Indeed, I would argue that 'knowledge of good and evil', 'knowledge of mankind' and 'self-knowledge' overlap and are interwoven as, I believe, Socrates would have agreed. What I did argue is that moral knowledge is a matter of the person's relation to the values *in* which he believes. The relation which constitutes such knowledge is that of love, and having this love is being in a particular state of soul. It is through such love that one makes contact with good and evil. One cannot come to it, however, without shedding much of what one clings to in oneself and so changing. It takes inner strength and courage to be able to do so. It is this very state of soul which, in Plato's view, constitutes virtue.

Thus, while Plato identifies moral knowledge with that state of soul which constitutes virtue, a state of soul which characterizes the self, similarly, I have argued, self-knowledge is that 'organization' or 'orientation' of the self which constitutes its truth or authenticity. This is the logical parallel I tried to highlight in my comparison between self-knowledge and moral knowledge. The genuinely authentic person *is* the person who knows himself. I mean this as what Wittgenstein calls a 'grammatical remark'.

More can be said by way of bringing out why we should want to talk of 'knowledge' here and find it appropriate to do so – appropriate on the basis of what we mean by 'knowledge' in other connections. Thus, for instance, the person who is authentic or true to himself has made his values his own. This means, among other things, that his conscience, when he departs from those values, is very much part of himself, in contrast with what Freud called the super-ego. Hence, even when he finds certain decisions difficult and is uncertain of what to do, he is still a person who knows his own mind – at least in the sense that his mind is his own. He has sufficient certainty in himself to be able to bend to others, give way before them for their sake, take orders from a superior. The point is that he has a place on which he stands, he knows where he stands. Melanie Klein would describe this in terms of his relation to his 'inner objects', but we are not concerned with this now.

Knowing where he stands is at least part of what we mean when we say that 'he knows who he is'. This 'knowing' has its foundation in the kind of relations he has had with his parents as a child, as they shape his present relationships. They play an important role in what he is able to give and what he is able to receive from the people with whom he interacts, and what part of himself he is able to put into the different activities of his life.

Again, such a person 'knows what he wants and where he is going', and this is part of his 'knowing himself'. Here it is important to be clear that one finds out what one wants not by looking within but by turning outwards. It is the self-illusions a person feels compelled to maintain as well as vestiges of his early narcissism that keep him from turning outwards. It is the person himself who then finds what he wants. Such a person 'knows what he wants' and pursues his ambitions and interests in the light of his moral beliefs and personal limitations.

This is the kind of self-knowledge which psycho-analysis tries to promote in the analysand and it does so (we have seen) through the promotion of the kind of inner change which constitutes insight into the self. Each such inner change, when achieved, liberates the patient to reconsider his early postures and solutions to his conflicts as these reappear in his current life and particularly in the trans-ference in analysis. It is the 'inner work' that he engages as a result of opening up, together with the reconsideration and revision of his early fixed positions which lead him to greater knowledge of himself.

7 SUMMARY

The main contribution of this chapter is the distinction I made between the kind of insight that pscyho-analysis aims to promote in the patient and the self-knowledge to which the patient comes by means of the inner work he undertakes as a result of this insight. I characterized the former as an 'enlargement of consciousness' and the latter as an 'enlaregement of the self'. But we have seen that the former also involves some enlargement of self. The two changes are continuous and overlap to some extent.

In the former the changes in those patterns which constitute the patient's feelings and desires go beyond changes in the aspect under which he sees them. They involve changes in his responses to things, and in that sense are changes in *him*. But the patient's modified responses maintain sufficient continuity with those former patterns which constitute his unconscious feelings and desires for the change not to amount to a change in his feelings and desires. Thus the patient changes in one respect but not in another: he becomes more open with his feelings and less anxious about owning them, but he is still a person who has the feelings and desires he has had all along.

It is for this reason that I prefer to talk of an 'enlargement of consciousness' here and to reserve the expression 'enlargement of the self' for those more radical changes whereby the patient comes to feel in new ways about things and finds growth. But even where I talk of an enlargement of consciousness we have a change that goes beyond the change in the aspect under which the patient sees himself when his unconscious feelings and desires become conscious. For he is already a less anxious person, perhaps a braver one too, and he has certainly given up strategies of defence which have played a part in shaping his relationships with others.

My reason, nevertheless, for insisting on the distinction was to bring out the more positive aspects of the work which engages the patient in the healing process. What is being healed is the patient's self, and it needs healing because it is split or divided in certain ways, because it is false in certain respects, because it is cut off from what would be a source of life, nourishment and growth to it, and because it is in pain. The more positive aspects of this inner work are what will concern us in the following chapter.

9

Healing and Growth of the Self

1 PSYCHO-ANALYSIS AND THE NEUROSES

In the earlier part of our discussion we saw that there are not neuroses in the sense in which there are physical illnesses. Rather, there are people with 'neurotic' problems and difficulties. These are problems *in* them, *personal* difficulties, and they do fall into certain recognizable patterns. But only up to a certain degree. And the closer one focuses on them the more do the categories under which they are classified turn out to be rather bogus labels of convenience. Tolstoy wrote in *Anna Karenina:* 'All happy families are alike but an unhappy family is unhappy after its own fashion.' This is equally true of people's neurotic problems and difficulties.

It is for such problems and difficulties that people seek psycho-analytic help – ostensibly at any rate. I say 'ostensibly' not to suggest that they do not seek help for these difficulties, as obviously they do. But these difficulties are only the outward sign of their inner discontent and conflict, and they are, partly at least, the consequence of their way of dealing with these. So in their request for help they are asking not only for relief from their ostensible difficulties but also for a solution to their deeper discontent and inner conflicts. Yet they are often unprepared to alter their way of dealing with these deeper problems, and furthermore they do not necessarily have a very clear notion of what they are letting themselves in for in seeking psycho-analytic help. So part of the process of being helped consists of a modification of their attitude in asking for help, the way they are prepared to receive it and their willingness to participate in the work.

In the course of this modification their focus shifts from their outward difficulties, the conscious psychological problems for which they sought help in the first place, to what lies underneath them, their deeper discontent and inner conflicts, and the postures they have adopted by way of a *modus vivendi*. This shift of focus is what I called 'insight' – insight into oneself. It opens up the possibility for the patient of being able to reconsider and revise his mode of living with his inner conflicts, to re-experience them and bring to bear on them emotional resources from which he has so far kept them isolated. This latter is what I called 'inner work'.

It is this affective work which enables the patient to come together, perhaps for the first time, to find greater inner unity and to start growing again in his new experiences. This is what constitutes 'the healing and growth of the self'. The changes involved often bring about a resolution of the difficulties for which the patient sought therapeutic help: either his difficulties disappear as a result of the changes that he undergoes or what constitutes them no longer troubles him. This may be called 'the cure of his neurosis' where the difficulties are sufficiently patterned to enable the psycho-analyst to talk of a neurosis.

2 WHAT MAKES A PERSON SEEK ANALYSIS?

Before considering this 'inner work' let us briefly review the kinds of ostensible psychological problems for which people seek analytic psychotherapy. The first thing to note is that it takes some self-awareness to be conscious of such problems *as* problems so as to be able to seek help for them.

Though the categories of problem for which psycho-analytic help is sought merge into one another, one could put these problems, in a rough and ready way, under the following headings:

1   Various forms of self-dissatisfaction – that is, dissatisfactions with the *self*, with oneself. One may, for instance, feel a sense of inferiority, or worthlessness, or feel oneself to be a poor sort of person morally or otherwise. One may desperately try to compensate for this and be dejected by one's failure to do so. This sense of one's own inferiority or worthlessness or unacceptability may mar one's relationships in the way, for instance, that one seeks other people's regard and approval. It may mar them, alternatively, in that what one gives others is

itself infected with this sense of one's own worthlessness or unacceptability. It is obvious that such dissatisfactions would make life problematic.

2   Various forms of dissatisfaction with *one's life*. It may appear limited or empty; one may feel one is wasting one's time, have no absorbing interests, find little fulfilment in the things one does. Obviously one would have to feel some responsibility and think of oneself as at fault and the cause of this state of affairs in order to be able to seek help.

3   Various kinds of incapacity that leave one with unsatisfied *needs*. One may be shy or awkward, one may continuously rub people up the wrong way, etc. One may, in consequence, find oneself isolated and yet feel that one is oneself the cause of this. (The needs that one is unable to satisfy may themselves be neurotic needs that may diminish and disappear in the course of the analysis.)

4   More passively, one may suffer from a feeling of *helplessness*, ineffectuality, impotence. One may feel that one makes no difference to other people, that one is not needed by anyone, that as far as others are concerned one may as well not exist.

5   Various kinds of *failure* for which one feels responsible and that one believes reflect badly on one, such as a series of broken marriages or relationships.

6   Specific distressing fears and incapacitating anxieties. I am thinking of cases where the emphasis is on the *distress* itself and where people most of all crave relief from the distress.

7   Specific *troubles* that one keeps finding onself in and that one feels unable to avoid, such as associating with the 'wrong' sort of people, picking up 'bad' habits and, as a result, losing out on things that one aspires to.

These are broad categories with vague contours, and there are psychological problems that it would be difficult to know where to fit in this scheme. The classification is not meant to be of *practical* value. Its main purpose is to highlight how much the problems in question have to do with a 'breakdown' of the *self* – its chronic discontents, incapacities, failures, pains – and some failure in its *development*. It is this that makes life and relationships problematic – isolation, emptiness, feelings of failure, envy, guilt, dejection and depression – in a way that makes people ask for *personal* help –

involving the desire to communicate, to be listened to, to receive attention and care. It is a combination of these desires, together with some recognition of personal failure and the wish to do something about it – though this is in conflict with a wish to maintain palliative strategies – that makes a person seek psycho-analytic therapy.

I repeat, the *ostensible* problems and difficulties are various and there is a sense in which they defy classification. They are best presented as Freud presented them, namely as case studies. As such the presentation bears some affinity with the art of the novelist. As for the underlying source of these problems, it is Freud's view that this is something that came into being in the past, in the person's early childhood, and has been preserved into the present.

Sources of psychological problems certainly vary from person to person and from family to family. But it is possible to highlight some patterns – patterns of relationship, conflict and consequent affective postures and indentifications. In different combinations, they recur in human life, though they take different forms in different cultures. It is on the particular combination in each case that each person's personality, character and neurotic problems are founded. The person himself builds up his personality and problems by reacting to this fixed base, trying to avert some of its pains, to compensate for some of its consequences, to accommodate his desires to its demands.

This is not a once and for all process, and each of his reactions and postures has further consequences to which he tries to adapt. Because these reactions are directed at the consequences, direct or indirect, of what lies at the foundations, because they are modes of adjusting to it, they have the effect of preserving it. This is what makes the base on which a person builds his personality a fixed one. By accommodating his life to it he gives these foundations solidity. Thus, a neurotic personality, one that creates its own problems, is a complex structure that tends to preserve itself. This is what makes psycho-analytic penetration to what lies at the roots of the person's neurotic problems such a difficult and painstaking task.

3   FREUD: THE OEDIPUS COMPLEX AS THE KERNEL
OF THE NEUROSES

Freud held the Oedipus complex to be the kernel of the neuroses (1949b, p. 283). In other words, he held that a person's neurotic problems are founded on his conflict-ridden triangular relations, in the family setting, with his two parents in his early childhood, that is between the ages of three and five. The shape the relations take in reality, as well as a person's apprehension of them, on account of what he brings to them from his earlier development, and what his parents themselves contribute to them, together constitute the character of almost the whole of his world. The child finds his being through them. Yet they present him, inevitably, with difficulties, and the whole prospect of his development depends on how he overcomes these difficulties and on what good he can retain from what he receives in these relationships.

Overcoming them involves some relinquishment of dependencies, the toleration of some painful feelings and the growing out of them, the holding together of strong feelings that are painful to hold together, giving them a chance to work on each other. To succeed the child needs external support as well as inner security, based on the care he has so far received and the trust that his environment has nurtured in him. Otherwise he will try to evade the challenge, neutralize the pain, compensate for the failure, and so preserve the difficulties while pretending they do not exist.

I now turn to a brief consideration of Freud's account of the conflicts and difficulties that constitute the Oedipus complex, and of what defusing and overcoming them amounts to. This is part of Freud's account of the early emotional-sexual development of the individual. Freud regarded sexuality as one of the most important co-ordinates of a person's identity. It is certainly not the only one, but in appreciating its importance it is crucial to see the way in which a person's particular sexuality – I mean the very particular form it takes – goes through his emotional life and sentiments, indeed the whole of his affective orientation. It is this particular form which is finally established in the course of the individual's Oedipal phase – what conflicts beset him, how he faces them and how far he succeeds in resolving them. Thus Freud saw this phase as 'the peak of infantile sexuality' (1949a, p. 104n). After the 'passing' of the Oedipus complex comes the 'latency period' (from five to twelve years of age) when the child's sexual interests go into a dormant stage, his other interests develop and his character and sexual identity are consolidated.

Freud's account of the early part of the child's development dwells on two of its aspects, that he does not sufficiently relate to each other – not explicitly at any rate. These are the young child's relation to his own body, the way his life centres on the pleasures and pains – but especially pleasures – he finds in various parts of his body and their exercise, and, secondly, his relation to his mother. Up the age of three Freud sees no difference in these respects between the developments of the young boy and the young girl. In so far as he brings the first aspect into focus he describes the child as 'auto-erotic', because he finds 'sexual gratification' in parts of his own body. Here Freud distinguishes between three pre-genital stages – the oral, anal and phallic stages.

But the young child or infant is in constant interaction with his mother and greatly dependent on her. Indeed, at first, in Freud's view, the infant does not differentiate himself from his mother – not clearly at any rate. In this symbiotic relationship he feels fused with her, taking her to be an extension of himself. He has as yet no conception of himself as a distinct being, nor of his mother as one. In so far as he has no conception of anything distinct from himself that can stand opposed to his will in his feelings he is 'omnipotent'. I am referring to what finds expression in his affective reactions, to the way he deals with what he finds frustrating. Here Freud talks of 'primary narcissism'. I take what is in question to characterize the peculiar relation of the infant to his mother at this early stage of his development. Little by little he comes to differentiate himself from his mother. Changes in his external circumstances may prod him on – such as weaning or the arrival of a brother or sister. But when they are experienced as traumatic they may hinder him, making him emotionally cling to his mother all the more.

Round about the age of three, when the child's interest in his body begins to shift towards and come to centre round his penis in the case of the boy, or the clitoris in the case of the girl, the father begins to assume prominence in the child's emotional life. This is what Freud called the 'phallic stage' – three to five years of age – under the first 'auto-erotic' aspect, and the 'Oedipus phase' under the second 'object-relations' aspect. In other words, the child's phallic phantasies and preoccupations give content to his or her relationships with mother and father, and to his or her understanding of and reactions to their relationship with each other.

So far the mother has been the object of the child's attachment and phantasies and a source of emotional sustenance. The father's entrance into the emotional life and awareness of the boy takes on a disruptive appearance there. He is apprehended as a disproportionately powerful rival, and dreaded on that account, while at the same time he is also loved in response to the caring attention he is perceived to give to the child. This constitutes the boy's 'ambivalence' towards his father, who may be seen as, and may in fact be, a figure of authority, one who stands in the way of the child having and doing what he wants, and also a helper, and even friend. His ambivalence divides the child within himself, pulling him in opposite directions.

Normally, the entrance of the father into the emotional life of the girl at this stage has a different effect. She renounces her interest in the clitoris and in her love turns from mother to father. It is the loved mother who now assumes the role of the dreaded rival to the girl who, according to Freud, wishes to bear him a child as a gift and token of her love.[1] But she continues to love the mother all the same and so has ambivalent feelings towards her.

Thus it is the discovery of the difference between the sexes which initiates the Oedipus complex in girls. This discovery has the opposite effect on boys. It arouses the wish to eliminate the father as a rival and the corresponding fear of being punished by castration.

Besides his love for his father, and alongside his negative feelings towards him, the boy also looks up to his father and makes him a model in his development. He tries to emulate him and craves his approval. Freud calls this a relationship of 'identification'. Affiliated to it is the process of 'introjection' in which the child takes into himself a particular attitude of the parent, a measure or standard by which the parent judges and upon which he acts. What we have here is a form of imitation. What is thus 'taken in' nevertheless retains some independence. That is, the child remains as imitator, while what he imitates continues to exercise a spell over him, benevolent or malevolent. It is as if the parent's voice establishes itself within the child, upholding and guiding him; but it also commands him when he is tempted to disregard it, scolds and even persecutes him in more extreme cases. Equally, the child sometimes sees those feelings he finds unacceptable in himself reflected in his parents. Thus he may see his own anger in his father, without recognizing its source, and fearing his father all the more for it. This is what Freud calls 'projection' and it obviously has a defensive use. Just as identification and idealization can have too.

Here then we have emotions, the cravings and reactions peculiar to

---

[1] Much light is thrown on the question of how a child of this age can know the facts of procreation in Freud's case study of Little Hans (see 1977, pp. 229–57).

them, and the conflicts between them that can assume dramatic proportions in the child's affective imagination – especially when there is little else in his life as yet to give him a sense of proportion. Freud describes the conflicts, preoccupations and turmoil of this stage of life very vividly in his discussion of Little Hans (see 1977, especially pp. 289–92).

While he holds that all children go through this turmoil and these conflicts, he also holds that many come through them to a greater or lesser extent. He thus talks of 'the passing of the Oedipus complex'. The boy gets over his jealousy of his father by identifying himself with him and detaching himself from his mother. He continues to love his mother but becomes less dependent on her. This is part of growing up towards full manhood. The girl, correspondingly, detaches herself from her father and gets over her jealousy of her mother by identifying herself with her.

Although this passing of the Oedipus complex is part of growing up, it is Freud's view that the conflicts in question are never resolved and that what the child keeps of his parents within himself remains to some extent distorted and exaggerated by his ambivalence and his defensive idealizations. These parental figures in his affective memory thus continue to keep him dependent and in conflict. They become a permanent part of him to which he has to make further adjustments. He may constantly feel guilty, for instance, and react to it in defiance, he may deny his dependence by becoming a rebel. The 'inner figures', that is, his parents in the shape in which they survive in his affective life, distorted by phantasy, play a leading role in shaping the growing adolescent's sexual identity and his later adult relationships. They are thus the source of his neurotic problems and difficulties. In short, *how* he resolves these early conflicts will either create what is benign and supportive in the rest of his life or be the source of internal strife and a problem-ridden life and relationships. Where the latter predominates we have the root-cause of neurotic problems.

What psycho-analysis attempts to do is to get the patient to eliminate his defences, that is, give up some of his postures which protect him from what he finds painful, so as to get to these early inner conflicts. The patient is thus moved towards facing these afresh, either by reliving them in the transference or by reliving them in other relationships which he brings to the analysis. There is still a difference between enacting his early conflicts in the present and seeing them for what they are. Direct transference interpretations are meant to help him to recognize the imprint of the past in what he acts out in his current life and in the analysis. Facing his early conflicts afresh in this way gives him the opportunity to revise his early 'solutions' of them, to get over these painful feelings bound up with them that are interfering with his present relationships, and in the process to grow up to a less dependent orientation. This will involve a humanization of the super-ego and so change its relation to the ego. It may increase the patient's ability to put more of himself into his sexuality and to find more meaning in his sexual relations.

It is clear that what is in question is not simply the disappearance of his current difficulties, but a resolution of what has kept the patient divided in himself, wrapped up in inner conflicts and unable to make full use of his own resources since his early life.

4   MELANIE KLEIN – I: OUR ADULT WORLD AND ITS ROOTS IN INFANCY

The picture I have sketched out in my summary of Freud's views on the relation between the Oedipus complex[2] and people's neurotic problems has been elaborated and added to, especially by Melanie Klein. I would like to consider her additions and modifications for the light they throw on what is involved in the kind of healing that psycho-analysis seeks to promote. The language in which she makes these additions and represents the steps taken by the infant and young child in his emotional development, when properly understood, is both illuminating and of philosophical interest. In it we can see either a subtle modification of Freud's concepts or the development of a trend implicit in them. Whichever view one takes – and I do not think there is much difference between these two alternatives – it is clear that her contribution is a *development* of Freudian psycho-analysis.

She developed particularly Freud's concepts of introjection and phantasy in interesting ways and used them with great penetration. She saw those activities of the young child which Freud characterized as 'auto-erotic' in terms of the child's *relationships*, prima-

---

[2] For my consideration of Freud's grounds for regarding the Oedipus complex as universal and for his estimate of its significance see Dilman, 1983, chapter 2.

rily with the mother, and filled in gaps in Freud's picture of the development of adult human emotions and the formation of moral sentiments. In all this she concentrated mainly on the development of the infant's relation to his mother in the first year of his[3] life prior to the Oedipal conflicts which Freud highlighted.

In Melanie Klein's view there is, from the start, a relationship of give and take between the infant and the breast from which he derives physical and psychological sustenance. The infant's first love is thus for the breast: a natural, primitive response of pleasure to it for the sustenance with which it provides him. It involves a naîve trust which at this early age is simply the lack of any suspicion. This trust is not something which the infant or child learns; it is the suspicion which he learns when things go wrong in certain ways – when he is let down or feels so on account of his own negative feelings which get in the way.

His need of the breast for its milk and warmth normally contains an element of greed, though the degree to which it does so varies from one infant to another. The greed, especially when combined with envy – another early primitive emotion wholly identified with certain reactions of the infant – undermines his trust, disrupts the feeding, and interferes with the sustenance and support he obtains from the breast. At an extreme his world becomes as cold and uncaring as his own greed; spoilt by his envy, the milk he has taken is felt to have lost its sustaining value. Indeed, psychologically its sustenance is diminished, and in extreme cases destroyed. He feels he has taken in something bad; he may spit or sick it out. He also tries to rid himself of this badness by projecting it onto the breast. That is, in his feelings he turns the breast into something bad and hateful. This defensive projection faces him with a new fear, since it turns the breast into a frightening thing.

Here is one movement, making up a vicious circle, countering an opposite one whereby a benign atmosphere is achieved, one in which the infant's love and trust predominate. In the latter case, the breast, as the centre of the infant's world, is a source of support and sustenance. The greed and envy, in contrast, poison his relationship with it. Melanie Klein sees this as a conflict between the life and death instincts, one furthering a sustaining relationship, leading to

---

[3] I use the masculine pronoun here for stylistic simplicity. At this stage of life the infant's sexuality has not yet taken a masculine or feminine identity.

greater strength of the infant's ego, the other making for a destructive relationship and hampering growth.

In this predicament, at first, the infant splits and tries to keep apart his good and bad feelings, his love and hate, greed and gratitude, trust and envy. He does so by keeping apart the two aspects under which he is aware of the breast affectively, thus fostering the impression that there are two qualitatively different breasts around which his world revolves, one good to him, caring and sustaining, and the other bad, uncaring, cruel and retaliatory. Melanie Klein calls this type of primitive defence 'schizoid'. Originally it is not a defence but a mode of apprehension that the infant grows out of as he acquires the notion of permanent objects which retain their identity through various kinds of change. In so far as the infant experiences the persecution that emanates from the bad breast as retaliatory, that is, as called for by his own destructive greed, the infant feels he is being punished. Here we have the earliest and most primitive form of guilt and conception of punishment – what may be called 'persecutory guilt': a primitive expectation of vengeful punishment because of one's badness.

As the infant derives sustenance and strength from his good relationship with the breast–mother, he will be able to dispense with his schizoid mode of dealing with his early conflicts – to a greater or lesser degree. He will, that is, allow his good and bad feelings to come together. He will come to see that what he has attacked and spoilt in his affective apprehension is *the same* breast as the one on which he has depended for care and sustenance. In short, he will come to see that he has spoilt and done harm to the very thing he depends on and loves. To hurt the bad breast is bad enough, for the infant fears that it will hurt him in return; but to hurt the good breast is much worse and fills the infant with dismay and dejection. This is the primitive version of the feeling of having destroyed goodness, of having injured what one loves.

Having given up his earlier schizoid position the infant is now able to contain his bad feelings and contemplate their consequences, without finding them mirrored in the world. Where previously he saw persecution he now finds a devastation of something cherished brought about by his own badness. Consequently, some of his paranoic fears give way to feelings of guilt and depression – what may be called 'depressive guilt': feeling sorry for having hurt, broken or injured what one needs and loves, for having harmed what has been good to one, and so feeling bereft of anything good on which one can fall back.

Once more the infant may accept these feelings or he may evade them by returning to the earlier splitting – the schizoid position. Or he may pretend that all is well since what he has attacked is not worth cherishing – 'manic defence'. Again, the extent to which he can accept these painful feelings depends on the preponderence of his good feelings. In so far as he can accept them, he will want to make up for and repair the harm he feels he has done, make restitution for it. He will give up sulking, forgive offences to which he has reacted with anger, play his part in restoring a good relationship, and receive what he is given with gratitude. What Melanie Klein calls 'the working through of the depression' I understand to be the assimilation of these painful feelings that combine love and hate, until (as she puts it) the love mitigates the hate through restitution and forgiveness. This heralds a change in the inner affective world of the infant.

It is worth noting that this story which Melanie Klein tells of the infant's world in the first year of his life is in terms of his relationship with what tends to his needs – the mother–breast – the give and take between them, and the way this is furthered or hampered by the infant's love and hate, greed, envy and guilt, desire for reparation and gratitude.[4] As she puts it: 'As I see it, object relations start almost at birth' (Klein, 1960). There is as much ground for arguing that this relation has a moral dimension as for arguing that it has a sexual character.

Certainly, in what her story depicts we have the primitive precursors to the moral life. These are the common shared reactions on which the diverse moral practices and institutions found in different societies are based. In them is to be found an important part of our common human nature, what makes us accessible to the forces of good and evil in human life, what gives them a foothold in us.

More important for our present purposes, the story also depicts those affective moves in the infant's life in which he *overcomes* difficulties that hamper his development towards greater inner unity

---

[4] There is no logical space as yet for jealousy, since that presupposes an awareness of a third person, the father, and the relationship which excludes the subject. That comes later at the Oedipus stage.

and emotional independence. These are what psycho-analytic therapy hopes to bring into motion in the patient who in his affective life has tied himself up into rigid positions. It is these responses that will free him, not insight by itself. Insight is what puts the patient in touch with those aspects of himself which, in turn, call for these responses, set these affective tendencies into motion – to forgive, make restitution, mend, grieve, etc. It is the key that unlocks the processes of healing.

When I speak of 'processes' here I do not mean 'what goes on in the patient', on the model of digestive processes for instance, but what the patient engages in, effective tendencies which he enters into and makes part of his emotional life, responses to what he has himself been doing or is involved in which he follows through. But before I turn to a consideration of the role of such 'processes' in the patient's 'recovery', I would like to defend Melanie Klein's conception of the infant's 'inner world' and elucidate the sense in which it is 'at the root' of the world he comes to share with adults in his emotional and intellectual development.

5 MELANIE KLEIN – II: THE INFANT'S INNER WORLD
AS THE BASIS OF HIS ADULT PERSONALITY

I say 'defend' because it is open to some philosophical criticism. Is not our adult world, the public world in which we live, made possible and largely shaped by the complex culture of the society in which we have developed and live? Do we not owe much of our being, all that we value and aspire to, indeed our whole way of thinking to that culture? Do we not enter the world of this culture very largely through language, through learning to speak? So, someone may ask, how can that world have its roots in prelinguistic infancy? Indeed, how can an infant, prior to all this, be said to have an 'inner world' at all? For is not our 'inner world', everything that we can imagine for instance, made possible by the public world in which we live and the public language that we speak? Does not even the madman's inner world derive its reality from and depend for its content on the outer world in which members of the society to which he belongs live?

The world of phantasy in which Dr Schreber lived at the height of his paranoic psychosis contained God, for instance, and it involved highly sophisticated conceptions which he had acquired in the public life of real interactions with other human beings, a life in which he had once occupied the position of a high-court judge. Thus we could say that the inner world he describes in his book was logically parasitic on the outer world with which he had lost contact in his psychosis. Should we not, therefore, say that only a man who has lived and shared in a public life with other human beings can have an inner world to retire into, and that only he can construct phantasies in which certain emotions flourish?

I would endorse much of this (see Dilman, 1986, chapter 4). But I do not think that it invalidates Melanie Klein's claim that the infant at first lives largely in a world of phantasy, an inner world from which he emerges as he develops self-awareness and comes to recognize his mother as a separate person. For to claim that he lives in an inner world of phantasy does not mean that he engages in imaginative activities, such as day-dreaming, or that he gets caught up in yarns that he spins, coming to believe them to be true. Rather, at first, there is no public world for the infant, and no distinction for him between truth and falsehood, fact an fancy. He has various cravings, such as hunger and thirst, bodily feelings and certain rudimentary perceptions which develop quickly in the course of his interactions with what lies around him. He has also a developing repertoire of affective responses to it in its relation to his needs, their satisfaction and frustration.

Thus his elementary perceptions, bodily feelings and expectations both arouse certain primitive emotions in him and are, in turn, appraised from the point of view of these emotions – found pleasurable, liked, wanted, rejected, feared, etc. If, for instance, the hungry infant is kept waiting he may feel starved and the anger engendered by his frustration may, in turn, evoke a fear that he will be punished, indeed treated in the image of the wishes contained in his anger. That is, he may suffer his own pangs of hunger as if he were being attacked. Being starved and persecuted: this is part of the 'language' he understands. I am referring to what one may call the 'language of the emotions' – the language of anger and hostility for instance. Understanding that 'language' is possessing the primitive inclination to respond to the frustration of one's desires in an angry way, finding this natural, expecting certain consequences, and recognizing these responses in others. The question, 'Am I really being starved?' does not as yet have any reality for the infant and cannot arise for him at all. He has not yet learned to ask this sort of question.

So if one says that the infant at this stage lives largely in an inner world of his own, what is meant is that the significance of his as yet elementary perceptions is determined by his primitive emotions, his expectations are dominated by these, and there is no question for him whether he is right or wrong. It is from this state that he emerges by learning to make sense of things, to distinguish between appearance and reality, and to appraise his perceptions and beliefs with regard to their reality and truth.

In this sense, then, there is nothing logically incoherent in the idea of the temporal priority of an inner world, the world from which the infant emerges in his emotional and intellectual development. This is the world of the emotions, the world of the unconscious and its phantasies, to which, Freud tells us, we can gain access in ourselves 'under the conditions of dreaming and of neurosis, that is to say, when the processes of the higher system Pcs [in other words, our everyday, adult mentality] revert to an earlier level by a certain process of degradation (regression)' 'The Unconscious', 1950, vol. iv, p. 120).

In his *Esquisse d'une Théorie des Emotions* (1948) Sartre brings this out very well. He speaks there of how in certain situations of urgency, danger, desire and frustration 'consciousness throws itself into the magic world of emotions, in this way degrading itself . . . The person who is in the throes of an emotion resembles the person who goes to sleep' (translation mine, p. 42). Sartre compares emotional transport with dreaming and hysteria (p. 43) and says that 'one should speak of a world of emotions in the same way as one speaks of a world of dreams or of worlds of madness' (p. 44). This is no other than the world of the unconscious, of magic and phantasy, into which men at times 'suddenly find themselves plunged' when 'the superstructures laboriously constructed by reason collapse' (p. 46).

In the case of the infant, the significance of his elementary perceptions is very largely determined by his primitive emotions. The phenomenon in question is one with which we are familiar in adult life. Thus, Sartre has said that an emotion, such as anger or fear, transforms the object or situation to which it is directed.[5] He discussed this same phenomenon in his later work *L'Etre et le Néant* in connection with sexual desire and brought out well the way it

[5] Proust has said that the emotion 'metamorphoses' its object.

transforms the person desired under the aspect of her physical appearance – here the person desired being a person conscious of the desiring person's own existence in the way she is aroused in her flesh. To return to the kind of example Sartre discusses in his *Esquisse*, the frightened person may see a harmless shadow as a peculiarly menacing object. The character that the shadow assumes in the person's affective awareness has no equivalent in the world of reason. One cannot understand what makes the shadow so frightening in terms of categories of reason, of a cause and effect relationship for instance. One can only understand it by entering, through imagination, the magic world of th emotions, the world of dreams, fairy tales and other children's stories (see Dilman, 1984a, chapter 3).

When strong emotions such as fear, envy and anger are touched off in people their awareness is thus transformed and they revert to an earlier mode of response and apprehension. The normal modes of assessment in their possession slip away from them, they regress to a primitive mode of mentality which dominated their life in infancy. The appearance that things take on when one is under the sway of such a mentality *is* the inner world of phantasy, which Melanie Klein has described in the case of the infant in the first year of his life.

The infant emerges from this inner world as he learns to think and reason, to make sense of things, to form opinions about what goes on around him, to consider their accuracy and veracity, to deliberate and act with intention – in short, as he becomes a human agent, conscious of himself and of others around him as such agents. Freud described this as the passage from the pleasure to the reality principle. Nevertheless, this inner world, as shaped in the course of his early interactions with an undifferentiated mother–breast, remains with him throughout his adult life and contributes to the form and colour of his affective life. This inner world, as described by Melanie Klein, is the repository of the infant's early relationships as he experienced them, and the effects and needs alive in these relationships. What is in question is thus a person's earliest 'affective memory'. Melanie Klein sketches out its relatively stereotyped possible contents.

When I say that a person's early relationships and experiences remain with him and shape his later affective life, I mean such things, for instance, as that he may remain susceptible to feelings of guilt which leave him no peace of mind. His constant attempts to either placate or defy those to whom they are directed limit the kind of relationships he is capable of making and what he can find in them. What, in consequence, he has to go without may become a constant source of pain and frustration to him to which he responds, in turn, in ways shaped once more by his early experiences.

If, on the other hand, he could, in analysis, re-experience the relationship in which his guilt was born, he might come to feel sorry and so become less defiant for instance. If he could, further, follow up in his actions and responses what goes with feeling sorry, he may come to feel less guilty and also become more giving in his relationships. He may, in consequence, begin to find greater sense and fulfilment in his relationships.

There are many different possibilities and many different 'personality structures' that may grow out of a person's early relationships and experiences. This is the sense in which 'our adult world' has 'its roots in infancy' as Melanie Klein means this. So where these 'structures' make life problematic, devoid of fulfilment and a source of misery, psycho-analysis tries to modify them by descending into the patient's early phases of development where the 'movements' that constitute 'normal development' have remained frozen.

Thus, the patient has to find in himself the capacity to feel concern, for instance, to grieve, to make amends and actually mourn the harm he feels he has done. He has to acknowledge concern for what he has hated and feel the pang of remorse. He has to forgive others in himself the injuries that have turned into grievances, the insults that he has continued to resent. These are normal, natural reactions which have been blocked, and the patient will find them in himself unless his early experiences have been so bad that he has never developed these capacities – or, to put it differently, unless these capacities have been destroyed in him, nipped in the bud. These are just two instances of what I called 'inner work', the kind of work which actually changes those inner affective constellations that lie at the root of those 'structures' that make life problematic and painful. Life, of course, has its problems without these particular 'structures'. But the 'structures' in question recreate some of these problems for the particular individual or prevent him from coming to terms with them when they come his way.

This is only a rough sketch of the kinds of affective constellation formed in early life which the inner work in which the patient engages thaws out and changes. It is this which constitutes the 'healing of the self', for the constellations in question are those that preserve conflicts of ambivalence, splits within the self, envy, hatred, guilt and later jealousy, and other affective attitudes which repel affection and block generosity, creativity and the satisfaction of deep needs of the self.

6 PROCESSES OF HEALING: INNER WORK AND OUTER RESULTS

At the time when he was collaborating with Breuer, Freud relied explicitly for therapeutic results on 'abreaction' and he described its effect as 'catharsis'. If a painful incident from the past, generating strong emotions which have been repressed, is recalled, the whole frame of mind in which it was experienced is brought back into consciousness. The patient has thus the opportunity to shed tears which he had checked at the time, to give vent to the anger which he had been afraid to express, to come out with resentments that had been smouldering in him, poisoning his relationships.

In this way the affective atmosphere he carries about with him is cleared, the tensions generated by it are defused, and feelings pent up in him spend themselves out like a smouldering ember that is exposed to air. Freud likened the process to the excavation of Pompeii. Brought into contact with air its antiques are threatened with disintegration: 'Their burial had been their preservation: the destruction of Pompeii was only beginning now that it had been dug up' (1979, p. 57). It is in this way that, Freud thought, exposed to consciousness the neurotic structures of the personality are subject to destruction: 'everything conscious is subject to a process of wearing away'.

Breuer had wondered why 'long-forgotten experiences should exert so intensive an influence, and their recollections should not be subject to the decay into which all our memories sink' (Freud and Breuer, 1950, p. 5). He pointed out that by burying them a person deprives himself of the opportunity of translating them into an 'energetic reaction' – 'ranging from crying to an act of revenge'. It is this, he pointed out, that enables the affect to be lived out: 'an insult retaliated, be it only in words, is differently recalled from one that had been taken in silence'. Silently endured, it becomes a 'grievance' (ibid.). As such the person craves a restitution which he can never get, since he cannot ask for it.

So he is locked into a particular posture or attitude from which he is unable to free himself. He cannot say 'go to hell', exact an apology, or get his own back. Instead he swallows the insult and continues to smart under it. Here psychotherapy tries to bring about a change in the patient that will enable him to defuse his emotions, to let out the venom they generate. This is a change towards greater self-confidence, one that involves a change in his relationships with other people.

Abreaction is thus part of the process through which such a release is achieved, one which the psychotherapist tries to bring into motion. It involves the patient in 'letting to' and 'living out' a past affective experience instead of withdrawing before its demands. The catharsis, which Freud compared to the lancing of a boil, is healing in the sense that it relieves the patient of something that has been poisoning his relationships and causing him pain.

Freud came to see that usually what is thus healed in the person is only part of a complex structure, and that it would take more than the abreaction of repressed affect to loosen and modify it. It is true that the abreaction of affect does contribute to the change that takes place in the patient in the course of psychotherapy and so is *a* process of healing. But it is itself made possible by changes in the 'structure' of the patient's personality, and Freud turned his attention to these changes which he represented in terms of the relations between the ego, the super-ego and the id.

It is these that led him to focus on the inner conflicts that make up the Oedipus complex and on their resolution. We see the way he worked on these especially in four of his case studies: Dora, Little Hans, Paul Laurenz the Rat Man and the Wolf Man. He emphasized the reliving of these conflicts in the absence of the psychological pressures before which the patient, as a young child, resorted to measures which prevented him from growing out of them. As a result the patient's perspective on his parents changes. He gives up idealizing or denigrating them, recognizes the role of projection in his estimate of them. He is freed from those dependent relationships which make him jealous, possessive, resentful, submissive, placatory or overbearing, constantly needing to prove himself, etc.

Certainly, the healing in question involves a decrease in feelings of anger, jealousy, resentment and guilt, and a corresponding increase in generosity and expansion of interest in other directions. As a result the patient gains the ability to have more satisfactory relationships and begins to find greater fulfilment in life. In connection with the notion of healing here we need to recognize that there are some feelings which, though very much part of human life and capable of contributing to its richness, *in excess* are a scourge. For they contain within them, as part of their intrinsic nature, seeds of self-division as well as of conflict with others. Greed, envy, jealousy, hatred and certain forms of guilt ('persecutory guilt') are among these. Also, of course, certain extreme forms of guilt, grief, fear and depression are debilitating. The healing of the self, therefore, would encompass gaining some freedom from such affective excesses, a modification in some of these feelings, and a sense of proportion which allows greater contact with what goes on around one. I am not, of course speaking of the eradication of these feelings. That, even if it were possible, would equally curtail such contact.

Those processes in which such changes are wrought in the case of different people are, I believe, those very ones the prototype of which Melanie Klein isolated in infancy – those that make for emotional growth and the development of the individual. When I speak of 'healing processes' I have in mind the 'following through' of certain natural affective responses, following them through in their commitment for the future in the teeth of some inner reluctance. That is why I spoke of this 'following through', which comprises the various processes of healing, as 'inner work'. In such work one moves forward by relinquishing certain affective positions or orientations, such as narcissism, by giving up defences and tolerating what one finds painful. The work consists of resisting temptation, bearing what is painful, following through affective responses in the teeth of some anxiety. What sustains a person in such inner work are (Melanie Klein would say) his good feelings, those in which his trust and hope originate. These are part of the heritage he has received from his parents.

These processes of healing include the following:

1   Giving up idealizations or denigrations and letting what one finds 'good' and 'bad', spelt out in detail, come together in one's apprehension of those who matter to one.
2   Repenting, grieving and making amends or offering to repair the damage one has or feels one has done to others, especially loved ones. This has the result of lessening 'depressive guilt' and increasing the ability to receive the good one is given, to

  acknowledge it with gratitude, to keep it and find sustenance
  in it. This, in turn, reduces envy and the movements that
  spring from it: certain forms of egocentric ambition and
  destructiveness.
3 Forgiving those one feels have injured one, giving up the
  grudges one has kept against `them. This will lead to the
  dissolution of one's resentments and to the growth of greater
  trust in those one has forgiven and greater concern for them.
4 Mourning the loss of what one relinquishes, something that
  was good at the time one was attached to it, and in this way
  keeping something of it within one. This is what enables a
  person to change the character of his relationships, to accept
  losses, without giving up his loyalties, denying the good he has
  received, or turning his back on loved ones. It gives the self a
  'substance' which shows in what the person is able to give to
  others, in the commitments he is able to undertake, in the
  privations he can withstand, and in his relative indifference to
  the attractions of the moment. For the self to have no such
  'substance' is for the person not to have a place on which to
  stand, not to have anything he can call his own.

These processes are directed at past relationships that have
remained active in the patient, continuing to shape his present
relationships and life. These are past relationships that determine the
'structure' of his personality. Melanie Klein speaks of them as alive in
him and mirrored in the relationships between figures of his inner
world. They are, to a large extent, the substance of his dreams as they
are taken in analysis.

The modifications these processes affect in the patient find
expression in what he can now bring into his present life and
relationships. What he does there in bringing them in contributes
further to the work of the healing processes and is conducive to
growth.

It is in these ways that in analysis, when resistances are peeled off,
defences given up and the deeper layers of the personality reached,
the patient finds the opportunity to undo the consequences of his
earliest emotional positions, to move out of them, and to grow in his
interactions with what lies at hand in his present life. What he can do
is, of course, limited by what he has been given in the first place, what
experiences he has had, and other 'accidents' of fortune and heredity.

If there is enough in him to make the therapy work he will learn to accept these limitations of self and fortune and make the best of what he has. This, I believe, is an equally important aspect of the healing that psycho-analysis makes posible. It is what I understand Freud to have meant when he said that 'there is *other* misery in the world besides neurotic misery – real unavoidable suffering' (1949b, pp. 319–20), and that 'much will be gained if we succeed in transforming your hysterical [and more generally neurotic] misery into everyday unhappiness, against which you will be better able to defend yourself with a restored nervous system' (Freud and Breuer, 1950, p. 232).

7   SELF-KNOWLEDGE: INSIGHT AND CURE

In an interesting book entitled *Brother Animal*, Paul Roazen tells the story, from the early days of psycho-analysis, of Victor Tausk's involvement with Freud and the psycho-analytic movement and the way it ended in Tausk's suicide. It contains an account of Tausk's love life and his emotional failures, his dependency on Freud, the way he sought to contribute to the movement, and to be analysed by Freud in order to find a solution to his emotional problems: his inability to accept the commitment of a loving relationship with a woman and his dependent need to be accepted by a father substitute, someone he could look up to and wanted to be the equal of. He chose Freud to be this substitute. The book also contains a subtle analysis of why Tausk committed suicide and Freud's responsibility in this sorry affair. Freud did not accept him for analysis but arranged for a young colleague and protégé of his, Helene Deutsch, herself under analysis with Freud, to analyse him. She took him in analysis and three months later broke off the analysis on Freud's instigation. Soon after, Tausk, on the eve of a third marriage, committed suicide.

A philosophical colleague, who read this book with great interest, was impressed by the role that psycho-analysis seems to have played in Tausk's suicide. It raised the following question for him which he put to me: why should insight and self-knowledge be always beneficial? Does not Tausk's story give the lie to this idea? After all, did it not lead to his suicide? Could it not be that a patient in analysis does not like what he finds about himself? Could it not, in such a case, increase his depression and dejection?

There is a comment to this effect in the book itself: 'Freud had at first held the view that to make something conscious can only be to weaken it. But removing self-deception presupposes that the patient's ego is capable of integrating the new insight presented to it. Otherwise, psycho-analysis may simply strip away a patient's defences, leaving him sicker than he ever was' (1973, p. 173).

The truth here is that a person's defences are indeed part of his protective equipment. They are intricately bound up with his particular identity and play a part in holding him together. To be stripped of them may be necessary for a psychological or spiritual rebirth, but it is to have one's old 'psychic wounds' reopened, which can be extremely painful. If it happens too suddenly it would leave a person with very little to hold on to, and this can be very bewildering. In a talk entitled 'Reflections on Captivity', C. J. Hamson writes about one kind of 'extreme situation'[6] where this happens:

> Some . . . got back into their character with comparatively small difficulty. Some . . . did seem to me to maintain their character almost continuously and almost intact. But for most that character took on the appearance of a mask which unaccountably they had affixed to themselves; and now that it had slipped they could not bring themselves to recognize the face of their nativity. This was a cause of great anxiety . . . What was it our nature to be now that the shell in which we had lived, the shell which we had taken to be our skin, had been broken into fragments? Into what contact with what objects had we come, now that we no longer were safely insulated within the thick carapace of our accustomed modes of living and our accustomed selves? Here was the process of cautious exploration – intermittent and slow. Almost everybody sometimes ran away into the past . . . many escaped into the El Dorado of the day of their return home . . . But most managed . . . to come to terms with themselves, to bear to uncover their eyes and to look . . .
>
> . . . It seemed that there remained a spring within us which we had not managed finally to break in our previous way of living, despite our best endeavours. It had not broken in the stress and the calamity which supervened upon us; and if much had to be discarded of what had seemed to us to be our own selves – I think the prisoner suffered in himself a denudation as great as that of his external possessions – if

[6] The expression comes from Bruno Bettelheim (1962).

much had to be abandoned as too great a bulk to carry through the
narrow gate of prison, yet from what was left (miraculously almost, as
it seemed) could come a creature less encumbered surely and not more
blind, a creature perhaps more likely to be capable of life.

In such 'extreme situations', which may throw light on what takes
place in the course of psycho-analysis, a person experiences habitual
modes of behaviour in which he feels comfortable to become
inoperative. Or he is tempted, in a way he has never been tempted
before, to depart from them, to resort to a mode of behaviour that he
regards as both shameful and totally alien to the values and standards
that define him in the way he apprehends himself. He experiences a
limit to the hold of such values on him. This changes his view of
himself and he may find it difficult to accept what he comes to see of
himself.

In the case of Tausk, who was desperately engaged to find himself,
to be accepted, and to take on commitments without thereby
jeopardizing his freedom and independence, the impression that
seems to have got through to him was that he was unacceptable, that
he was mediocre, that he had failed those who had depended on him
and whom he had loved, and that he would continue to fail them:

> It may have been only when Freud finally brushed him aside that
> Tausk was forced to realize how his tie to Freud had masked his own
> inability to grow into independent manhood. But he had known all
> along that his difficulty in establishing a secure relationship with a
> woman was due to his inability to bear another person's dependency.
> Tausk's own dependencies were anxiety-ridden. Running from so
> many different women, Tausk was fleeing from his own inner
> passivity. (p. 115)

> We do not know what happened later that night between Tausk and
> Hilde . . . He must have realized . . . that although he had fallen in
> love with her partly to escape his dilemmas, he was nevertheless going
> to have them with him to the end. She was his hope, the last tie
> binding him to life. He had been using her to free himself from
> Freud, and presumably he realized that night that for him there was
> no way out. Despite his terrible longing for love, he found that he
> could not love Hilde.
>
> His involvement with Freud had eaten up his emotional energy,
> and he had failed in his search for a solution to his conflict . . . With
> this woman [Hilde] he had wanted more than ever to succeed in love,

yet he knew that he had seen it all happening to him before. But this time he was left without Freud as well. (pp. 121–2)

He himself wrote in his will before committing suicide:

> The recognition that I cannot gladly enter into a new marriage, that I can only keep myself and my beloved fiancée in conflicts and torments, is the true conscious motive of my suicide. (p. 126)

Roazen comments that 'Tausk had sought salvation in psycho-analysis, for himself and for those he loved' (p. 127). When that failed him, he lost all hope. But certainly he did not have and was not given the opportunity to work out his conflicts in psycho-analysis. His analyst was young and inexperienced, not detached from him and not independent in herself. She had known him outside the analysis and she discussed him in her own analysis with Freud who knew Tausk and who was not sympathetically disposed towards him. Freud interfered with this analysis and indeed was instrumental in bringing it to a premature end.

It was not so much what he found out about himself that led to his suicide as the dashing of his hopes. Given his volatile personality, his hopes had been unrealistic. He had invested too much in his psycho-analysis. But these hopes were dashed rather brutally, and a combination of outer circumstances and inner predispositions left him without any support or safety net when he needed it most.

The philosophical point I want to make is that there is no base-line to self-knowledge, as it were, beyond which one appears to oneself as one finally and irrevocably is in oneself, and has been all along. Finding oneself, as we have seen, certainly involves the shedding of illusions and the coming to a more realistic assessment of one's past actions and behaviour. Certainly one may, and more often than not one will, find what one comes to see as unflattering, unpalatable, painful, difficult to accept. But this is not, logically speaking, the end of the line, even though it may, in fact, feel as if it were. One may discover more to oneself which may change the aspect under which this appears. More than this, one need not go on from here in the way in which one has inexorably done so up to now. One may break loose from this pattern, change, develop potentials one has not recognized in oneself before.

We have seen how this, too, is part of finding oneself. Indeed, without it, merely being stuck with what one finds unpalatable does not constitute finding oneself. For if what one finds is unpalatable, then there is something further to be done: one will either modify it in the future or learn to live with it. If one can do neither, then one has not been able to resolve one's inner conflicts.

To return to Tausk. He had certainly come to see things about himself which filled him with dismay. What drove him to suicide, however, was not the dismay, but the despair of not being able to do anything about it and of there being no one to help him, to give him support in his hour of need. He could not find within himself at the time anything that would make a difference to this state of affairs.

His failure stared him in the face: 'he knew that he had seen it all happening to him before'. But there is nothing final about failure. If one cannot make a go of what one has tried time and again, one *can* at least turn in a different direction, succeed at something else, learn to accept and live with the failure. Relinquishing something that has meant a great deal to one is never easy to accomplish and calls for a basic trust in oneself – or, as Melanie Klein would put it, 'in one's inner objects'. My point is that the kind of despair that made Tausk take his own life, however much it may have sprung from insight into his past, cannot be identified with self-knowledge.

We have already seen that the process through which a patient in analysis sheds his defences, though it may be likened to the peeling of an onion, is not one of coming to face one's real self, or coming to self-knowledge. But not because, like the onion, which has no solid core, there is no such thing as 'the real self'. Rather, one's real self is what one comes to in resolving one's inner conflicts and growing in one's interaction with the outside world. One's real self does not exist ready-made prior to this. What the patient moves towards in shedding his defences is an undiluted experience of his old inner conflicts. It is this that enables him to take on the 'inner work' through which he is healed in himself and in the process finds himself. If we describe what he finds as his 'real self', this is because in being it he is at last authentic, that is, himself. 'Real' here means 'authentic', as opposed to 'false', 'made to measure', 'trimmed to satisfy certain requirements', 'held under certain restraints'.

Before leaving this topic I should like to return to the way I have separated the inner changes that belong to gaining insight into oneself and those changes that the patient achieves through the inner work which psycho-analysis frees him to undertake. I said before that there is no hard and fast line between these two. After all, the giving up of habitual defences, which appear as resistances in analysis, is itself part of the inner work in which the patient engages. And whether or not what he gives up is a defence or resistance depends on the context in which it is considered. I described grieving, forgiving, making amends as 'healing processes'. But the postures and movements that a person reverses in them are themselves defences or protective measures.

Therefore, if the giving up of defences *is* gaining insight into oneself, it should be remembered that it is also, and at the same time, what constitutes the healing of the self. So what I have called 'enlargement of consciousness' and 'enlargement of the self' in the last chapter merge into one another. Perhaps one should say that insight and healing, even if they are not the same thing, overlap at least to some extent, and where they do they are identical in the sense of being the same changes in the person seen under two different aspects.

Healing recapitulates steps in the early development of the 'normal' child which the patient side-tracked himself from taking in his childhood, missing his way towards authenticity. Psycho-analytic therapy is an attempt to provide him with the opportunity of taking these steps in the present. The key it uses is insight into the self in that it supports the patient's desire for greater authenticity. It does so by helping him to follow this desire. Its way of helping him to do so is by spelling out this desire for the patient whenever it makes its appearance in what the patient says or does and by pointing out the obstacles that stand in its way for the patient to re-evaluate. In thus gaining insight into himself the patient finds he can follow through those responses to his inner plight which constitute what I have described as 'processes of healing'. It is through these that he works his way towards greater inner unity and greater autonomy in action.

8　PHILOSOPHICAL CONCLUSIONS

It is sometimes said that in physical, medical treatment the physician provides the appropriate treatment and for the rest relies on nature to take its course. It is the natural processes of the body that heal the condition from which the patient is suffering, and not the medication that the physician administers or other of his interventions.

There is a certain parallel to this in psycho-analytic therapy. The 'processes of healing' on which the psycho-analyst relies are 'natural' in the sense that they belong to the 'normal' development of the infant and young child, that is, when this development is not impeded. They are 'processes of growth', that is, processes that contribute to the growth of the child in the course of his interaction with the environment which surrounds him – primarily his family and its particular ethos. Without such interaction, of course, there is no growth, emotional or intellectual. For it is through such interaction that the infant, and later the child, receives the 'materials' for his growth – love, support, interest, guidance, understanding, standards, praise, rebuke and punishment. What I called 'processes of growth' refer to what enables him to receive and assimilate these, make them part of himself and find sustenance in them. They represent his contribution to his own growth.

Psycho-analytic therapy unlocks these processes, when blocked, by the insight it makes available to the patient. We saw in the last chapter *what* this insight amounts to, and in the two previous chapters *how* it is made available. It seeks the patient's collaboration in enabling him to come to such insight and for the rest leaves him to find his own solutions to his problems and to heal himself in the way we have examined.

It is this healing of the self which results in the amelioration or disappearance of his 'neurotic difficulties' and in the growth of his ability to tackle or deal with the problems of his particular life.

I have examined the sense in which these neurotic difficulties are embedded in the 'structure' of his personality and are the outcome of his early interactions and experiences. I have also elucidated the sense in which what I have called 'processes of healing' are 'processes'. In talking of 'processes' here I am not falling into the philosophically objectionable language of 'mental processes'. What is in question is what I have also described, alternatively, as 'inner work'. I have explained why I talk of 'work' here and the sense in which the patient is engaged in doing something that has the form of work or labour – much in the sense in which we talk of 'creative work' and 'pains of labour' in childbirth.

I have characterized this work as 'inner' because it is directed at the person's own emotions, attitudes and affective orientation. What one may call 'outer work' by way of contrast, such as a person engages in when building a house or making a cabinet, is what others can engage in jointly with him – they can carry the bricks, mix the cement, cut the wood. Here they would be jointly engaged in the *same* piece of work. But the inner work I have been concerned with, in contrast, is what a person carries out 'in the solitude of his own heart'. Here, while others can help him in what he is engaged in, they cannot do the work for him, or in his place. I expressed this earlier when I said that another person can hold me together when I am falling apart, but he cannot make me whole (see pp.81–3 above). What such work achieves is the 'healing of the self'. I have described its results as 'outer results' in the sense that they are changes in the patient's present life and relationships.

This distinction is not the same as the philosophically objectionable dichotomy between the inner and the outer which I have criticized elsewhere (see Dilman, 1986, chapter 4). It corresponds to the distinction I have made in this chapter and earlier between the patient's conscious psychological problems, the ones for which he seeks psychotherapy, and their unconscious sources, which belong to the past and at which this inner work is directed.

10

Self-control and Autonomy

1 THE DILEMMA BETWEEN IMPULSE AND REPRESSION

We have seen that the removal of the patient's repressions is a central aspect of psycho-analytic therapy. But to what purpose is the patient helped to give up his repressions? Would this not deliver him to the mercy of his impulses? There is much that can be misunderstood here, and it is easy to think that Freud was advocating a life of impulse and pleasure, making light of what he regarded as 'the higher things in human life' (1933 p. 95), namely the patient's moral ideals.

Freud explicitly repudiated any such idea: 'now who has given you such a false impression of analysis?' (1949b, p. 361). He distinguished between 'repression' and 'suppression' or 'self-restraint'. In maintaining his repressions a person acts blindly or unconsciously and he is not fully behind what he denies himself. In contrast, when he exercises self-restraint he is aware of the consequences of giving in to his immediate inclinations and of his own reaction to them. So in forgoing what he feels an impulse to do he pleases himself, he is behind the restraint he exercises. This presupposes that he has resolved his conflict and is acting as one. Freud here talks of 'self-control'.

But this notion, too, can be misunderstood and it may now seem that what Freud advocates is a life of conscious self-restraint. The idea here is that impulse is not itself subject to change and that all that we can do is consciously to hold it under control. This, at best, is a narrow view of what psycho-analytic therapy can achieve and it errs in the opposite direction to the earlier idea that psycho-analysis promotes a life of unbridled impulse. It is, however, encouraged by philosophical misconceptions to which Freud's own thinking was susceptible. For the idea of self-control as 'the conscious control of impulse in the name of reason' presupposes a conception of the self as inevitably divided between reason and impulse. Behind it lies a conception of reason as divorced from everything affective.

In Freud this takes the form of a dichotomy between nature and culture. It is true that what counted for him was the resolution of the patient's inner conflicts made conscious during analysis. This would secure a unification of the self so that both in what he does and in what he refrains from doing the patient acts as one and, therefore, autonomously. Nevertheless, some of the things Freud says are tainted by a 'rationalism' in which reason, as a cultural achievement, is seen as inevitably divorced from all affective inclinations conceived *en masse* as belonging to 'nature'.

Indeed, the dilemma I have presented is itself a product of Freud's philosophy of culture and of its place in man's life, and it belongs to the early days of psycho-analysis. It makes it seem as if the crux of the problem for therapy is whether or not the patient is able to find satisfaction in life, conceived of as the satisfaction of 'instinct', 'desire' or 'appetite'. This, it seems, is what psycho-analysis aims to bring about by the removal of repression. But men have to live in society and consider those with whom they have to live. So, the idea goes, if their life is to be tolerable they must exercise *self-control*.

There is much that is confused in all this, but the confusions are not intrinsic to the therapeutic goals of psycho-analysis (see Dilman, 1983, chapter 6). More immediately, what needs pointing out is that the trouble with repression is not so much that it involves the frustration of desire which erupts in neurotic symptons, as that it buries inner conflict and prevents movement and change. It is *this* which psycho-analysis aims to bring about by removing repression. Only then can the patient move towards greater fulfilment in life through the attainment of greater autonomy and the ability to pursue his interests and fulfil his obligations – those into which he has put his whole heart. This is not the mere satisfaction of desire and appetite. Rather, the patient comes to know what he wants, and this is not something separate from what he values.

2 FREUD ON REASON AND SELF-CONTROL

It is clear that Freud saw little to admire in a life of impulse and came to think of 'self-mastery' as 'the highest achievement attainable to any human being' (Puner, 1959, p. 199). He said that when repression is lifted both sides of the inner conflict become conscious and the patient re-experiences the conflict he had buried: 'An affective decision can be reached only when they confront each other on the same ground' (1949b, p. 362). The patient is then no longer divided in himself, pulled in two opposite directions. Freud describes this as his having gained 'self-control'.

But in that case why does the patient need to exercise self-control: if he has resolved his inner conflict, what is there left for him to check or control? Obviously, Freud is here thinking of 'self-direction', 'self-mastery' or 'autonomy': no longer divided in himself he comes to be in charge of his life. He is his own master: he doesn't have to tow the line, act in subservience to anything outside himself. He does not have to appease or placate a tyrannical conscience within – the super-ego. Nor is he subject to the tyranny of impulse, the appeal of the moment.

In 'Analysis Terminable, Interminable' Freud speaks of it as the 'taming' of instinct which, he explains, is not its disappearance. The demand it makes on the person is felt again, but 'it is brought into harmony with the ego and becomes accessible to the influence of the other trends in the ego, no longer seeking for independent satisfaction' (1950, vol. v, p. 326). Thus, in the case of sexuality, for instance, a man's or a woman's sexual inclinations become part of his or her personal relationships; he or she is able to put his or her personal feelings into it and find fulfilment in their satisfaction – not just the momentary satisfaction of a desire, the relief of a tension. Indeed, such a person's sexuality loses its impulsive character and assumes a significance it could not have had before.

In the case of man's aggression, to take another example, we have a similar 'integration' into the ego of what erupts as an impulse or spurt of anger. Of course, this 'integration' involves the operation of such 'healing processes' as I have considered in the last chapter: forgiving bad figures from the past still alive within one, making amends for the guilt one feels on account of the bad feelings one has nursed towards them. Here the person's anger actually diminishes and the aggressive energy bound in it can now be put into and find expression in constructive schemes which give meaning to his life. The anger he then feels when unfairly obstructed in their pursuit, for instance, no longer has the impulsive character that previously unhinged him from such activities. Now what it is directed at is no longer seen in narrow personal terms, as an affront to a self insecure in itself, for instance, and so needing to think of itself as deserving special consideration. He sees it instead as something that obstructs what he attaches value to independently of himself. This is what I take Freud to mean by the 'taming' of instinct – whether or not 'instinct' is the right word to use for sexuality and aggression.

What is central to it is the growth of the ego in strength and the change in its relations to the id and the super-ego. I have discussed this aspect of Freud's notion of 'autonomy of the will', as I called it, elsewhere (see Dilman, 1984b), and compared his account of it with those of Hume and, especially, Plato and Kant. I said there that in his therapeutic concern to promote such autonomy Freud aimed at healing different forms of dissociation between reason and the passions and that in his theoretical account of 'the divisions of the personality' he was groping for a way of expressing these disso-ciations.

Freud identified 'reason' with the ego and thought of a person who is 'able to use his reason' as someone who is not subject to compulsions, someone whose contact with what he acts on is not clouded with phantasy. The ego can face the demands made on it by the id, the super-ego and the environment from a position of strength or from one of weakness. From a position of strength it can endorse or repudiate such a demand. This is what Freud has in mind when he speaks of self-control. For when it endorses the demand, the ego acts on its own behalf: it does not give in to the id, submit to the super-ego, conform to other people's expectations, or act in obedience to public opinion. When it repudiates such a demand, it does so on the basis of values and long-term goals which it has made its own. From a position of weakness, in contrast, it complies with such a demand in a placatory way or 'runs away from it' by resorting to repression or reaction-formation. Here it does not act on its own behalf, whether the line it takes is repressive or submissive. This is how Freud conceives the contrast he makes between repression and repudiation, submission and endorsement.

Repression and other forms of control and defence, then, are expressions of weakness of the ego, and this weakness comes ultimately from the figures it has or has not been able to take into itself in its early life, during the period of its formation, through 'introjection' and identification, and from the kinds of realtionships it has or lacks with such 'inner' figures. Freud speaks of repression as something which the ego does in compliance with the super-ego, whereas in ordinary self-restraint it acts on its own behalf, knowing what it is doing: 'the whole process of decision on the point takes place with the full cognizance of the ego' (1949b, p. 248).[1] Here there is no division of will. Thus, where, for instance, a person forgoes doing something that attracts him for the sake of someone he loves he does not do so becaue he is afraid to incur his or anyone else's displeasure or disapproval. Giving it up is what *he* wants to do. Indeed, under its new aspect it no longer attracts him. However, even where something of the original attraction remains, the light in which it appears, given the things for which he cares, will give him sufficient reason to want to give it up. In either case, he is fully behind his choice not to go after it. What unifies his will, or keeps it one, is his love or regard for the person for whose sake he gives it up, or his genuine belief in values that cast an unfavourable light on the object that attracts him.

Thus, when the ego 'repudiates' a demand made by the id, it derives its strength from certain feelings and sentiments. These, in the above example, are the person's love for someone he cares for, and his regard for values in which he believes. In other words, if we identify the ego here with reason, we could say that it does not rule at the expense of the passions, but with their support. Freud compares the relation of the ego or reason to the id or passions with that between a rider and its horse: 'The horse provides the locomotive energy, and the rider has the prerogative of determining the goal and of guiding the movements of his powerful mount towards it' (1933, p. 108).

This is different from Hume. In Hume the passions determine a man's goals or ends, and reason can only choose the way or means to them. It is also different from Kant, for whom reason is an active principle and can give direction to a person's actions in disregard of his emotions. Whereas in Freud the ego has no motive-power of its own: 'In its relation to the id, the ego is like a man on horseback who has to hold in check the superior strength of the horse; with this difference, that the rider seeks to do so with his own strength while the ego uses borrowed forces' (1949d, p. 30).

When Freud said that 'the ego is not master in its own house'

---

[1] Of course, the action can be fully intentional without involving any 'process of decision'.

(1950, vol. iv, p. 353) he was thinking of its subservience to its 'three harsh masters'. But he would have said that when not subservient, the ego still cannot act without regard to its moral beliefs and other emotions without alienating them. I compared what Freud claims here with a remark to the effect that the American President 'cannot do what he wants', 'cannot do anything on his own and without the co-operation of the Senate and Congress'. To say this is not to deny the President's autonomy; it is to characterize it as a 'relative autonomy'. It is not to deny that he can act with vision and independence, that he can lead those from whom he derives his power rather than be led by them.

Freud, similarly, is saying that the ego can lead or be led by the horse it rides; but when it leads it still depends on the horse's 'locomotive energy' in the way that the autonomous President depends on his 'power base'. The President, if he is to lead, has to be in touch with, understand and respect, the different shades of opinion that give him the basis of his power, and he can still lead without manipulating that opinion. Similarly, Freud holds, for the ego. When he says that the ego is not 'master', he means that it is not an absolute monarch. He is, I think, opposing the kind of omnipotent conception of reason we find in Kant.

Hume rightly rejected such a conception of the sovereignty of reason. But because, like Kant, he divorced the concepts of reason and passion from each other, he was wrongly forced to embrace a conception of reason as a slave of the passions. Freud, himself, felt some of these conceptual pulls but, in his therapeutic work, he managed to take a view of reason which steered clear of these excesses.

Thus when, for instance, a person avoids giving in to a temptation and obeys the voice of his conscience, he exercises 'self-control', acts with autonomy. But if one describes him as heeding 'the voice of reason', it should be noticed how different that voice is from the one depicted by Kant. For his moral sentiments are very much active in that voice. Indeed, one could say that the voice in question is as much a voice of his sentiments as it is a voice of reason. For there is no division between the two.

I have described the reasons such a person has for resisting temptation as 'affective reasons' and explained the way reason and moral sentiments are internally related in such a case (see Dilman, 1984b, part II). In Kant, however, because 'reason' is forever divided from 'inclination' it represents the voice of the super-ego which models itself on an absolute monarch – one of Freud's 'three harsh task masters'.[2] Where a person acts in subservience to his super-ego he acts out of the fear of punishment and his main concern is to placate an overstrict conscience, one which has over-reached itself and no longer represents his moral concerns. In contrast, where he obeys his genuine conscience, he is being reminded of what he, himself, believes. So in heeding it he acts out of genuine conviction and is fully behind what he does.

There is a similar difference between the ego acting in subservience to the id, giving way to impulses of lust, for instance, and the case where it endorses some powerful emotion. Only in the latter case will the emotion be consolidated into a genuine affective relaitonship in the context of which the ego is fully behind the actions it undertakes. The forces it uses are 'borrowed forces' only in so far as the sexual affections and moral sentiments which enter into the person's decisions and actions belong developmentally with the id and the super-ego in Freud's conceptual scheme. Freud talks of them as 'borrowed' to remind us that the ego's strength depends on its association with the id and, let me add, with the super-ego too. In dissociation from them it remains weak. They are *not* 'borrowed forces', however, in so far as the ego is not dissociated from the id and the super-ego, so that the 'force' it derives from the sentiments in question is its own force. This is the case where 'the instincts are tamed' or 'civilized', and the super-ego is 'humanized'.

In both these cases, where the person heeds the voice of his conscience and where he endorses a powerful emotion of sexual love or attraction, the ego is not subservient. Nor does it dictate and, in that sense, 'control', if that implies a division between what controls and what is controlled. Rather, it carries along with it aspects of the personality which are themselves 'tamed' or transformed in this new relationship with the ego.[3]

'The ego does not dictate; its voice is never tyrannical. When it seems to be, it is always the super-ego that is speaking through its

---

[2] Here the notion of self-control reverts to that of the control of the self by a part of it which has remained 'unintegrated' or 'dissociated'.

[3] 'Taming', like 'control', is not the word Freud wants since it implies a form of emasculation. I have used the word 'civilizing' to characterize the kind of transformation that is in question here. But, paradoxically, Freud's own account of the process of civilization completely fails to do justice to it. Thus see Freud, 1949g, and my criticisms in Dilman, 1983, chapter 6.

mouth.' Tyranny, in Freud's view, flourishes only in an unequal partnership, it is the expression either of a lack of self-sufficiency and the compensatory desire to exploit or of weakness and the fears to which this leaves vulnerable. This state of affairs, however, is the result of the ego's dissociation from other aspects of the self. It is precisely this condition of th ego which Freud describes as its subservience to its 'three harsh task masters'. This is the reason why, in Freud's scheme, when a person's voice is tyrannical it is never the voice of the ego but always that of the super-ego.

There is thus a difference between the self-restraint that, say, a bank robber shows in planning a robbery and the self-restraint shown by a person who is saving money for someone he loves or a cause in which he believes. The robber's motive for the self-restraint he shows is greed, and while a person can be behind his greedy actions he can never find lasting fulfilment in the satisfaction of his greed. Indeed, as Socrates has argued in the *Gorgias,* the pursuit of greed is self-impoverishing. Hence, while the greedy person may show remarkable self-restraint in the pursuit of his greedy schemes, he is *ruled* by the greed which motivates him. It is the trait of an immature, self-insufficient personality. The self-restraint he shows on occasions, hower consistently, is not, therefore, an expression of what Freud would call 'self-control'. Indeed, greed is the antithesis of self-restraint and the desires that spring from it are in themselves immoderate and, therefore, incompatible with self-mastery.

Tyranny or domination and subservience constitute a dichotomy *only* from a common basis of weakness and inner poverty, where domination is a reaction-formation or a quest for compensation. A person who has real strength does not need to dominate. Thus Freud suggests, broadly speaking, that there are three possible relations in which the ego (or reason) can stand to the id (or 'the passions'). In Kant there are only two such relations: that of master or absolute monarch – 'the autonomy of reason' – and that of slave – 'the heteronomy of reason'. The three relations, in Freud's view, are the following: (i) the ego can try to make itself independent of the emotions, reject their contribution as dangerous and corrupting, and see its role as being that of subduing them. Here it enters into the service of the super-ego; (ii) it can idealize the passions and enter into their service; (iii) it enlists the support of the emotions, derives sustenance and vitality from them, or, as Freud puts it, 'borrows' their energy. This calls for their 'integration' rather than their 'repression', and it involves the transformation of both reason and the emotions in the direction of greater personal autonomy: 'where id was, there ego shall be'. It should be clear that the main reason why Freud talks of the ego using 'borrowed forces' is to remind us that the ego has no strength *on* its own, that is, in dissociation from the id, but not *of* its own.

There is a counterpart to each of these three relations in the case of the super-ego: (i) The ego can try to make itself independent of the super-ego, thinking of morality on the model of its demands, and so rejecting them as arbitrary dictates that can have no basis in reason, except perhaps on a purely prudential model. This is reminiscent of a form of 'rationalism' which regards morality as a kind of superstition and is close to Freud's *philosophical* conception of morality, outlined in the following chapter. (ii) It can enter into the service of the super-ego, making every word its command. Here we have the seeds of a form of 'moralism' which is antithetical to a genuine moral attitude. (iii) The third alternative is one on which Melanie Klein and her followers have focused attention. Freud was not able to give a clear voice to it.

In their view, the super-ego has a positive aspect in addition to the negative one emphasized by Freud. It contains love as well as inverted aggression and is thus capable of entering into a co-operative relationship with the ego. To enlist the support of this aspect of the super-ego the ego has to tolerate guilt and depression. If it can do so, not only will the original demands of the super-ego be transformed in their adoption by the ego, so that the person finds a new relationship to the moral values which inform his actions, but he will also find a greater concern for other people and a richer relationship with them: 'where super-ego was, there ego shall be'. This is the transformation of the super-ego into a genuine conscience. As such it becomes part of the ego and speaks with the ego's voice.

It is this third relation which psycho-analysis seeks to promote in both cases. Here the ego, from a position of strength, endorses or repudiates the demands made on it. It does not impose its will on the id or the super-ego – a state of affairs excluded in the Freudian scheme. That is why I find the word 'control' inappropriate. Rather, it 'borrows' their energy, makes sexual affections and moral sentiments its motive for action. It does not have to assert itself or seek for compensations. Indeed, we could say with Freud that the person 'loses some of his ego' (see Wortis, 1954, p. 80). 'When dissociated aspects of the self are integrated into the ego the person loses some of his ego.' There is nothing self-contradictory about this claim. The person in question is no longer afraid to let go. He can give himself to activities that absorb his interest, lose himself on occasions of enjoyment and celebration.

Freud sees this capacity of the ego to abandon itself to what arises from the id as an expression of its strength and its lack of narcissism. He believes that (i) when the ego stops loving itself and turns its love and interest outwards, and (ii) when it accepts the id and makes peace with the super-ego, it makes deeper contact with the outside world.

3   SELF-CONTROL, SELF-MASTERY AND MORALITY

Self-control is thus not the control of one part of the self by another, if that implies any fragmentation or dissociation of the self. Indeed, it presupposes its unity. In that case it cannot be something that one exercises all the time. For if it takes 'self-control' to do or avoid doing the things which other people do or avoid doing without having to exercise self-control, this means that the person in question is divided in himself with respect to the actions he does or avoids doing.

What Freud aimed at in his therapeutic work was to help patients to find greater unity of self. This involves the transformation of the parts integrated and so the growth of the self. What is thus achieved in the therapy is wider than self-control. The patient acquires the capacity for self-control, certainly, which capacity he exercises if and when the occasion arises. But normally, apart from lapses, he acts with autonomy and does not need to exercise self-control. It is only on special occasions that he has to do so. The need for it arises from particular situations in which he finds himself rather than any permanent inner conflict that divides him. We can say that such a person possesses self-mastery, in the sense that he is his own master in what he does.

Self-control, in contrast, is what a person exhibits in the face of provocation, temptation or danger. He keeps his temper, resists the temptation, does not run away. That is, he is not overwhelmed by the moment, does not lose touch with considerations that weigh with him normally. When, on such an occasion, he is told 'use your reason', this means 'you will regret it later' or 'you will blame yourself'. He is being reminded of something he knows, asked to think of it himself. The trouble is that the temptation or the fear makes this difficult. He has to make a link which the emotion of the moment has temporarily weakened or severed, a link with part of himself.

Anybody could on some occasions fail to exercise self-control. The provocation, the temptation, the danger may be too great for him. The person who lacks self-control, on the other hand, is one who fails consistently and systematically. In this case what we have is a weakness of the self rather than an excess in the provocation or temptation to which he is subjected. But this is a relative judgement which presupposes certain norms of what a person can be expected to withstand. Putting aside the difficulties raised by such norms, we see that a person who lacks self-control is one who is impulsive, lacks courage or staying-power. We have a range of possible cases here, but they do not cover the whole spectrum of 'weaknesses' or 'deficiencies' that psycho-analysis attempts to treat.

The impulsive person is one who is overwhelmed by the moment because his desires do not form part of a coherent structure. The person who lacks courage, for instance, does not have the kinds of relationship in his inner life to sustain him in the face of danger. He 'goes to pieces' too easily. The person who lacks staying-power is not sufficiently attached to interests and concerns to give him the motive to keep working or trying in the face of distractions or difficulties. In contrast, the person who has the capacity for self-control has a sense of himself or identity that is rooted in concerns and loyalties that give him an inner unity, an affective sense of continuity, over which the moment has little hold and which its exigencies cannot easily undermine.

Thus, take the case of a happily married man tempted by the charms of a woman he meets by chance. Thinking of his wife and of his life with her gives him a perspective from which those charms are resistible. This is one instance of the exercise of self-control. It presupposes, of course, a sensibility of such charms. But this sensibility is not itself a weakness so long as it is not indiscriminate. When it becomes so it ceases to be a sensibility. Thus, the husband in question will not normally be tempted by the attractions of the opposite sex, and he will exercise self-control on those occasions when he is really tempted. Otherwise he is either not happily married or, more seriously, there is something wrong with him. For instance, he may be unable to sustain the commitment of marriage. What such a person needs is not so much to develop 'self-control' in order to remain faithful to his wife as to come to know what he wants: does he want to commit himself to one person or have a life with a different centre in which he has a series of relationships.

We have already seen that to find or come to know what one wants is not to discover one's unconscious desires, though it does involve facing and coming to terms with them. It is finding values one can give one's heart to, interests to which one can give oneself, developing concerns that give coherence and unity to one's life. Psycho-analysis can assist in this process by helping a person to face what it is that damages his capacity to care, to give or commit himself to something outside. It is only there, and as a bonus, that a person will discover what gives unity to his life and so to him as a person, and in doing so achieve autonomy. If he can do so, he will have acquired the capacity for self-control, for he will have something worth fighting for, something that will give him a reason for persevering in the face of difficulty, for resisting what threatens to undermine it.

What is in question is a notion which such philosophers as Socrates, Spinoza and Kant have attempted to elucidate: self-mastery, or being in charge of one's life and actions. I am confident that this is the notion in which Freud was interested. Its rendering into English as 'self-control' has this excuse: it is a condition of the self in which the self, in contrast to something external to it or a part dissociated from it, is in charge or control of its actions and life – that is, those of the person in question.

It is not an accident that the philosophers I mentioned treated this as a *moral* notion, focusing on the self in its relation to its moral beliefs. Because of his defective philosophical conception of morality Freud failed to highlight the moral core of this notion. I speak of a 'moral core', for how can a person achieve mastery over himself unless he has something to live for, something that transcends him and gives sense and order to his life, something he considers worthwhile and wants to give himself to? Surely, this is what it is hoped he will move towards in his therapy as his inner conflicts come up for revision.

Unless a person cares for certain things, attaches importance to certain values, cherishes certain ideals, how can he have any mastery over himself? Unless he has any lasting interest outside himself, how can he control his momentary inclinations? Without such a framework, which the things for which he cares gives him, would he not simply be a prey to impulses of the moment? Self-mastery certainly implies the subordination of one's desires to some order, an order that makes sense to the person in the light of what he cares for. It is from there that the motive for self-dicipline arises – from what one loves, is attached to, values and cherishes. Without it there can be no 'self-control' or self-mastery, and no 'progress' in psycho-therapy.

It is important not to misconceive an opposition to repression, such as is central to Freudian therapy, as an opposition to discipline. Freud gave us an account of the role that the father's position of authority plays in the formation of the super-ego. But he did not sufficiently emphasize the importance of discipline in the child's learning and development and of its supportive role in the formation of sentiments. Fear and repression have unfortunate results in the child's development certainly, but so do indulgence and spoiling. A child who has always been allowed to have his own way will not learn to consider others and will have problems in his relationships with them. Indeed, his relationships will be the poorer since he will not have learned to put much into them.

Part of the process of acquiring the capacity for self-control in one's development thus involves accepting the discipline of one's parents and making it one's own. Such self-dicipline, which needs to be dis-tinguished from the regime of the super-ego, is an essential part of being in charge of one's own life and actions. The important thing about the discipline from which one learns self-discipline is the spirit in which it is given, whether it is supportive of the child's growth or crushes his initiative. It is not discipline as such that damages the child's development, but the repressive way in which it is administered.

In analysis, it is true, the patient is asked to put discipline aside in his free-associations, but only in order himself to come to it in what he finds out about himself. Certainly, moving towards greater self-control and self-mastery involves as much moving away from too impulsive a personality, one which knows little discipline, as moving away from too compulsive or too inhibited a one, one that has been crushed by a discipline it has been unable to make its own. Such a person is able to go after what he wants and genuinely approves of and he is not afraid to enjoy what he finds there. But to do so is not to pursue self-gratification.

Indeed, the very notion of a person 'knowing what he wants' presupposes that he considers certain things important or worthwhile, others trivial or nasty, that he has affections, loyalties and interests in which his personal identity is rooted. In their absence wanting degenerates into momentary desires and appetites which exist independently of the person's conception of himself, and their satisfaction does not bring fulfilment to the self. Such a person could not understand why he should check the satisfaction of his desires except because an external authority that he fears says so, or because otherwise his survival will be put at risk.

So the self-mastery which Freud aimed at in psycho-analytic therapy presupposes self-knowledge, and that involves having come to know what one values and wants. The transformation of affect and impulse which Freud called 'the taming of instincts' requires that there should be more to the patient than 'instinct', 'appetite', 'impulse', that he should care for certain things and be capable of those natural reactions that go with caring or are part of it – gratitude, compassion, sorrow, guilt, repentance, reparation, forgiveness. These are moral reactions. The person who is capable of self-mastery thus has to be a moral agent; his having moral beliefs and attitudes are essential to the possibility of his being able to exercise self-control.

4 CONCLUSION AND FURTHER QUESTIONS

We see that Freud believed in the desirability of working towards the abandonment of repression in his patients not because it leads to the satisfaction of desires that have remained unsatisfied, but because it opens the way to an inner work in the course of which there is the hope of resolving inner conflicts and achieving greater autonomy.

Repression freezes, immobilizes, locks a person in a state of inner conflict. It restricts or limits his affective contact with what goes on around him. At the opposite extreme, an impulsive person, metaphorically speaking, doesn't stay long enough in one place to find any nourishment there or to make a contribution to it. He, too, cannot grow.

The task of the therapy offered by psycho-analysis, therefore, is not simply to help the patient give up his defences, abandon his repressions, but also to hold him together while he works at his problems. Not only must the soul be purged of deception, it must also be allowed to find its own pattern, develop attachments, concerns and interests, an order to its feelings, and so find a unity to itself. These three things, authenticity, autonomy and inner unity, are three aspects of the same thing, and its achievement has remained a goal for psycho-analytic therapy.

But where does the patient find the values, concerns and interests which unify his life? Does he come to them in the course of his analysis? Are they in any way implicit in the outlook and work which constitutes the therapy? Could it be that 'the humanization of the super-ego', 'the taming or civilization of instinct', 'the unification of sensuality and affection', 'the mitigation of hate by love', 'forgiveness and making reparations' are value-laden goals? If so, how does working towards any such goal square with the analyst's 'moral neutrality'? These are the questions to which I now turn in the following final chapter.

11

Values in Psycho-analytic Therapy

1 FREUD, ANALYSIS AND MORALITY

Philosophically, Freud could make little of morality and presented it in negative terms. Thus, in his *New Introductory Lectures*, after having pointed out that man is not 'merely a sexual being, but has nobler, higher feelings', he goes on to say that the super-ego is 'as much as we have been able to apprehend psychologically of what people call the "higher" things in human life' (1933, p. 82). His descriptions of the super-ego speak for themselves. It is that aspect of ourselves, primitive and archaic, which, through identification with an external authority, apprehended as arbitrary, has taken over its tyranny, real or imaginary. It is thus external compulsion internalized (1949f, p. 3). As such, Freud sees it as the means by which civilization holds in check the aggressiveness that opposes it. The super-ego takes over this propensity to harsh aggressiveness which, as Freud sees it, the ego would like to exercise against others and directs it onto the ego. This aggressiveness is thus what energizes it into action when it forbids or compels the ego to act, or punishes its failures and transgressions. The feelings of guilt with which it punishes the ego are thus self-centred in character, their content being made up of the dread of losing love. The motive of moral action, in this view, is fear (see 1949g, pp. 41–5).

This is obviously a poor picture of what is high and noble in men and, indeed, in this view men are indifferent to the claims of morality and only fearful of the consequences of disregarding these claims: 'Ethics means *restriction* of instinctual gratification' (1940, p. 25; see also 1949g, p. 41). Since, according to Freud's hedonism, this is what all men seek and need in order to be happy, morality becomes one of the main sources of human misery. Indeed, not only is morality 'at variance with men's nature' (1949g, p. 87), but 'the more a man checks his aggression the more tyrannical becomes his ego-ideal' (1949d, p. 109). The result is that the fiercer a man's ego-ideal or morality the less his capacity for love and joy (1949b, pp. 360–1; see also Jones, 1937).

Although, in this view, morality is on the side of repression, Freud thought of it as of some 'value' or benefit to humanity. Moral values are useful and even necessary for regulating human behaviour, lessening conflicts between people and ensuring for them a relatively peaceful co-existence: 'All that is co-operative, creative is purchased at the price of renouncing instinctual gratification' (1949b, p. 108). Thus, while there is no more reality in moral values than there is in any convention, conditioned by the accident of historical circumstances, they have nevertheless a pragmatic function. They serve men who need each other and live in sociey: 'the word "culture" describes the sum of the achievements and institutions which differentiate our lives from those of our animal forebears and serve [the] purpose . . . of regulating the relations of human beings among themselves' (1949g, pp. 49–50; see also 1949f, p. 9).

Freud's whole idea of morality is crude and riddled with philosophical confusion. I have criticized it elsewhere (see Dilman, 1983, chapters 4 and 5) and so will content myself with indicating, in broad outline, what is wrong with some of its strands. I will single out three of these: (i) Moral values are imposed on men. Men 'internalize' them and in their name repress some of their longings. But they pay a high price in their neuroses for doing so. (ii) Men are deceived in believing in these values. For there is no reality in them. (iii) Still they are useful and, indeed, it is doubtful that men could have got on with each other without them. They are, thus, a mixed blessing.

Morality can, of course, be an instrument of repression. But is there any *a priori* reason why it *must* be so? It is true that the values in which we come to believe exist independently of us. We acquire them in the course of our upbringing and development. Even when they are 'internalized', however, in the sense in which Freud means this, they *may* remain 'external' to our will and actions, in the sense that we comply with them not because of what we see in them, but because this is what an external authority demands from us. That is, we act, at best, merely out of habit or conformity, for the reward of approval and the consequent feeling of solidarity with others, or out of the fear of punishment. As is well known, the possibilities of self-deception here are numerous.

But men can, and at least at times also do, act out of genuine moral conviction. That is, they come to see something in the values they have been brought up to accept and they find what they see appealing. It is this that moves them to act on particular occasions or to refrain from acting when tempted or compelled to do so, and not the fact that they have been told to heed these values. What moves them then is no longer external compulsion but their own will.

This is what it means to have genuine moral convictions. When this is the case the values in which a person believes are no longer 'imposed' on him, and his moral actions come from him, not from some part of him that is the instrument of some alien will. What a person's moral beliefs demand is obedience, self-restraint in particular circumstances, self-control, even self-denial, but never repression – except in the case of moralities for which the individual is of little value. If men feel guilty and repress those inclinations that make them feel guilty, it is not their moral values that are at fault. For those values demand that they should restrain such inclinations, not that they should pretend that they have no such inclinations. Often they demand more than this: that they should be 'better' men, that they should so change as to no longer be attracted by what these values show in a poor light. If they genuinely believe in these values, if their moral beliefs truly define their identity as individuals, such a change would be one that is in the direction of greater, not lesser, authenticity.

In the last chapter we saw that repression and self-mastery stand opposed to one another. Perhaps I should point out that self-denial is not the same thing as 'repression'. A person who represses a desire or inclination simply pretends that it does not exist and continues to be a slave to it. What rules him is the fear of what he represses. It is for himself that he is afraid. Whereas self-denial is always for the sake of some good that transcends the self; otherwise it would not be a denial of the self.[1] It demands self-mastery and full awareness.

The idea of morality as an instrument of repression goes hand in glove with Freud's hedonism, namely the idea that what men want, seek and find happiness in is pleasure: 'The force behind all human activities is a striving towards the two convergent aims of profit and

---

[1] As Plato puts it in the *Phaedo* it would be a form of self-indulgence.

pleasure' (1949g, pp. 57–8). 'Every culture must be built upon coercion and instinctual renunciation' (1949f, p. 11). It is, therefore, 'hard for men to feel happy in it [civilization]. In actual fact primitive man was better off in this respect, for he knew nothing of any restriction on his instincts' (1949g, pp. 91–2). Hence the idea that it is part of the business of psycho-analysis to reverse this exchange where it has gone too far and resulted in neurosis. This idea, too, is confused and I have criticized it elsewhere (see Dilman, 1983, chapter 6).

As for Freud's idea that moral values are of benefit to men in so far as they secure men's co-operation and regulate human affairs, part of the trouble with it is that it represents the agent's moral values as externally related to the conduct that they are supposed to regulate. It does not recognize how much these values themselves add to men's problems and conflicts (see Winch, 1972, p. 172). It is true that men's moral beliefs may restrain them from doing what they might otherwise do and even still feel some temptation to do. But this need not, and often does not, serve needs they have independent of their moral beliefs – such as the need for security. Even if it did, however, it would still have little to do with the importance men attach to the values in which they believe, values such as honesty, decency, justice, kindness. What gives these value in the eyes of those who believe in them does not, in this way, lie *outside* them. It is to be found *in* them, in what they mean to men in the kind of life they live.

This is where their *reality* is to be found; not in some supposed independent existence which supports them or to which they correspond. If one seeks it there one will be forced to conclude, with Freud, that men's moral beliefs are illusions, since they are not based on an independent reality in this way at all (see 1949f, p. 59).

Freud cannot see what it could mean to speak of a moral belief as 'true' except in the way that a scientific hypothesis may be true. So the only positive alternative he can find is to claim that commonly-held moral beliefs are at least useful. They may be useful illusions, but in so far as they are believed they are pieces of wishful thinking: 'we call a belief an illusion when wish-fulfilment is a prominent factor in its motivation, while disregarding its relations to reality' (1949f, pp. 54–5).

Another part of the trouble with Freud's idea of morality as useful for securing men's co-operation with each other lies in his thought that this is something that needs to be manufactured at all. Behind it is Freud's idea of an original human nature in respect of which men are essentially pleasure-seeking and antagonistic towards each other. In this view there is nothing in human beings that breeds a genuine interest in others of their kind other than the need for sexual pleasure and self-interest. Since all love is sexual in character and all sex is pleasure-seeking, something *external* is needed to enable men to work together. This is provided by a morality that absorbs men's aggressive energies and curbs their rivalry.

But this whole presupposition about men's original nature, which pre-exists their culture and resists its civilizing 'effect', needs criticism (see Dilman, 1983, chapter 6). Men's co-operation does not need to be something that is produced externally. Common work, shared identities and genuine concern for others provide the basis for such co-operation. The basis for dissent and conflict lies in men, certainly, but so does the basis for co-operation. It lies both within men and outside them, in the movements to which they give themselves and within which they find their identities. There is, therefore, no reason to suppose that concern and co-operation need to be 'imposed' on men from outside.

To what extent do these views characterize psycho-analytic therapy itself? Is the psycho-analyst's 'moral neutrality' conditioned by Freud's philosophical presuppositions about the nature of morality? We have seen the sense in which psycho-analysis is a *non-directive* psychotherapy: the patient's decisions and solutions are allowed to come from him, they are not imposed on the patient. The analyst's moral neutrality belongs with this. It is also part of the importance that Freud attached to the reserve that the analyst should exercise with regard to aspects of his own life and personality: otherwise the patient's transference would not remain pure and the analyst's preceptions of the patient would be adulterated by what comes from the analyst himself. Thirdly, Freud was afraid that in a relationship like that between the analyst and the patient there may be the temptation for the analyst to assume a form of 'moralism' which would inhibit the patient's self-disclosure and collaboration.

So it is, at least partly, therapeutic considerations that lead the analyst to assume an attitude of 'moral neutrality' towards the patient. But taking up this attitude has nothing to do with Freud's philosophical scepticism with regard to morality. If the analyst does not express any moral judgements in the course of an analysis this does not mean that he regards making moral judgements as such with suspicion. His reserve is bound up with the character of the enterprise in which he is engaged. He may have moral views on what the patient tells him he is doing. He may reserve these views, however, in order to avoid taking on a role that the patient is trying to force on him. Instead, he will usually draw the patient's attention to this and search for his reasons for doing so.

In any case there is a difference between 'moralizing' and holding strong moral views. It is the former that the analyst wishes to avoid, thus also avoiding taking sides with the patient's super-ego. 'Moralism' involves censure and lack of sympathy. It is an attitude of rejection. But it is possible to condemn an act while at the same time feeling compassion for the agent. In this way one refuses to turn away from him without making light of that in him which the action condemned engages. Though he did not articulate it clearly this, I believe, is the kind of attitude which Freud favoured as an ideal for the therapist.

It is important to recognize, however, that this is itself a *moral* attitude, one of concern. In it the analyst feels at one with the patient in his suffering rather than above him. If, beyond this, he reserves his moral judgement, this is to let the patient himself appraise what he sees about himself and respond to it with his own values. Such reserve need not be a form of dishonesty or insincerity. Whether or not it is depends on the circumstances and on the person's motives for doing so. The analyst is supposed to be alert to his own motives.

The same distinctions apply to the patient's moral views about himself. The question of whether his moral convictions are genuine or spurious, that is, an aspect of his defences so that in holding them he deceives himself, is a very real one. The analyst needs to gauge this matter with tact and sensitivity. It is, of course, true that an *a priori* suspicion, which may stem from the analyst's philosophical presuppositions, may lead him to treat any moral scruples expressed by the patient in a cavalier way. But a thoughtful analyst ought to be able to avoid such insensitivity, his 'better sense' ought to see through his 'bad philosophy'.

Over and above this there may be times in the analysis when the analyst urges the patient to put his perfectly genuine moral views aside. The prominence he gives them in connection with certain matters being discussed in analysis may be an expression of his reluctance to go into them more deeply, to see them under a new aspect. Thus, his genuine moral views may come to constitute a barrier to a new way of looking at certain things, one which would open up new questions which at the moment he just shelves. If the analyst then asks the patient to keep his moral judgements in abeyance or tells him that they do not constitute a 'fruitful' way of looking at what is under discussion this is not to impugn their reality or to treat them lightly.

In short, then, the analyst's 'moral neutrality', his refusal to be drawn into making moral judgements or siding with the patient's super-ego is not part of the philosophical scepticism about morality we find in some of Freud's writings. Indeed, while the analyst's 'neutrality' is itself part of a wider moral attitude integral to the whole conception of treatment in analysis, the *a priori* scepticism about morality, which he may share with Freud, is no more than philosophical baggage. The views on which it is based are not part of the 'theory' of psycho-analysis.

Certainly, the core of the psycho-analyst's therapeutic work consists of exposing the patient's illusions about himself, and often about others as well. But this does not include undermining his moral beliefs by exposing them as illusions. Some of them may be illusions in the sense that the patient does not really believe in them but hangs on to them for defensive purposes. That is, they may have no 'truth' for him and thus fail to be true in the only sense in which moral beliefs can be true. They may be no more than remnants of what was once imposed on him. But there is no *a priori* necessity why they should all be illusions in this sense. The idea that they are so is itself a piece of philosophical 'illusion' which Freud embraced in some of his theoretical writings.

But, I repeat, it is not itself part of the practice of psycho-analytic therapy. Indeed, how can it be so when all psychotherapeutic practice is concerned with changing people and, therefore, must regard certain forms of human existence as 'better' or 'worse' than others?

Besides, what makes the genuinely moral aspect of a person is often that part of him from which the solution to his problems arises. I do not mean simply his genuine conscious ideals but his deep affective reactions of concern in the face of his own greed, envy and selfishness, for instance. For the analyst to undermine any of this is not only for him to depart from his 'moral neutrality' but, more seriously, it is to interfere with the 'inner work', which alone leads to the patient's ultimate 'cure'.

2 JUNG: IS FREUD'S A PSYCHOLOGY WITHOUT A SOUL?

Jung appreciates this in his criticisms of Freudian psychology and psychotherapy (see Jung, 1966). His main criticisms are that Freudian interpretations are 'one-sided', 'reductive', relevant only to those in 'the morning of their life', and in a broad sense 'materialistic', and secondly that, while providing insight may be very well and to the point, it is not enough: Freudian therapy fails at least a certain category of patient by doing nothing to 'develop the psyche' or 'educate the will'. He writes:

> Freudian psycho-analysis is limited to the task of making conscious the shadow-side and the evil within us. It simply brings into action the civil war that was latent, and lets it go at that. The patient must deal with it as best as he can. Freud has unfortunately overlooked the fact that man has never yet been able single-handed to hold his own against the powers of darkness – that is, of the unconscious. Man has always stood in need of the spiritual help which each individual's own religion held out to him. The opening up of the unconscious always means the outbreak of intense spiritual suffering. (1966, p. 277)

Jung sees man's morality, his moral inclinations and apprehensions, as being confined to his consciousness. His unconscious, in contrast, is his 'shadow-side'. He says that 'the end-product of the Freudian method of explanation is a detailed elaboration of man's shadow-side such as had never been carried out before. It is the most effective antidote imaginable to all idealistic illusions about the nature of man' (p. 46). But, he points out, it is an illusion to think that only this side of man is real and that his conscious motives and ideals are a mere defensive cover-up, reaction-formations or rationalizations: 'Freud's method of interpretation rests upon "reductive" explanations which unfailingly lead backward and downward, and it has a destructive effect if it is used in an exaggerated and one-sided way' (p. 47). Psychology has learned from Freud that 'human nature has also a black side', but it would be naïve to suppose that 'what is radiant no longer exists because it has been explained from the shadow-side' (p. 47).

In the same vein he writes that the Freudian school 'deserves reproach for over-emphasizing the pathological aspects of life and for interpreting man too exclusively in the light of his defects' (pp. 134–5). He adds: 'Freud's teaching is definitely one-sided in that it generalizes from facts that are relevant only to neurotic states of mind; its valdity is really confined to those states . . . Freud's is not a psychology of the healthy mind' (ibid.). One example would be Freud's identification or near identification of a genuine moral conscience with the archaic super-ego. Another example would be Freud's reduction of love to sex, or his representation of 'chaste love' as 'a sublimated form of carnal love' (see Weil, 1953, p. 69, and also Guntrip, 1977, p. 79).

But more than this Jung finds Freud's conception of the pathological, or of neurosis iteslf, one-sided and defective:

> What could seem more plausible . . . than to seek the specific cause of the psycho-neuroses, not in the mystical notion of the 'soul', but in a disturbance of impulses . . . This is Freud's standpoint when establishing his well-known theory which explains the neuroses in terms of disturbances of the sexual impulse. (p. 257)

Jung argues that in many cases the root of neurotic trouble is not to be found in impulses which would run riot but for repression, but rather in a lack of spiritual framework in the light of which they are ordered:

> Disturbances in the sphere of the unconscious drives are not primary, but secondary phenomena. When conscious life has lost its meaning and promise, it is as though a panic had broken loose and we heard the exclamation: 'Let us eat and drink, for tomorrow we die!' It is this mood, born of the meaninglessness of life, that causes the disturbance in the unconscious and provokes the painfully curbed impulses to break out anew. (p. 269)

So Jung holds that it is this spiritual condition to which the therapist needs to direct his attention. He argues that not only does Freud neglect doing so, but that he shows no recognition of the spiritual in man. Further, the kind of interpretations psycho-analysis offers actually alienate analytic patients from a spiritual standpoint: 'Freud's theory of sexuality and Adler's theory of power . . . are hostile to spiritual values.' As methods of treatment they 'hinder the realization of meaningful experience . . . This means that the great majority of [their] patients are necessarily alienated from a spiritual standpoint' (p. 263).

'A psycho-neurosis', he writes, 'must be understood as the suffering of a human being who has not discovered what life means for him . . . The patient is looking for something that will take possession of him and give meaning and form to the confusion of his neurotic mind' (p. 260). He says a little way above that 'it is only the meaningful that sets us free' (p. 259). When Jung says that mere insight is not enough it is at least partly this that he has in mind: 'Mere insight into themselves is sufficient for morally sensitive persons who have enough driving force to carry them forward; for those with little imagination for moral values, however, it does not suffice' (p. 49).

Freud, as we have seen, was primarily concerned to increase the patient's insight into himself. The patient thus, in the course of his analysis, comes to notice certain patterns in his behaviour, for instance, he comes to recognize the role of such behaviour in his 'psychic economy'. He comes to see that in them he is defending himself against acknowledging certain painful truths about himself, learns what these truths are, and comes to appreciate how his running away from them constrains him in certain directions and limits his life. In short, he is made to see what obstructs his life.

It is this that Jung finds insufficient, however much to the point it may be. He holds that the patient lacks something and is looking for it in his perplexity and confusion. It is this the therapist must help him find. Freudian therapy, he argues, may release the patient from what holds him back; but it does not point forward, it does not help the patient to discover a new direction. This is what many patients need, especially those who are in the second stage of their lives, have found social and material success but have not found this to be enough. Jung talks of this as 'education of the will' and 'development of the psyche':

> It is obviously not enough for him [the patient] to know how and why he fell ill, for to understand the causes of an evil does very little towards curing it . . . The crooked paths of a neurosis lead to as many obstinate habits . . . [and] these do not disappear until they are replaced by other habits . . . The patient must be, as it were, prodded into other paths, and this always requires an educating will. (p. 52)

Jung also emphasizes 'the individual case' and the 'relative validity' of all viewpoints in psychology and psychotherapy: 'The needs and necessities of individuals vary. What sets one free is for another a prison – as for instance normality and adaptation' (p. 56). 'It would be an unpardonable error to overlook the element of truth in both the Freudian and Adlerian viewpoints, but it would be no less unpardonable to take either of them as the sole truth . . . I hold the truth of my own views to be equally relative, and regard myself also as the exponent of a certain predisposition' (p. 65). He then makes several distinctions, one of these being that between 'a psychology of the morning of life' and one 'of its afternoon' (pp. 66–7).

> As a rule, the life of a young person is characterized by a general unfolding and a striving towards concrete ends; his neurosis, if he develops one, can be traced to his hesitation or his shrinking back from this necessity. But the life of an older person is marked by a contraction of forces, by the affirmation of what has been achieved, and the curtailment of further growth. His neurosis comes mainly from his clinging to a youthful attitude which is now out of season. Just as the youthful neurotic is afraid of life, so the older one shrinks back from death. What was a normal goal for the young man, inevitably becomes a neurotic hindrance to the older person. (p. 67)

Jung's claim is that, therefore, the aims of the therapy must be different in the two cases and so too the means appropriate to their achievement. He takes the goal of Freudian therapy to be 'normality' and 'adaptation' and says that for those whose aspirations and problems are spiritual this would be a restriction: for a man 'whose neurosis unfits him for normal life to be "normal" is a splended ideal', but for those 'who have far more ability than the average . . . restriction to the normal signifies . . . unbearable boredom, infernal sterility and hopelessness' (p. 55). 'The course the physician then adopts [for such people] is less a question of treatment than of developing the creative possibilities that lie in the patient himself' (p. 70). 'We Occidentals had learned to tame and subject the psyche, but we knew nothing about its methodical development and its functions' (p. 62).

Not only must the aims of therapy differ according to the kind of problem a person is seeking help for but the therapy must also cater for the kind of need which the patient has but is unable to satisfy. Thus, some people's attitudes are 'essentially spiritual', those of others 'materialistic'. 'It must not be assumed', Jung points out, 'that such an attitude is accidentally acquired or springs from some misunderstanding' (p. 68). In other words, it would be an expression of narrowness and a symptom of philosophical confusion to assume that such an attitude might be an error, or that it is reasonable or unreasonable. The only question, in every single case, is whether it 'exists in its own right', in other words, is authentic, or 'is perhaps only a compensation for the opposite' (p. 69).

So what the therapist needs to do is help the patient to develop within the framework of whatever attitude is authentic to him: 'The shoe that fits one person pinches another; there is no recipe for living that suits all cases' (p. 69). Jung believes that Freudian therapy does not recognize and does not cater for the needs of those whose attitude to life is 'essentially spiritual'. He even characterizes Freudian therapy as a 'rational' therapy because (as he claims) it does not recognize spiritual concerns and aspirations as a positive force in human life. He argues that 'problems' of life do not have answers in the sense that mathematical questions and questions regarding means to agreed ends do: they are 'questions which allow of more than one answer, . . . answers that are always open to doubt' (p. 109). He then goes on to connect the possibility of such problems with what is distinctive in human life as distinct from animal life, one of instinct, one in which there is no logical space for deliberation and introspection. In other words, human life is inherently problematic, its problems being the product of man's civilization and consciousness: 'It is the growth of consciousness which we must thank for the existence of problems; they are the dubious gift of civilization' (p. 110). He then goes on to distinguish the existence of problems from a neurosis: 'People whose own temperaments offer problems are often neurotic, but it would be a serious misunderstanding to confuse the existence of problems with neurosis . . . The neurotic is ill because he is unconscious of his problems; while the man with a difficult temperament suffers from his conscious problems without being ill' (p. 116). And a little further down he points out: 'The serious problems of life . . . are never fully solved. If it should for once appear that they are, this is the sign that something has been lost. The meaning . . . of a problem seems not to lie in its solution, but in our working at it incessantly. This alone preserves us from stultification and petrification' (pp. 118–19).

Jung stresses the importance of the personality of the therapist and how much he is himself influenced by the contact he makes with his patients: 'the relation between physician and patient remains personal within the frame of the impersonal, professional treatment' (p. 56). 'The meeting of two personalities is like the contact of two chemical substances: if there is any reaction, both are transformed' (p. 57). 'You can exert no influence if you are not susceptible to influence' (ibid.). The therapist must thus be open towards the patient and be himself in the treatment. He must not shrink from contact with disturbing aspects of the patient's personality, hide himself behind his profession, or keep the patient at arm's length by judging him: the doctor must be the man through whom he wishes to influence others (p. 59). Here Jung contrasts 'being' with 'mere talking'.

> The patient does not feel himself accepted unless the very worst in him is accepted too. No one can bring this about by mere words; it comes only through the doctor's sincerity and through his attitude towards himself and his own evil side. If the doctor wants to offer guidance to another, or even accompany him a step of the way, he must be in touch with this other person's psychic life. He is never in touch when he passes judgement . . . [But] to take the opposite position, and to agree with the patient offhand, is also of no use, but estranges him as much as condemnation. (p. 270)

It is clear that Jung attaches therapeutic importance to the contact itself, which the therapist establishes with the patient, the genuineness of the relationship, the integrity of the therapist and the working of the patient at his problems. For, otherwise, the therapist has no 'solutions' to offer and no 'methods' by which to proceed (see p. 261).

This then is a brief summary of Jung's critique of Freudian psychotherapy. It is not clear to me whether or not for Jung psychotherapy is something that goes beyond the treatment of neuroses, that is, of conditions other than those that constitute neuroses. Often this seems to be the case. He speaks of neuroses as illnesses and contrasts them with conditions of meaninglessness in which people feel 'I am stuck',[2] and not 'I am sick'. Jung says of such people that they 'are suffering from no clinically definable neurosis' (p. 70) and that what the therapist does is not to 'treat' them but to 'develop the creative possibilities that lie in the patient

---

[2] This is what Tolstoy called an 'arrest of life' (see 1961).

himself' (ibid.). 'Among my patients . . . there is a considerable number who came to see me, not because they were suffering from a neurosis, but because they could find no meaning in life' (p. 267). It is not a physician whom these patients need to see: 'We can hardly expect the doctor to have anything to say about the ultimate questions of the soul' (p. 262). Someone who has something to say here is not someone who has an 'answer': 'I do not know what to say to the patient when he asks me: "What do you advise? What shall I do?" I do not know any better than he' (pp. 70–1). 'I was soon forced to tell him that I, too, had no answer . . . Such a confession is often the beginning of the patient's confidence in him [the psychotherapist]' (p. 267).

If Jung distinguishes such cases from those of people suffering from a 'clinically definable neurosis', does this mean that he regards the latter as calling for 'treatment' in *contrast* with 'the development of their creative possibilities'? Jung's answer to this question is neither clear nor unequivocal. But on the whole he thinks that, even where the soul is not involved, psychological trouble calls for an approach that goes beyond medical practice:

> The latest advance of analytical psychology makes an unavoidable problem of the doctor's ethical attitude. The self-criticism and self-examination demanded of him radically alter our view of the human psyche. This cannot be grasped from the standpoint of natural science . . .
> What was formerly a method of medical treatment now becomes a method of self-education, and therewith the horizon of our modern psychology is immeasurably widened. The medical diploma is no longer the crucial thing, but human quality instead . . . Analytical psychology is no longer bound to the consulting room of the doctor . . . It is freed from its clinical origins and ceases to be a mere method for treating the sick. It is now of service to the healthy as well. (pp. 61–2)

'The healthy as well' – in other words, the healthy *and* the sick. There are two distinctions which Jung makes, even if they are not sharp distinctions: one between physical and psychological illness, and in particular neurosis, and the other between neurosis and spiritual perplexity. He is saying that, logically, neurosis is in the same space as spiritual perplexity.

So far so good. But he seems to me to go too far when he suggests that all neuroses arise out of certain spiritual conditions: 'Disturbances in the sphere of unconscious drives are not primary, but secondary phenomena . . . The causes of a neurosis lie in the present as well as in the past; and only a still existing cause can keep a neurosis active' (p. 269). After all, he himself distinguishes between a psychology of the morning of life and one of its afternoon. The neuroses of the young, he tells us, arise out of a clinging to childhood and a fear of life; the neuroses of the middle-aged arise out of a clinging to youth and a fear of old age and death. This is, of course, very general, but certainly here Jung recognizes a difference. The questions which the neruoses of the young raise are: what is he afraid of in life and why? What is it that he clings to in childhood and why has he remained so dependent? These are, surely, some of the questions raised by Freud himself. As for the middle-aged, the questions which their neuroses raise are: what is it about old age that frightens them? Why are they so frightened of taking their leave of life? What is it in life that they are clinging to, what do they get out of it and why do they crave it so compulsively?

These are the questions examined by Tolstoy in his story 'The Death of Ivan Ilytch'. He finds the cause of Ilytch's suffering in the character of the latter's life, in the things he lived for, in his greed and materialism, in the way he always put himself first and had no real consideration of others, even those closest to him, and in the way this condition alienated him from all spiritual values. In a book entitled *Sense and Delusion* Professor Phillips and I debated, among other things, the question of whether Ilytch's depression was the cause or product of the life he led. In my original paper, 'Life and Meaning' – chapter 1 of the book – I had taken the view that it was part of the cause of such a life. Phillips corrected my one-sided view by arguing that it was its product. The question is the same as the one raised by Jung.

I would now say that the relation in question is more complicated than either of us put it and goes both ways. Ivan Ilytch's middle-aged life was conditioned both by his early youth and childhood *and* by his social environment and its 'values', his relationship to the latter being itself conditioned by the kind of person he was as a result of his early family experiences. In the latter connection I am thinking of his susceptibility to outside influence, of his conformism and its sources, and of the way what he borrowed and copied was made into a vehicle for the pursuit of his greed as well as a refuge from anxieties that flowed from the emptiness of his life and his own insubstantiality.

That is, the emptiness of his life and the depression that goes with it are together both a primary and a secondary phenomenon. They have their source both in the condition of soul whose foundations lie in the past and in the form of life, outside Ivan, constituting his present environment. Certainly, this life which Tolstoy portrays him as sharing with those around him, the life of those belonging to a particular social milieu, is devoid of spirituality and the possibilities of creativity. It is bound, therefore, to stunt the spiritual development of one who makes it his own. This would inevitably lead to such *psychological* consequences as Tolstoy portrays so vividly in his story.

On the other hand, why should a person be so ready to take over the life of his milieu and live it so uncreatively? Why should he ape or conform to its 'values' so completely and uncritically? Surely, the psychology with which he comes to it at this stage of his life has something to do with it, the psychology which was formed at an earlier period of his life. This seamless interaction between the outer and the inner stretches back to a person's early childhood. So while Jung is right in thinking that it will not do to reduce the spiritual to the psychological, it is equally a mistake to regard a person's psychological problems as a mere product of his spiritual condition.

A person's 'psychological state' and 'spiritual condition' are normally interwoven and each plays a part in shaping the other. It is not even always possible to distinguish between the psychological and the spiritual, to say where the one begins and the other ends. Often they are two aspects of the same thing, or the same thing seen under two different aspects. Thus, while Ivan Ilytch's greed and egocentricity certainly belong to his psychology, are they not, at the same time, an important feature of his spiritual condition, depending on our point of view?

Jung is right about the 'reductionist' tendency in Freud's thinking. Whether or not, and to what extent, it is an essential part of psycho-analysis as a therapy is another question. But it is a bias in the opposite direction to suppose that psychological disturbances are always rooted in the absence of a framework of values which would give sense to a person's life and order his actions. Prior psychological conditions may poison a person's relationship to any such framework at source, destroying the possibility of its playing a positive role in his life.

Jung himself makes a connection between the young man who has difficulty in growing up and the middle-aged person who cannot accept his age:

To the psychotherapist an old man who cannot bid farewell to life appears as feeble and sickly as a young man who is unable to embrace it. And as a matter of fact, in many cases it is a question of the selfsame childish covetousness, of the same fear, the same obstinacy and wilfulness, in the one as in the other. (pp. 128–9)

What Jung focuses on here are what makes growth and change problematic, since that involves the relinquishment of what feeds the self and affords protection to it. At the bottom of the neurotic problems of both the young and the middle-aged, therefore, lies what Freud called 'weakness of the ego', the conditions for such weakness lying in the person's early childhood. In 'The Death of Ivan Ilytch' Tolstoy brings out well how much Ilytch's social environment blinded him to a perspective that might have enabled him to change in such a way that he lost these cravings, and how much these cravings themselves fed on each other and made him unwilling to give up life as he had known it, fearful of the psychological and spiritual dangers to which that would expose him. It is Freud's view that it is the same cravings, dependencies and compulsions, the same anxieties and fears, that constitute a resistance to change in different periods of a person's life.

But to return to Freud's 'error', 'one-sidedness' and 'reductionism', his neglect of the spiritual: is this an essential aspect of Freud's vision and of psycho-analytic therapy? My own view is that it is a product of philosophical confusions which could be cleared up without thereby having to give up what is distinctive in psychoanalytic therapy as I have depicted it in earlier chapters. Thus, despite what Freud said about religion, for instance, I see no reason why a psycho-analyst should not respect a patient's religious convictions when they are genuine. This really is the only question he should address himself to, as he does in other matters: are they genuine or are they part of the patient's defences? Is the patient authentic where his religious convictions influence or determine his actions or is he deceiving himself?

One may argue, of course, that Freud's theoretical framework does not permit a psycho-analyst to take his patient's religious convictions seriously and for what they are. Thus Phillips writes:

For Freud not *any* resting point would do as a final explanation . . . Psycho-analytic explanations lead back to themes which have a sexual character, or which relate to the destructive tendencies of the death instinct. (1976, p. 64)

This is a comment on what Jung called the 'reductionism' and 'one-sidedness' of Freudian thinking. It is there, and both Jung and Phillips are justified in their complaint. My point is that psychoanalytic therapy contains much to which Freud's 'reductionist' views of religion and morality are peripheral. What is in question is Freud's 'philosophical baggage', which can be jettisoned without changing the character of the therapy.

Of course, a psycho-analyst who is influenced by these views may undermine what needs nurturing in a particular patient. There is no guarantee against this. To avoid it a psycho-analyst needs a sensitive imagination, a capacity for critical thinking, and the kind of breadth that comes from culture. As for the patient 'whose neurosis involves religious ideas' (Phillips, 1976, p. 63), if he is to benefit from psycho-analysis his analyst would have to be someone who has an understanding of these ideas and is able to appreciate what it means for them to go deep in a person's life.

Jung, however, thinks that Freud's 'one-sidedness' is *integral* to psycho-analytic therapy: 'Freudian psycho-analysis is limited to the task of making conscious the shadow-side and the evil within him [the patient]' (p. 277). He identifies the unconscious, which Freudian therapy aims to make conscious, with 'the powers of darkness'. That is why he thinks that uncovering it is not enough and that if the patient is is to be helped the analyst should give him something more positive which would enable him to contain or come to terms with what has been unleashed. Jung has every excuse for thinking so, given Freud's early views of the unconscious. For, in those views, every man in his unconscious is inevitably selfish and morally indifferent or amoral.

However, Freud later came to recognize that there is no limit to what man may deceive himself about. He came to see that the unconscious is not co-extensive with the id, that aspects of the ego iteslf are often unconscious. Those who developed his thinking came to see that a person may be afraid to face not only what is bad in him or what he has been made to think is bad, but also what is decent. Just as a man may be afraid to accept his sensuality, for instance, so equally he may be afraid to recognize and give way to his tenderness. Just as he may be afraid to acknowledge his anger and aggressiveness, he may also be afraid of those sentiments in him which open him up to other people, lower the boundaries which separate him from them.

Therefore, while Jung is right to think that 'the opening up of the unconscious always means the outbreak of intense suffering' he is wrong to think that it is always and only 'the powers of darkness' that are thereby unleashed in the patient. For to admit one's care, for instance, or to allow oneself to feel tender, is to drop one's boundaries, to lower one's defences, to expose one's vulnerabilities, those from which one insulates oneself by whatever power one acquires and exercises. If, especially, one has been selfish, greedy, cruel or callous, to acknowledge one's concern is to court much pain in the form of remorse, sorrow, guilt and grief. One may have reason, therefore, to repress what is good in one as well as what is evil. Thus, often in analysis, when the patient's unconscious is opened up, what is 'positive' and 'healing' in him is also released. In learning to accept it and make it part of himself, however painful or frightening this may at first be, the patient finds a direction in life. His life acquires a direction it never had before. In this way he finds his way *himself*, without the guidance of his analyst.

It is not even true, strictly, that analysis 'simply brings into action the civil war that was latent [in the patient] and lets it go at that'. For, while it is true that the analyst refrains from giving the patient guidance, the routine of the analysis and the analytic relationship itself provide him with a 'holding' environment in which he can risk dropping his defences, exposing his vulnerabilities and facing what divides him in himself without falling apart.

Could a person whose early relationships and experiences have left him with a stunted interest in and concern for others be said to be 'disturbed'? What can a psycho-analytic therapy have to offer him? This is perhaps one kind of case where Jung's criticism of a non-directive therapy such as analysis appears to be most justified. Certain forms of delinquency fall within this category, and also those whose later experiences have severed their links with any moral values and spiritual concerns which might have taken root in their lives – that is, those who have never developed any roots to give them a stable identity and those who have been uprooted from those they once had.

I don't think that Freud would have spoken of a 'neurosis' here. For where there is a neurosis a person has got knotted up, given his past history and circumstances, on account of his sensitivities and vulnerabilities. Whereas the trouble with a person who lacks an enduring concern for others is not so much excessive vulnerabilities as indifference. Where his childhood experiences have left him with little ability to take an interest in others and feel for them he cannot have full relations with people. He may 'enjoy' a certain 'freedom' which the lives of most of us exclude, but those needs which, nevertheless, draw him to others constantly result in conflict with them, anger and frustration. Being human he cannot altogether avoid entering into relationships, but his relationships are always 'disturbed'. Whatever life he makes for himself never sustains him; he thrashes about, gets into trouble, and life passes him by without leaving anything for him to hold onto.

Jung is right about what such a person lacks and his need for 'guidance', and it may be that psycho-analysis cannot help him. One thing is clear though, and I am sure Jung appreciates this, namely that no 'external' guidance can solve such a person's problems. Perhaps his only hope is a genuinely accepting relationship in which the other person, friend, priest or therapist, avoids all the 'mistakes' of his early environment that have brought him to his present plight. Here the guidance comes purely from the example which the other person provides within the relationship in being himself. It is in the course of contact with such a person that he may 'learn' what he failed to learn in his childhood. But then is this not the kind of therapy that psycho-analysis offers through the transference? I admit that Freud's thinking contains both dogma and philosophical confusion; but there is more to the therapy he has developed than is contained in his descriptions of it.

3 FROMM AND MONEY-KYRLE: SELF-KNOWLEDGE AND ETHICAL TRANSFORMATION

At the end of last chapter I asked: where does the patient find the values, concerns and interests that give unity and direction to a person's life? I considered Jung's criticism of Freudian therapy that it is at its weakest when the patient is a person who has lost his way spiritually and, therefore, needs direction. Jung's criticism was that psycho-analysis cannot provide such a direction because it is based on a reductionist philosophy of human motives and moral values. I argued that while this reductionism is in Freud's thinking, it is not an essential part of Freudian psychotherapy. The special form of treatment that Freud has developed for those with neurotic problems through personal contact and emotional work stands on its own and is separate from the reductionism that Jung criticized in Freud.

Jung's was one answer to my question, namely that Freudian psychology is spiritually bankrupt and bound to undermine the patient's values. The answer at the other end is that the transformation that psycho-analysis brings about in the patient, when successful, is an ethical transformation and returns him to certain values that are in him by virtue of his very humanity. These are also the values implicit in the psycho-analytic outlook. In their own different ways Erich Fromm and Roger Money-Kyrle have held this kind of view (see Fromm, 1950 and Money-Kyrle, 1955).

Certainly, the kind of transformation that takes place in a person as he sheds his self-deceptions and advances in self-knowledge is an *ethical* transformation. This means that it involves a change in his relation to the values that enter his life, directly or through the culture in which that life bathes. But the view under consideration goes further than this and claims that, irrespective of the individual concerned, psycho-analysis always returns the patient to the *same* set of values, those that are 'inherent'[3] in human nature. Thus, Money-Kyrle speaks of a certain convergence in the values of those who have had a deep analysis in contrast with the variety one finds among those who have not had such treatment (1955, p. 422).

Erich Fromm, who comes to this question from a somewhat different angle, describes a man's conscience, when genuine, as 'man's recall to himself' (1950, p. 158). 'Humanistic conscience', as he calls it, is, he says, 'our own voice', 'the voice of our true selves which summons us back to ourselves, to live productively, to become what we potentially are, the voice of our living care for ourselves' (ibid.). Thus it calls man to the values on which his very humanity is founded.

Fromm characterizes such a conscience as anti-authoritarian, as does Money-Kyrle, and he contrasts it with the Freudian super-ego which 'imposes' its values, those it has acquired through 'identification' with an outside authority, on a resisting self or 'ego'. One task

---

[3] The term is Marion Milner's, a Kleinian analyst, who contrasts 'inherent morality' with one that is 'implanted'. See Milner, 1977, p. 67.

of psycho-analytic therapy is to free the self from this tyranny. If, as Freud claimed, the super-ego were the only guardian of morality in the person, then it would be true that psycho-analysis undermines the patient's morality. But, Fromm and Money-Kyrle argue, since it is not, what psycho-analysis does is to liberate the patient from an authoritarian conscience or super-ego, and its morality, leaving his conscience free to become 'humanistic'. Such a person develops an allegiance to 'humanitarian' values, that is, to a morality of love rather than one of force. Only such a conscience is genuine, it is implied, and only the morality to which it gives voice is 'authentic'.

In a different way, Ernest Jones (1937) says something similar. He misleadingly describes the attitude of one whose super-ego is pronounced as a 'moral attitude',[4] thus, like Freud, identifying any morality with the 'morality of the super-ego', or what Fromm calls 'authoritarian morality'. He contrasts it with the attitude or orientation of someone who is free from the tyranny of the super-ego, calling this an 'attitude of love' but, unlike Fromm and Money-Kyrle, failing to recognize that it is a particular type of *moral* attitude. It is *this* attitude and, therefore, this morality which psycho-analysis promotes. As the patient is 'liberated' he moves towards such an orientation naturally and of his own accord.

To return to Fromm, there is a certain ambiguity in the notion of conscience as 'man's recall to himself' which his thinking exploits. It is certainly true that when a man of genuine moral convictions is tempted to turn away from the path to which they point, his conscience 'tells' him that what is attracting him at the time is not what he, *himself*, wants and that if he gives in he will *himself* come to regret it. In other words, the desire which he experiences does not have its source in what forms part of his identity; he does not condone it. It stands outside the network of beliefs, desires and relations which draw the framework within which he experiences life and flourishes. The path of its satisfaction is not part of the way he has made his own. In this sense, Fromm is right, a man's conscience recalls him to himself, that is, to *whatever* values he has genuinely made his own.

He is wrong, however, in the suggestion that a man's conscience always recalls him to one and the same set of values in relation to which *only* a man can be true to himself. The idea is that only these values are the values of an authentic morality, all other moralities

---

[4] He should have called it a 'moralistic attitude'.

being *oppressive* and *illusory*. No doubt Fromm thinks of instances of such alternative moralities in these terms, and he has a perfect right to do so. But he finds them oppressive and thinks of those who believe in them as deceived only from where he himself stands *morally*. His judgements are not themselves morally neutral.

It is not the self, in its authenticity, that determines a man's values, but the other way around: it is in relation to the values that a man makes his own, whatever they may be, that he finds his authenticity. In other words, putting aside the question of whether or not a person can be authentic without any morality,[5] authenticity alone does not make a man moral. What a man's conscience recalls him to are his *values*, those he has made his own but is in danger now of forgetting or betraying. True, that constitutes a recall to himself, but only because the values in question determine who he is, what he wants and what constitutes flourishing for him.

Both Fromm and Money-Kyrle are right to emphasize that psycho-analysis frees its patients from the tyranny of the super-ego. I have described this earlier as the 'humanization' of the patient's super-ego. I meant that the patient becomes more accessible to the consideration of other people and to feelings of compassion, less ready to condemn them at the drop of a hat and more ready to forgive them. But I see no reason why the liberation of the patient from the tyranny of his super-ego should result *necessarily* in his embracing what Fromm and Money-Kyrle call a 'humanistic' morality. An 'authoritarian' conscience and morality may be perfectly genuine.

What psycho-analysis does is to free a man to become more genuine or authentic – and this includes greater authenticity in his moral convictions and attitudes. But I don't see that it needs to determine the content of this authenticity, the direction in which it is to be found. This depends on the patient, his particular background and individuality. It is true that, as in all other relations in life, he may learn from his contacts with the analyst and his values may change in the process.[6] True, the very kind of relationship that analysis promotes is in many ways anti-authoritarian in character. Growing in that relationship is, therefore, bound to promote growth in an anti-authoritarian direction. But this is not because this is 'the

---

[5] A question that Plato raises in connection with Polus in the *Gorgias*.
[6] This should not be confused with indoctrination.

true direction', 'the only authentic path'. If one so describes it, one ought to be clear that one is expressing one's own moral beliefs. Otherwise one risks falling a prey to the kind of 'moral narrow-mindedness' that psycho-analysis is meant to combat. If one is not careful philosophical confusion can turn into moral oppression.

The question of moral oppression and tolerance is a difficult and complicated one. But it is a confused oversimplification to think of oppression as on the side of an authoritarian conscience and of tolerance as necessarily on the side of a humanistic one. Any kind of conscience can be seen as oppressive in a moral conflict by someone who does not share its beliefs. After all, moral values set limits to human actions that would appear as limitations to someone with whom those values carry no weight. And a conscience that upholds them forbids actions that transgress those limits and is the source of the guilt, shame or remorse which a person feels upon ignoring them. It endorses and supports the punishment of those who disregard them in their actions. None of this is the prerogative of an authoritarian conscience only.

There is, of course, a difference between this kind of 'oppression' and the kind of oppression that uses morality as a pretext, or the oppression of fanaticism, though it is not always easy to tell them apart. When a person's conscience uses the morality he has acquired as a child to oppress and persecute him then such a person is in the grip of self-deception. He does not recognize the true character of the relationship between his ego and super-ego, their respective attitudes, and the way this colours his relationships with other people and his outlook on life. Philosophical confusions apart, I am convinced that it is his deep perception into just this that led Freud to think, mistakenly, that morality is a curse and a deception, one in the name of which people oppress each other and themselves become its slaves.

As for tolerance, this does not mean never saying no, making no moral judgements, having no strong feelings of moral aversion. Just as freedom is not the same thing as licence, so, equally, tolerance is not the same thing as indifference. It stands opposed to fanaticism. There are, of course, some moralities, those for which the individual has little value, which attach little value to tolerance. Obviously, psycho-analysis cannot have a peaceful co-existence with such a morality, since its efforts are directed to bettering the life of the individual for the individual's sake. But it is a mistake to think of all authoritarian moralities as being like this.

What Fromm and Money-Kyrle call 'humanistic' or 'humanitarian' conscience is a conscience, identified with a particular set of values: love *versus* force, regard for the individual as an end in itself, tolerance of differences in beliefs and attitudes, authenticity of self, honesty in human relationships. If they contrast this with an 'authoritarian conscience', the main difference they have in mind is that for the latter type of conscience the autonomy of the individual is not what is of primary importance; obedience is. But there are problems in this way of putting it, since the autonomy of the individual is a necessary condition for *any* form of authentic moral conduct, except in the case of moralities that disregard the individual. But spiritual moralities, such as Christianity, which advocate the renouncement of self are no exception to this. For they are concerned with the individual, with his soul, and the selfless obedience that they make into a central virtue still has to be willed by the agent; it is not enough that he obeys slavishly. So perhaps we should say that the main difference Fromm and Money-Kyrle have in mind is that in a humanitarian morality the free development of the individual is a central value, whereas in an authoritarian morality it is subordinated to the particular values that it regards as central.

Of course, there need be nothing inauthentic about the conscience of one who has allegiance to an authoritarian morality. For there is nothing servile about obedience *as such*, and nothing oppressive or repressive about authority *as such*, though Fromm and Money-Kyrle think otherwise. That is why they see the change in a person's conscience away from an authoritarian character as a liberation. My point is that allegiance to an authoritarian morality need not be a form of bondage. Whether or not it is so depends entirely on the character of the authority and on the nature of the individual's relation to it.

As for the distinction between 'inherent' and 'implanted' morality, we should remember that most of what constitutes an individual's morality is 'learned'. It comes to him from outside, from the society in which he is brought up and lives. But this does not make it into something 'implanted' into or 'grafted' onto him. For it is through this 'learning' that all of us become the individual human beings we are. What are 'inherent' in us are our primitive propensities, which this learning uses, some of which it develops and shapes, while it stunts others, depending on the morality in question. I am thinking of such propensities as the propensity to take a friendly interest in others, to show concern for them, to forgive injuries received, as well as to resent this and seek revenge, to identify oneself with the strong, to despise the weak, as well as to feel sorry for them, etc. We have a wide range of mixed reactions here, some of which could be characterized as 'moral reactions'.

It could, therefore, be said that we have the *seeds* of morality in us from the start. But that is not to say that we are born with an 'inherent' morality. Indeed, what kind of morality these seeds will develop into depends on the soil in which they grow and the kind of watering they receive. The soil in question is the culture and moral environment in which we are brought up, and the watering is the care and attention we receive in the personal relations through which we develop in our most formative years.

The upshot of our discussion then is twofold. First, the idea that Freudian analysis is hostile to morality and risks undermining the patient's values has some justification and some reality to it. The source of this hostility, however, lies in the philosophical confusions in Freud's thinking. While these confusions can make a difference to analytic practice if the analyst himself is vulnerable to them, they are not an integral part of psycho-analytic therapy. There is no need, no logical necessity, for its practice to be reductionist or hostile to moral and spiritual values.

Second, and on the other side, the idea of a morality inherent in human nature, to which psycho-analysis opens up the patient, is equally confused. But again this does not mean that there is no truth behind this idea. The truth is that there are certain primitive 'moral' reactions to which most people have a natural propensity, reactions which, with certain variations, transcend the boundaries of the diversity of cultures in human societies. These reactions spell certain psychological dangers for people just as much as their sexual propensities do. Therefore, a therapy which strengthens a person ('the ego') against these dangers and also frees him from the 'false' morality of the super-ego would make these moral reactions accessible to him. Such a change would amount to an ethical transformation in the patient.

In addition, the very character and ethos of psycho-analytic practice, the kind of concern and attitude of the analyst towards his patient, presupposes certain values that are bound to have some impact on the patient. This does not mean that the patient acquires these values blindly, but he is certainly exposed to their appeal. Indeed, to some extent, in so far as he enters the analytic relationship, he accepts these values, however provisionally. I now turn to a consideration of them.

4 PSYCHO-ANALYTIC THERAPY AND ITS VALUES

We have tried to understand the reasons why, on the whole, a psycho-analyst refrains from considering the patient's problems from a moral point of view and from making moral judgements in the course of the treatment. This is not to say, however, that his approach to the patient, as a psycho-analyst, is entirely neutral. Indeed, we have seen that his 'moral neutrality' is itself a moral attitude. Besides, the very notion of the patient as a person who needs psycho-therapeutic help is value-laden and cannot be articulated without bringing in certain moral notions. The patient needs help because he has failed in certain ways and in certain directions. The very attribution of such 'failures' to him brings in certain ideals of development and well-being. Third, the notions of 'giving and receiving help' in questions differ, in ways we have seen, from the notion of 'repairing a faulty machine' and also that of treating a person for some specific disease or physical ailment. Fourth, the peculiarity of psycho-analytic therapy is that it is founded on the promotion of personal truth or authenticity, and so makes claims on the patient's honesty, demanding that he should be truthful with the analyst. It is well known that one cannot be truthful as a means to some further end. One has to have regard for the truth and be prepared to put it first whatever the consequences.

So the treatment itself, which, as we have seen, does not by-pass the patient as a person and involves his responsibility, demands a particular moral orientation from him. The patient is asked to be truthful in what he relates about himself and to suppress nothing in what he says, but as the treatment progresses he learns to be honest with himself and in his relationship with the analyst. That relationship, so central to psycho-analytic treatment, has itself a particular character and makes demands on the patient's moral integrity. It is true that the patient is left free to be as it comes to him. But the analyst refuses to play his 'games', to enter into the kind of relationship that suits the patient. Instead, he spells out the patient's aims and strategies, and points out the way that he turns away from a more authentic existence in playing these 'games' and pursuing these ends. It is, in the end, only a desire for greater authenticity, born out of a regard for an authentic existence, that makes him change. If all that spurred him on were the desire to avoid the pain and discomfort of his neurosis he would simply go on looking for a 'less inconvenient', 'more satisfactory' neurosis. This is often what people do under the pressures that life exerts on them on account of their neurotic problems. Psycho-analysis is an attempt to break this mould.

It can only succeed because the relationship is different from those in which the patient's neurosis flourishes or is aggravated. It offers him something new; that is, he learns something new about himself from the relationship, and this involves learning new attitudes and new values. The values in question may not be new to him at all, but he learns what it means to keep faith with them and the difficulties this involves. In the process he develops a regard for them he did not have before.

One of these values is independence, self-reliance, freedom or autonomy. He learns to establish himself in his relationships with others on a more equal footing. He gives up his false attitudes towards them, exaggerated attitudes of false modesty and of false pride. He learns to consider and respect others without fearing to displease them. He learns to be open with them, to listen to them, without fearing to think for himself and be what he is. Above all, he learns to be close to the people for whom he cares without seeking to merge his identity with theirs or to incorporate theirs into his. This, at the same time, is coming to value individual autonomy.

While this is a distinct value, it is compatible with different moral outlooks. For instance, there is no necessity why someone who has regard for individual autonomy should be an 'individualist' in the narrow sense and give priority to the freedom of the individual over the demands of affection. Certainly, he does not learn always to put the needs of his own development as an individual first, but only to keep his ground in the face of meddlesome interference. Above all, he learns to keep his head and judge what to do, where to give in and where to hold his ground.

In *Freud and Human Nature* I said that the psycho-analyst is not 'morally partisan' in the sense that he is not tied down to one specific set of values (1983, p. 187). Certainly, in psycho-analysis the patient learns self-respect and the courage to be himself. But he also learns to respect others, to be giving in his relationships, and to value generosity. Winnicott's notion of 'mature dependence' captures well the balance between these two values which can come into conflict with each other. Put it like this: on the one hand the patient comes to learn the value of independence and of relationships in which others recognize his separateness and respect him as an individual, while on the other hand he learns to acknowledge the value of a life of contact and give and take with others, enriched by affection, humour, concern, and sustained by loyalty.

Analysis, when it works, enables him to grow out of infantile and selfish orientations, particularly in his most intimate relationships. Many of the feelings and attitudes in question, such as greed, envy and jealousy, are such as to keep him in bondage and curtail his autonomy. With luck, what he discovers in himself and the support he finds in the analytic relationship help him to 'grow out' of such attitudes and develop a different orientation. This liberates him from cravings that thrust the self to the centre of the stage, cravings of an ego that has remained weak, hungry and infantile. It also enables him to realize what he values for itself.

Authenticity, honesty or being truthful with oneself and others; autonomy or the freedom to be oneself, to think for oneself and act on one's own behalf; respect and concern for others, the ability to establish relationships of affection, loyalty and friendship; creativity, however modest, in the pursuit of one's interests, and all attendant capacities such as initiative, trust and generosity are the central qualities which are valued in the kind of orientation implicit in a psycho-analytic approach and promoted by psycho-analytic therapy. Such qualities of character as manipulativeness, domineeringness, vanity, cruelty, servility, meanness, egocentricity, possessiveness, mere conformity, all attitudes that are false or compulsive, such as certain forms of submissiveness or overbearingness, and such traits as signal a failure to attain certain standards of character, such as irresponsibility, fickleness and cowardice, are viewed with disfavour in the light of these values. The 'authoritarian' attitude, to which both Fromm and Money-Kyrle refer, is seen as violating some of these values, particularly those of individual autonomy, criticism and independence of thought.

It is no accident that the kind of change and character transformation that is considered as being in the direction of 'cure' – cure of the complaints for which the patient has sought psychotherapy –

is at one and the same time an ethical or moral transformation in the direction I have indicated. I differ from Money-Kyrle in holding that this is partly because of values implicit in psycho-analysis itself, which the patient learns and seeks to realize in the course of his treatment. I agree that he does discover and develop the seeds of certain virtues in himself, at least if he is lucky. But I disagree that this is enough to account for the kind of transformation in question. It is interesting that the seeds of these virtues are the source which analysis taps in the patient in seeking to help him. We have seen that to activate them by putting the patient in touch with them is 'healing' in the sense that these 'healing processes' in the patient lead to a greater unity within him, a freedom from cravings that are divisive and enslaving, and also greater contact and more friendly relations with others on a more equal footing.

There are, of course, other values than these for which a person may have a perfectly genuine regard. In the case of some of them, a person, whatever his problems, would hardly consider a personal analysis or be favourably disposed to it. Conversely, the 'solution' to his problems, if he finds any, would hardly be what psycho-analysis would see in a favourable light. But it would be wrong to draw the conclusion that psycho-analysis is something like a sect or religion, preaching its own particular dogmas. That would be a grotesque caricature of the matter. For, while it has a distinctive outlook and its own broad values, it neither preaches these nor is it interested in converting anyone. It helps those who seek its help by teaching them to approach their problems *critically* and to respect and practice truth, honesty or authenticity in their lives and to show regard for the separateness of others.

Bibliography

Berger, Louis, 1981. *Freud's Unfinished Journey*. Routledge.

Bettelheim, Bruno, 1962. *The Informed Heart*. The Free Press of Glencoe.

Champlin, Steve, 1981. 'The Reality of Mental Illness', *Philosophy*.

Custance, John, 1951. *Wisdom, Madness and Folly*. Victor Gollancz.

Dilman, Ilham, 1979. *Morality and the Inner Life, A Study in Plato's 'Georgias'*. Macmillan.

—— 1983. *Freud and Human Nature*. Blackwell.

—— 1984a. *Freud and the Mind*. Blackwell.

—— 1984b. 'Reason, Passion and the Will', *Philosophy*.

—— 1986. *Love and Human Separateness*. Blackwell.

—— and Phillips, D. Z., 1971. *Sense and Delusion*. Routledge.

Dostoyevsky, Fyodor, 1956. *Crime and Punishment*, trans. David Magarshack. Penguin.

Drury, M. O'C., 1973. 'Madness and Religion', *The Danger of Words*. Routledge.

Eliot, George, 1956. *Middlemarch*. Houghton Mifflin.

Eliot, T. S., 1955. 'Burnt Norton', *The Four Quartets*. Faber.

Ferenczi, Sándor, 1950. 'On the Technique of Psycho-analysis', *Further Contributions to the Theory and Technique of Psycho-analysis*. Hogarth Press.

Field, Joanna – see Milner, Marion below.

Freud, Sigmund, 1933. *New Introductory Lectures on Psycho-analysis*, trans. W. J. N. Sprott. W. W. Norton.

—— 1940. *Moses and Monotheism*, trans. Katherine Jones. Hogarth Press.

—— 1947. *The Question of Lay Analysis*, trans. Nancy Procter-Gregg. Imago.

—— 1948. *An Autobiographical Study*, trans. James Strachey. Hogarth Press.

—— 1949a. *Three Essays on the Theory of Sexuality*, trans. James Strachey, The Alcuin Press.

—— 1949b *Introductory Lectures on Psycho-Analysis*, trans. Joan Rivière. Allen and Unwin.

—— 1949c. 'Contributions to the Psychology of Love', *Freud on Sex and Neurosis*, ed. Sandor Katz. Garden City, New York.

—— 1949d. *The Ego and the Id*, trans. James Strachey. Hogarth Press.

—— 1949e. *An Outline of Psycho-analysis*, trans. James Strachey, Hogarth Press.

—— 1949f. *The Future of an Illusion*, trans. W. D. Robson-Scott. Hogarth Press.

—— 1949g. *Civilization and its Discontents*, trans. James Strachey. Hogarth Press.

—— 1950. *Collected Papers*, vols i–v, trans. Joan Rivère. Hogarth Press.

—— 1954. *Psychopathology of Everyday Life*, trans. A. A. Brill. Ernest Benn.

—— 1977. *Case Histories I: 'Dora' and Little Hans'*, trans. Allix and James Strachey. Penguin.

—— 1979. *Case Histories II: 'Rat Man', Schreber, 'Wolf Man', Female Homosexuality*, trans. James Strachey. Penguin.

—— and Breuer, Joseph, 1950. *Studies in Hysteria*, trans. A. A. Brill. Beacon Press.

Fromm, Erich, 1950. *Man for Himself*. Routledge.

—— 1960. *Psycho-analysis and Zen Buddhism*. Unwin Paperback.

Glover, Edward, 1955. *The Technique of Psycho-analysis*. Baillière, Tindall and Cox.

Guntrip, Harry, 1970. *Your Mind and Your Health*. Unwin Paperback.

—— 1977. *Personality Structure and Human Interaction*. Hogarth Press.

Hampshire, Stuart, 1961. 'Feeling and Expression', Inaugural Lecture. H. K. Lewis and Co.

Hamson, C. J., 1955. 'Reflections on Captivity', *The Listener*, 19 May.

Horney, Karen, 1937. *The Neurotic Personality of Our Time*. W. W. Norton.

Hume, David, 1967. *A Treatise on Human Nature*, ed. L. A. Selby-Biggs. Oxford University Press.

Jaspers, Karl, 1956. *De la Psychothérapie*. Presses Universitaires de France.

Jones, Ernest, 1937. 'Love and Morality', *International Journal of Psycho-analysis*.

—— 1954. *Sigmund Freud: Life and Work*, vol. i. Hogarth Press.

Jung, C. G. 1953. *Psychological Reflections*, ed. Jolande Jacobi. Routledge.

—— 1966. *Modern Man in Search of a Soul*, trans. W. S. Dell and Cary F. Baynes. Routledge.

Kant, Immanuel, 1959. *Fundamental Principles of the Metaphysic of Ethics*, trans. T. K. Abbott. Longman.

Klein, Melanie, 1953. 'Love, Guilt and Reparation', *Love, Hate and Reparation*, Two Lectures by Melanie Klein and Joan Rivière. Hogarth Press.

—— 1957. *Envy and Gratitude*. Tavistock.

—— 1960. 'Our Adult World and its Roots in Infancy'. Tavistock Pamphlet.

Kubie, L. S., 1950. *Practical and Theoretical Aspects of Psycho-analysis*. International University Press, New York.

Laforgue, René, 1937. 'Exceptions to the Fundamental Rule in Psychoanalysis', *International Journal of Psycho-analysis*.

Laing, R. D., 1985. *Wisdom. Madness and Folly, the Making of a Psychiatrist 1927–57*. Macmillan.

Milner, Marion (pseudonym Joanna Field), 1952. *A Life of One's Own*. Penguin.

—— 1977. *On Not Being Able to Paint*. Heinemann.

Money-Kyrle, Roger, Roger, 1955. 'Psycho-analysis and Ethics', *New Directions in Psycho-analysis*, ed. Melanie Klein, Paula Heimann, R. E. Money-Kyrle. Tavistock.

Oatley, Keith, 1984. *Selves in Relation, An Introduction to Psychotherapy and Groups*. Methuen Paperbacks.

Overstreet, Harry and Bonaro, 1954. *The Mind Alive*. W. W. Norton.

Peters, R. S., 1958. 'Freud's Theory', *The Concept of Motivation*. Routledge.

Phillips, D. Z., 1976. 'Freudianism and Religion', *Religion Without Explanation*. Balckwell.

Plato, 1955. 'Phaedo', *The Last Days of Socrates*. Penguin.

—— 1973. *Gorgias*. Penguin.

Proust, Marcel, 1954. *A la Recherche du Temps Perdu*, vols i–iii. N. R. F., Bibliothèque de la Pléiade.

Puner, Helen Walker, 1959. *Freud: His Life and His Mind*. Dell.

Reich, Wilhelm, 1950. *Character Analysis*, trans. Theodore P. Wolfe. Vision Press.

Roazen, Paul, 1973. *Brother Animal*. Penguin.

Sartre, Jean-Paul, 1943. *L'Etre et le Néant*. Gallimard.

—— 1948. *Esquisse d'une Théorie des Emotions*. Hermann.

Suttie, Ian D., 1948. *The Origins of Love and Hate*. Kegan Paul, Trench, Trubner.

Szasz, Thomas S., 1967. *The Myth of Mental Illness*. Delta

Tolstoy, Leo, 1956. *Anna Karenina*, trans. Rosemary Edmunds. Penguin.

—— 1959. 'The Death of Ivan Ilytch', *Ivan Ilytch, Hadji Murad and Other Stories*, trans. Louise and Aylmer Maude. Oxford University Press.

—— 1960. 'Father Sergius', *The Kreutzer Sonata and Other Stories*, trans. Aylmer Maude. Oxford University Press.

—— 1961. *A Confession*, trans. Aylmer Maude. Oxford University Press.

Weil, Simone, 1953. *La Pesanteur et la Grâce*. Gallimard.

—— 1962. 'Human Personality', *Selected Essays 1934–43*, trans. Richard Rees. Oxford University Press.

Winch, Peter, 1963. 'Moral Integrity', Inaugural Lecture. Blackwell. Reprinted 1972, *Ethics and Action*. Routledge.

Wisdom, John, 1952. *Other Minds*. Blackwell.

—— 1965. *Paradox and Discovery*. Blackwell.

Wittgenstein, Ludwig, 1963. *Philosophical Investigations*, trans. G. E. M. Anscombe. Blackwell.

—— 1969. *The Blue and Brown Books*. Blackwell.

Wortis, Joseph, 1954. *Fragments of an Analysis with Freud*. Simon and Schuster, New York.

Index